TIME
FOR KIDS
ALMANAC
2009

PRODUCED BY

PRESIDENT: **Julie Merberg**
EDITOR AND PHOTO RESEARCHER: **Sarah Parvis**
ASSISTANT EDITOR AND PHOTO RESEARCHER:
Kate Gibson
SENIOR CONTRIBUTOR: **Jeanette Leardi**
SPECIAL THANKS: **Sara Newberry, Patty Brown,
Pam Abrams**

DESIGNED BY
Georgia Rucker Design

TIME FOR KIDS

PUBLISHER, TIME FOR KIDS MEDIA GROUP:
John Stevenson
MANAGING EDITOR, TIME FOR KIDS MAGAZINE:
Martha Pickerill
EDITOR-IN-CHIEF, TIME LEARNING VENTURES:
Jonathan Rosenbloom
SENIOR EDITOR, TIME LEARNING VENTURES:
Curtis Slepian

Time Inc.
HOME ENTERTAINMENT

PUBLISHER: **Richard Fraiman**
GENERAL MANAGER: **Steven Sandonato**
EXECUTIVE DIRECTOR, MARKETING SERVICES:
Carol Pittard
DIRECTOR, RETAIL & SPECIAL SALES:
Tom Mifsud
DIRECTOR, NEW PRODUCT DEVELOPMENT:
Peter Harper
ASSISTANT DIRECTOR, BRAND MARKETING:
Laura Adam
ASSOCIATE COUNSEL: **Helen Wan**
SENIOR BRAND MANAGER, TWRS/M: **Holly Oakes**
DESIGN & PREPRESS MANAGER:
Anne-Michelle Gallero
BOOK PRODUCTION MANAGER:
Susan Chodakiewicz
MARKETING MANAGER: **Alexandra Bliss**

SPECIAL THANKS:
Glenn Buonocore, Margaret Hess, Suzanne Janso,
Robert Marasco, Dennis Marcel, Brooke Reger,
Mary Sarro-Waite, Ilene Schreider, Adriana
Tierno, Alex Voznesenskiy

Copyright 2008
Time Inc. Home Entertainment

PUBLISHED BY TIME FOR KIDS BOOKS
Time Inc.
1271 Avenue of the Americas
New York, New York 10020

ISSN: 1534-5718
ISBN 13: 978-1-60320-775-1
ISBN 10: 1-60320-775-9

TIME For Kids is a trademark of Time Inc.

We welcome your comments and suggestions
about TIME For Kids Books. Please write to us at:

TIME FOR KIDS BOOKS
ATTENTION: BOOK EDITORS
PO BOX 11016
DES MOINES, IA 50336-1016

If you would like to order any of our hardcover
Collector's Edition books, please call us at
1-800-327-6388.
(Monday through Friday, 7:00 a.m.–8:00 p.m. or
Saturday, 7:00 a.m.–6:00 p.m. Central Time).

TFK CONTENTS

TFK NEWS RECAP

WHAT IN THE WORLD HAS BEEN GOING ON?

The answer is *plenty.* Countless events and trends around the world contribute to the state of the nation and the world in 2009. Here are some of the highlights (and low points) of 2007 and 2008 that affect the world today.

Around the World

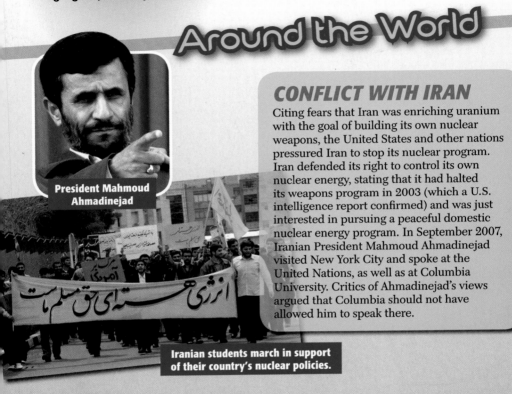

President Mahmoud Ahmadinejad

Iranian students march in support of their country's nuclear policies.

CONFLICT WITH IRAN

Citing fears that Iran was enriching uranium with the goal of building its own nuclear weapons, the United States and other nations pressured Iran to stop its nuclear program. Iran defended its right to control its own nuclear energy, stating that it had halted its weapons program in 2003 (which a U.S. intelligence report confirmed) and was just interested in pursuing a peaceful domestic nuclear energy program. In September 2007, Iranian President Mahmoud Ahmadinejad visited New York City and spoke at the United Nations, as well as at Columbia University. Critics of Ahmadinejad's views argued that Columbia should not have allowed him to speak there.

THE IRAQ WAR SURGE

The war continued but with a change: the 2007 addition of 30,000 U.S. troops. Known as the "troop surge," about 168,000 armed forces personnel boosted America's military presence in Iraq. At the start of 2008, the United Nations World Health Organization estimated Iraqi civilian casualties to be about 151,000. In addition, some estimates cited about 2 million Iraqi refugees displaced in other countries.

On March 24, 2008, the number of U.S. soldiers killed in Iraq hit 4,000. Approximately 30,000 American soldiers have been wounded.

TURMOIL IN PAKISTAN

Pakistan's President Pervez Musharraf declared a state of emergency in 2007 due to riots and protests opposing his leadership. Eventually he stepped down as head of the nation's military, but remained the country's president until democratic elections could be held. Former Prime Minister Benazir Bhutto returned to Pakistan from exile to challenge Musharraf's presidential bid, but she was assassinated on December 27, 2007. Many people believed the incident was not the work of terrorists, as Musharraf claimed, but instead a plot by his backers. The pro-Musharraf political party was soundly defeated in February 18, 2008. Because Musharraf was such a close ally of the United States, the election affected U.S. policy in the region.

Benazir Bhutto

Gordon Brown

NEW LEADERS ON THE SCENE

After a decade in office as Britain's Prime Minister, Tony Blair resigned. Blair had been a strong supporter of President George W. Bush's policies relating to fighting terrorism and attacking Iraq. His position was filled by his Labor Party colleague Gordon Brown. As the new Prime Minister, Brown immediately faced challenges of his own. Within days of his taking office, two car bombs were found in London, and an SUV driven by terrorists allegedly associated with al Qaeda crashed into an airport terminal in Glasgow, Scotland.

In Liberia, a Harvard University–educated economist, Ellen Johnson-Sirleaf, became the country's first female president and first elected leader since the end of Liberia's civil war in 2003, which lasted 14 years. She received 59% of the vote, defeating her challenger, soccer star George Weah.

France elected a new president, Nicholas Sarkozy, a conservative pro-American, who received 53% of the vote—6% more than his liberal rival, Socialist candidate Ségolène Royal.

9

Environmental Headlines

GLOBAL WARMING REMAINS CENTER STAGE

The world's attention returned often to the issue of global warming due to several important events. A Live Earth concert performed at eight different venues around the world on the same day, July 7, 2007 (07/07/07), was viewed by hundreds of millions of people. The extravaganza was supported by former U.S. Vice President Al Gore, whose own documentary about global warming, *An Inconvenient Truth*, won an Academy Award. Later in 2007, Gore and the United Nations Panel on Climate Change shared the Nobel Peace Prize. An environmental summit of more than 180 nations took place in Bali, Indonesia, in which the representatives pledged to work together to solve the world's climate-change issues.

Live Earth

California wildfires destroyed about 2,000 homes.

WILDFIRES AND DROUGHT

Nearly two dozen wildfires ravaged southern California, causing 14 deaths and the evacuation of 1 million people. More than 500,000 acres (200,000 hectares) of land were scorched. Meanwhile, a drought hit more than 40% of the United States, mostly in the Southwest and Southeast.

WHERE ARE THE BEES?

Beekeepers around the world began noticing something strange happening in their colonies. The insects would suddenly disappear and not return to their hives. This condition, called Colony Collapse Disorder (CCD), is having a major effect on flowering crops throughout the world. It's estimated that one-third of all the food humans eat comes from plants that need bees to pollinate them in order to produce vegetables, nuts, seeds and fruit—that is more than $14 billion in crops in the United States alone. How extensive is the CCD loss of bees? It is around 60–70% in the United States and around 40% in Europe—and the numbers continue to rise. Scientists don't know the cause of CCD, although some believe it is due to the overuse of pesticides and herbicides on plants.

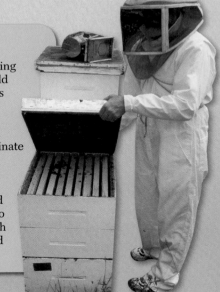

STEM-CELL RESEARCH

Stem cells are early versions of cells that have the potential to develop into specific cells throughout the body, depending on where they are placed. Scientists look to stem cells for help in curing, preventing or treating diseases such as Parkinson's, Alzheimer's, diabetes and even cancer. Many recent developments in stem-cell research are bringing scientists closer to the time when new human organs can replace damaged ones and certain diseases may be reversed or even cured.

A scientist at the University of Georgia works with frozen stem cells.

SHOOTING AT VIRGINIA TECH

On April 16, 2007, Virginia Tech student Seung-Hui Cho shot a total of 32 students and professors, then killed himself. It was the worst school shooting in U.S. history. Cho, who had a history of mental health problems, failed to submit to court-ordered treatment. The tragedy sparked a national examination of how security and mental health issues are handled on college campuses.

RECALL OF CHINESE PRODUCTS

An unforeseen and hazardous effect of trade with China was the recall of more than 19 million Chinese-made items such as cans of dog food, bags of shrimp, rubber tires, tubes of toothpaste and a wide array children's toys. Investigators found defects or high concentrations of lead, chemicals or other toxins in these products. As a result, consumer groups and politicians pressured manufacturers to increase regulation and inspection of products coming from overseas.

THE ECONOMY SLOWS DOWN

The U.S. economy began taking a downturn, caused by several factors. For one thing, many people bought new homes but couldn't pay for them when the interest rates on their home loans suddenly increased. This led to the foreclosure (when a bank takes possession of a house) of more than 2 million homes. Also, oil prices rose to more than $100 a barrel, and those high prices were passed along to consumers in their home heating bills and costs of gasoline for their cars. Congress responded to these challenges by passing bills that would increase cars' fuel efficiency and put more money in Americans' hands, in the hope that increased spending would stimulate the economy.

THE ISSUE OF IMMIGRATION

In 2007 and 2008, the question of what to do about the 12 to 14 million undocumented laborers in the United States occupied much of the nation's debate and political decision-making. Since most of these illegal immigrants are from Mexico, the Department of Homeland Security began work on a 1,952-mile (3,253-km) fence along the U.S.–Mexico border. The project included fences 15 feet (2.73 m) high made of sheet metal and concrete and, in some places, guarded by security cameras and radar. The most heated debate focused on whether or not to offer citizenship to those undocumented residents who already live in the United States.

Candidates Barack Obama and Hillary Clinton (below) and their supporters (above) during the primary campaign

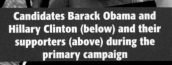

RACE TO THE WHITE HOUSE

The combination of earlier primary dates and a long series of televised debates made the 2008 U.S. presidential race a hot and unpredictable one. The race to the nominating conventions in the summer of 2008 included an incredibly diverse list of presidential hopefuls, including Vietnam War veteran John McCain, ordained Baptist Minister Mike Huckabee, Mormon Governor Mitt Romney, female Senator Hillary Clinton and African American Senator Barack Obama, among others.

After "Super Tuesday" on February 5, 2008, when 24 states held their caucuses or primary elections, Senator John McCain emerged as the likely Republican presidential nominee. Senators Barack Obama and Hillary Clinton fought a tight race for the Democratic presidential nomination.

Mike Huckabee and John McCain at a Republican presidential debate

The Republican candidates at the beginning of the primary season

13

Front-Page Gadgets and Sports

A NEW WAY TO READ

Amazon.com developed the Kindle, a hand-held reading device that enables readers to download nearly 90,000 online books. Each book costs only $10. The device is about the size of a paperback book, with a 6-inch (15.24-cm) screen, weighing 10.3 ounces (288.4 g). The font size and type of print can be changed by the user, and the device can store about 200 books on its hard drive. A memory card can hold hundreds more.

With the Kindle, a reader can search for phrases and names within the text of a book. Like a mini-computer, it also allows readers to subscribe to newspapers and read them, receive e-mail and surf the Web. It costs about $400.

A PHONE THAT'S MUCH MORE

Apple's release of its iPhone in June 2007 pushed the envelope of cell-phone technology. The 4.5 x 2.4 x 0.46–inch (11.4 x 6.1 x 1.17–cm), 8 GB touch-screen device puts users in touch, literally, with Wi-Fi, EDGE networking, music, photos, video and the Internet. At $400 apiece, millions of iPhones have been sold.

Jeff Bezos, founder of Amazon.com, with a Kindle

NOT-SO-SPORTING NEWS

In the recent past, several American athletes have admitted to the illegal use of performance-enhancing drugs. Some others have been accused of having unfair advantages because of suspected drug use. Among the controversial players were runner and Olympic Gold Medal–winner Marion Jones and 2006 Tour de France winner Floyd Landis. Both athletes were stripped of their titles. The Mitchell Report, a government investigation of steroid use in Major League Baseball, concluded that there was "widespread use of steroids" in the sport. Major League stars Barry Bonds, Roger Clemens and Andy Pettitte have all been accused of illegal drug use.

Barry Bonds

Marion Jones

Saying Goodbye

GOODBYE, HARRY POTTER

The publication of *Harry Potter and the Deathly Hallows*, the seventh and final volume in the Harry Potter series, caused hysteria at bookstores in the United States and the rest of the world. Booksellers struggled to supply enough copies of the wizarding tale to meet the incredible demand. It was another record-breaking release for author J.K. Rowling: 72 million copies of the book were sold worldwide in just 24 hours.

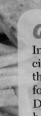

GOODBYE TO TRANS FATS, TOO

In a move to get Americans on a healthy eating track, several cities (including New York City, Philadelphia and others) banned the use of trans fats in restaurant kitchens. In addition, major food manufacturers and sellers such as McDonald's and the Walt Disney Co. said they, too, would be replacing trans fats with healthier substitutes.

THE WORLD SAID GOODBYE TO...

Lady Bird Johnson

Every year, we must say goodbye to some of the great minds and amazing talents that we've known and loved. In 2007 and 2008, the world mourned memorable writers, including Norman Mailer, Kurt Vonnegut, Art Buchwald and Madeleine L'Engle. Daredevil stuntman Evel Knievel, fashion designer Liz Claiborne, former Russian president Boris Yeltsin and former First Lady Claudia "Lady Bird" Johnson passed away. Astronaut Wally Schirra Jr. and Sir Edmund Hillary, the first man to scale Mt. Everest, died as well.

Evel Knievel

Heath Ledger

Probably the most shocking death was that of 28-year-old Heath Ledger, the star of films such as *Lords of Dogtown, The Brothers Grimm, A Knight's Tale* and *The Dark Knight*. On January 22, 2008, the Australian actor died after taking too many prescription drugs. He left behind a young daughter, Matilda, whose mother is actress Michelle Williams.

DEEP SEA DISCOVERIES

FROM **TFK** MAGAZINE

Imagine you are in a small craft, floating in total darkness, two miles beneath the surface of the ocean. Suddenly, a long string of glowing lanterns dripping with tentacles comes into view. It looks like a moving curtain of lights. A saucer-shaped object with rows of blinking jewels floats by. Then, a creature with huge pearly eyes, wicked teeth and headlights stares back at you. Is that an octopus with elephant ears over there? These are just a few of the wonders you will find in the deep ocean, or abyss (a-*biss*). "Many of these creatures are so rare that they have been seen and photographed only once," Claire Nouvian, author of *The Deep*, told TFK.

Many sea creatures, like the ctenophore (left) and the jellyfish (above), give off a bioluminescent glow.

Every year, more and more of these bizarre creatures are discovered. In October 2007, an expedition returned from the Celebes Sea near the Philippines. The scientists reported that they had used an underwater camera to search for new species and collected 100 different specimens. According to Larry Madin of the Woods Hole Oceanographic Institution in Massachusetts, one of their strangest finds was a jet-black jelly.

A WORLD OF TOTAL DARKNESS

Of all the places on the planet where life can be found, the largest habitat is the deep ocean. Scientists believe it may also be the most diverse. This watery world has been in complete darkness for 2 billion years and humans are just beginning to explore it. In fact, more people have stood on the moon than have reached the deepest point in the ocean.

Deepwater craft called submersibles are helping researchers explore the farthest depths of the seas. The earliest submersibles could move only straight up and down, like underwater elevators. But in the 1970s, scientists designed craft that they could steer.

DON'T CALL THEM MONSTERS!

The creatures of the deep look like nothing seen anywhere else. These marvels are perfectly adapted to the harsh, strange world of the abyss, and to nowhere else. Since one of the key features of the deep is permanent darkness, animals create their own "living light." The chemical process is called bioluminescence (bye-oh-loo-mih-*ness*-ens). Only a few land creatures, like fireflies and glowworms, have this ability.

To our eyes, many creatures of the deep look like monsters. The vampire squid, which seems to be armed with cactus-like spines, looks as scary as its name. This animal has not changed in 200 million years and can survive in water that holds little oxygen. Other deep-sea creatures may look fierce, but are only an inch or two long.

What really rules the deep ocean are not monsters, but the creatures called jellies. They are one of the earliest forms of life. Some large jellies may live for decades. And don't let their appearance fool you: Jellies are hunters, always on the prowl.

WHAT ELSE IS DOWN THERE?

The exploration of the deep is just getting started. The big question for many marine scientists is: What else is down there?

—By David Bjerklie

ANIMAL KINGDOM

PHYLUM CLASS ORDER FAMILY GENUS SPECIES

All creatures belong to a kingdom of life (see SCIENCE, page 177). Scientists further classify them according to the following subdivisions:

Each subdivision is smaller than the one preceding it. In this way, scientists can name every creature according to certain characteristics it shares with others and characteristics that are unique to itself. This categorization is called *taxonomy*. Here is the taxonomy for two very different animals.

HORSE

KINGDOM	Animalia	All animals share this kingdom.
PHYLUM	Chordata	These animals have backbones.
CLASS	Mammalia	Female mammals breastfeed their young. Almost all mammals give birth to live young.
ORDER	Perissodactyla	These mammals have an odd number of toes. Includes tapirs and rhinoceroses.
FAMILY	Equidae	These Perissodactyls have long legs to run fast and a single stomach to digest food quickly.
GENUS	Equus	This is the only genus in the Equidae family to survive to modern times. Includes horses, zebras and donkeys.
SPECIES	caballus	This species distinguishes horses from zebras and donkeys.

BALD EAGLE

GUESS WHAT?

Horses are related to hippopotamuses. They share the same kingdom, phylum and class. But the hippo's order, Artiodactyla, includes mammals that have an even number of toes. Artiodactyla includes cattle, goats, sheep, pigs, camels, antelope and deer.

KINGDOM	Animalia	All animals share this kingdom.
PHYLUM	Chordata	These animals have backbones.
CLASS	Aves	Birds have feathers and wings and lay eggs.
ORDER	Falconiformes	These are meat-eating birds of prey (raptors) that hunt in the daytime. Includes hawks, vultures and falcons.
FAMILY	Accipitridae	These Falconiformes usually kill the prey they eat.
GENUS	Haliaeetus	This genus includes all kinds of eagles: bald, sea, fish, snake, serpent and golden, to name a few.
SPECIES	leucocephalus	This species distinguishes the bald eagle from all other eagles.

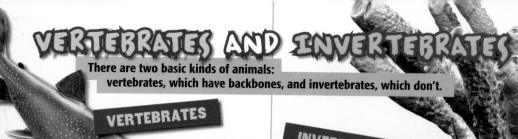

VERTEBRATES AND INVERTEBRATES

There are two basic kinds of animals:
vertebrates, which have backbones, and invertebrates, which don't.

VERTEBRATES

FISH are cold-blooded, live in water and breathe using gills. Their skin is scaly, and they lay eggs (except for sharks which give birth to live young). Salmon, goldfish, tuna and flounder are other examples of fish.

AMPHIBIANS are cold-blooded and begin life in the water, breathing through gills. When they are fully grown, they breathe through lungs and can walk on land. They lay eggs. Some examples of amphibians are frogs, toads and salamanders.

REPTILES are cold-blooded and have lungs. Their skin is scaly. Most reptiles lay eggs. Reptiles include snakes, lizards, turtles, tortoises, alligators and crocodiles.

BIRDS are warm-blooded and have wings and feathers. All birds lay eggs and, with the exception of ostriches and penguins, can fly. Eagles, canaries, parakeets and turkeys are other examples of birds.

MAMMALS are warm-blooded and, with the exception of the platypus, give birth to live young. Mammal mothers breastfeed their young. Most mammals have hair or fur and live on land (except for porpoises, dolphins and whales, which live in the water). Giraffes, lions, mice, wolves, chimpanzees and humans are all mammals.

INVERTEBRATES

SPONGES live in water and are immobile. They get their food by filtering tiny organisms that swim by.

COELENTERATES use their mouths not only for eating but also to eliminate waste. Around their mouths are tentacles that sting. Examples of coelenterates are corals, jellyfish and sea anemones.

ECHINODERMS live in the sea and have skeletons on the outside of their bodies called exoskeletons. They include sea urchins, starfish and sea cucumbers.

WORMS live in a variety of places, including underwater, in dirt and even inside other living creatures. Examples of worms include roundworms, flatworms and earthworms.

MOLLUSKS have soft bodies. To protect themselves, some mollusks have hard shells. Snails, slugs, octopuses, squid, clams, oysters, mussels and scallops are all mollusks.

ARTHROPODS have bodies that are divided into different parts. They also have exoskeletons, which means that their skeleton or supporting structure is located on the outside. Arthropods include crustaceans (such as lobsters, crabs and shrimp); arachnids (including members of the spider family, scorpions and ticks); centipedes; millipedes and all insects (such as butterflies, ants, bees and cockroaches).

Warm-Blooded or Cold-Blooded?

Warm-blooded animals (birds, mammals) are able to keep their body temperature constant. In cold weather, they turn the food they eat into energy that creates heat. In hot weather, they sweat, pant or do other things to help cool their outsides and insides. Most of the food warm-blooded animals take in is used to maintain their body temperature.

The body temperature of **cold-blooded animals** (reptiles, fish, amphibians, invertebrates) is the same as that of their surroundings. When it is hot, chemicals in their bodies react very quickly to help their muscles move, but these reactions slow down as the outside temperature drops. Because of this, they are able to be very active in hot weather but are sluggish at low temperatures. Most of the food cold-blooded animals take in is used to build their body mass.

ENVIRONMENTAL FOCUS | Coral Reefs

Coral reefs are places where coral live in colonies, usually in warm-water zones. They provide food and shelter for sea slugs, clams, jellyfish, sea anemones, sea worms, oysters, crabs, shrimp and many kinds of fish.

Although coral reefs might look like lifeless stone, they are actually made up of coral polyps, which are alive. When water temperatures get too high, or if pollutants enter the water, the coral bleach, or turn white, and die. Reefs are also threatened by construction on coastlines, swimmers, divers and natural disasters such as tropical storms. Marine biologists are looking for ways to save the earth's remaining coral reefs.

go *To read more about the plight of coral reefs, go to www.timeforkids.com and search for "coral reefs."*

TFK TOP 5 | Common U.S. Birds

Count them in! Every year American bird-watchers participate in the Great Backyard Bird Count. The yearly event asks them to report the number and kinds of birds they see in their area. Here are the birds that were reported most in 2008.

1. Northern cardinal
2. Mourning dove
3. Dark-eyed junco
4. Downy woodpecker
5. American goldfinch

Source: The Cornell Lab of Orinthology

Endangered Animals

Brown pelican

In 1973, the Endangered Species Act was passed by Congress to prevent various plant and animal species from vanishing from the earth. The U.S. Fish and Wildlife Service keeps track of the populations of all known species in the country. Some endangered species on the 2007 list are:

- gray bat
- Caribbean monk seal
- blue whale
- whooping crane
- brown pelican
- jaguar
- bighorn sheep
- gray wolf
- ivory-billed woodpecker
- leatherback sea turtle

Jaguar

GUESS WHAT? The bald eagle, which had been on the Endangered Species List since 1978, was taken off the list on June 28, 2007. At that time, there were approximately 10,000 nesting pairs in the United States.

ANIMAL FACTS: WEIRD BUT TRUE

Skunks can spray their foul odor about 10 to 15 feet (3 to 4.6 m), and it can be smelled from at least a mile (1.6 m) away.

The sex of an alligator depends on the temperature of the soil or sand in which the eggs lie. Temperatures between 90°F and 93°F (32.2°C and 33.8°C) will produce males. Temperatures between 82°F and 86°F (27.7°C and 30°C) will produce females. Temperatures in between will produce a mixture of males and females.

To make a pound of honey, honeybees visit about 2 million flowers and travel a total distance of about twice the circumference of the earth.

Record Breaker

Scientists discovered earth's oldest living creature: a clam brought up from a seabed off the coast of northern Iceland. By counting the rings of the clam's shell, they determined its age to be between 405 and 410 years old.

After courtship, the females of some species of black widow spiders kill their mates and eat them.

The female angler fish has a kind of spiny "fishing pole" sticking out of its head to lure prey swimming by. It wiggles a fleshy part at the end of this spine to make other fish think it's "food." Female angler fish can grow to about 47 inches long (119.4 cm), while the males are only about 2.5 inches (6.35 cm) long and attach themselves to the females' bodies.

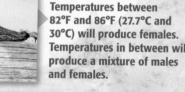

The sea squirt, an invertebrate resembling a grape, has a simple sort of "brain" that helps it locate a rock or other hard surface to attach itself to for life. Once it is attached, it "eats" its own brain within a few days because it is no longer needed.

Sea horses are really fish that look like horses with curly tails. The males assume the responsibility for holding and hatching the eggs by receiving them from the females and storing them in their pouches until they are ready to be born. The eggs hatch inside the male, who then squeezes them out.

When geese migrate, they fly in a V formation to cut down on wind resistance and save their energy. The formation also enables the geese to see one another as they fly. They take turns leading so that no one goose has to fly in the most difficult position the entire time.

Flamingos take in food by putting their heads upside down into the water. They use their tongues to push the water, which contains small creatures, into their beaks.

Sea otters have the thickest fur in the world, with about 1 million hairs per square inch (6.5 sq cm). That's more than 10 times the amount of hair on a human head.

TFK TOP 5 — Heaviest Land Mammals

The lion may be king, but elephants are the heavy favorites. How do other land mammals measure up?

1. Elephant: up to 15,000 pounds
2. Hippopotamus: up to 7,000 pounds
3. Rhinoceros: up to 5,000 pounds
4. Giraffe: up to 3,000 pounds
5. Water Buffalo: up to 2,600 pounds

Source: The San Diego Zoo

ANIMALS THAT SERVE

Humans first began domesticating dogs about 13,000 years ago. Around 5,000 years later, people domesticated sheep, cats and goats. Domesticated animals can be used as sources of food, work animals and pets. Today, animals serve other vital services for their human owners.

> **DOGS** continue to be the most versatile service animals.

- K-9 dogs (usually German shepherds) work with police officers and are trained to sniff for illegal drugs or for bombs and other explosives.
- Bloodhounds help track lost or missing persons by finding their scents after sniffing an item of clothing or other belonging.
- St. Bernards are famous for their mountain rescue skills.
- Labrador retrievers as well as other breeds act as guides for blind people.

Dogs are also used to help the deaf by alerting them when a phone, bell or alarm rings. Some dogs can even sense if their epileptic owner is about to have a seizure. These dogs alert their owners in time to take necessary precautions.

> **CAPUCHIN MONKEYS** are known for their dexterity, which means they are very coordinated and have skillful hands. They also have a long life span (about 40 years) and are quick learners. These attributes make them great "helping hands" for people in wheelchairs or who are unable to move in other ways.

> **MINIATURE HORSES** have been used as guide animals for blind people.

> **CATS** make great pet therapy animals, as do many dogs. Pet therapy animals are taken into hospitals and nursing homes to bring happiness and comfort to the patients and residents, who hold and pet them. In one well-known case, a cat named Oscar has been able to sense when nursing home residents are about to die. He lies in bed next to that person, providing warmth and comfort. Scientists suspect that Oscar can smell biological changes in people's bodies before they die.

> **PIGEONS** have been used as messengers for centuries, flying for miles with tiny rolled-paper messages attached to their legs. Messenger pigeons were used in ancient Greece and Rome, as well as throughout World War I. Today, pigeons are fitted with tiny vests to deliver blood samples or news photographers' film from remote places to either laboratories or newsrooms. Because of their keen eyesight, pigeons on rescue helicopters have also been trained to spot orange life jackets worn by people floating in the sea.

> **LEECHES** are invertebrates that attach themselves to other creatures and feed on their blood. They were used by physicians since about 500 B.C. to treat all kinds of ailments (this process was not often successful). Medicine has evolved greatly since then, but scientists *have* discovered medicinal properties in leech saliva. It acts as an anesthetic (which means it kills pain), as an anticoagulant (which means it keeps blood from clotting) and as a vasodilator (which means it increases blood flow in the arteries and veins). Doctors also use leeches to remove excess blood from bruises and surgical sites and to heal plastic-surgery patients' skin.

MEDICINE FROM ANIMALS

> Other animals are sources of medicine for humans. For example, the skin of the **AMAZON FROG** (*Phyllomedusa bicolor*) gives off a chemical that is used to treat depression, seizures and strokes. Some **EARTHWORMS** contain chemicals that can lower blood pressure and control allergy symptoms. The blood plasma of the **EUROPEAN** **HEDGEHOG** can help prevent uncontrolled bleeding and the omega-3 oil found in the tissues of certain **FISH,** such as tuna, cod, salmon and mackerel, can promote heart health in humans.

Ten Most Popular Dog and Cat Names

DOG NAMES	CAT NAMES
1. Max	1. Max
2. Molly	2. Chloe
3. Buddy	3. Lucy
4. Bella	4. Tigger
5. Lucy	5. Tiger
6. Maggie	6. Smokey
7. Daisy	7. Oliver
8. Jake	8. Bella
9. Bailey	9. Sophie
10. Rocky	10. Princess

Source: Veterinary Pet Insurance, Co.

TFK TOP 5 Pets

Perhaps you have a llama, a lemur or a lynx. But when it comes to pets, most Americans prefer those that bark or meow. More than a third (37%) of U.S. households have dogs, but cats are hot on their tail.

1.	Dogs	37%
2.	Cats	31%
3.	Birds	6%
4.	Fish	3%
5.	Horses	3%

Top 10 Dog Breeds

1. Labrador retriever
2. Yorkshire terrier
3. German shepherd
4. Golden retriever
5. Beagle
6. Boxer
7. Dachshund
8. Poodle
9. Shih Tzu
10. Miniature schnauzer

Source: American Kennel Club, 2007

WHO WORKS WITH ANIMALS?

There are many careers available to animal lovers. Here are just a few.

BREEDERS mate animals to obtain certain characteristics of health, appearance or longevity.

CONTEST JUDGES award prizes in animal competitions based on behavior and appearance.

FARMERS raise animals as sources of food and clothing.

JOCKEYS ride horses in races.

PET THERAPISTS use domesticated animals to comfort and entertain patients or residents in hospitals, nursing homes and other places.

RESCUERS save animals in danger of abuse or abandonment in domestic environments, or from injury or death during natural disasters.

TRAINERS teach animals to behave properly, to perform in entertainment venues (in circuses, on TV and in the movies) or to become service animals.

VETERINARIANS vaccinate animals and treat their diseases and/or injuries.

ZOOKEEPERS feed and maintain animals in zoos.

ZOOLOGISTS study and classify animals. There are different types of zoologists, such as ornithologists, who specialize in birds; ichthyologists, who study fish; herpetologists, who study reptiles and amphibians; and mammalogists, who specialize in mammals.

Offspring!

TFK GAME

Animals' offspring, or babies, have special names. Unscramble the names in the box and see if you can fill in the blanks for each furry friend.

1. A baby goat is called a ___ ___ ___.
2. A baby penguin is called a ___ ___ ___ ___ ___.
3. A baby kangaroo is called a ___ ___ ___ ___.
4. A baby seal is called a ___ ___ ___.
5. A baby deer is called a ___ ___ ___ ___.

ANSWERS ON PAGE 244

BABY NAMES
ejyo
idk
wfna
kccih
ppu

HOW DO ANIMALS COMMUNICATE?

Animals communicate with members of their own species or other animals for three basic reasons: to attract a mate, to form social bonds within their species and to scare off or escape from competitors or predators. Some communication methods include:

VISUAL: Many animals use their appearance to communicate. For example, some poisonous frogs have brightly colored skin to warn predators not to eat them. The male white-tailed deer grows antlers that tell other males how powerful he is. Many male birds are very colorful. Their bright colors are a sign of health used to attract female birds, who choose mates that can produce healthy offspring. Displays are another form of visual communication. The male peacock spreads his colorful tail feathers into a huge fan and wiggles it to attract a mate. The puffer fish, or **blowfish**, can swallow water and expand to twice its size to scare off a predator. Wolves and dogs bare their teeth to challenge others in the pack. To show that they are not a threat to others, they will lie on their backs or put their tails between their legs. Bees returning to the hive after finding a field of flowers do a figure-eight wiggling dance inside their hive to show other bees where the field is located. **Chameleons** can change the color of their skin to match the background of where they sit. This helps them hide from predators.

AUDITORY: Howler monkeys have loud calls to warn others in their group of approaching danger as well as to mark their territories. Male and female mockingbirds sing different songs during different seasons. They can imitate the calls of other bird species and even other animals and machines. They use complicated songs to attract mates and establish their territories. **Dolphins'** whistles and clicks make up a complex language that scientists are studying.

TACTILE: Baboons touch one another constantly, grooming each other's fur. This is not just an act of cleanliness. The touching helps the baboons form close bonds with other members in their group. Many baby animals, such as bear and lion cubs, tumble and play with their siblings as a way to establish a hierarchy of power among themselves.

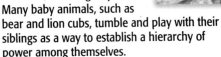

CHEMICAL: Members of the cat family, such as mountain lions and lynx, use scent from their glands to mark their territories. They urinate on leaves or against trees or scratch tree bark, leaving scent from their paws. The skunk has a powerful scent gland under its tail and defends itself against predators by spraying them with a foul odor that chases them away.

23

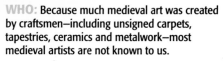
Art Movements

Different styles, or movements, of art have characterized certain periods of Western history.

CLASSICAL ART

Praxiteles'
Aphrodite of Knidos

WHEN: Beginning 500 B.C.

WHERE: From Greece to Rome to the rest of Western Europe and North Africa

WHAT: The ancient Greeks, who founded the Olympics, created statues and painted vases and pottery featuring symmetrical designs and idealized, athletic bodies. Many sculptures depicted nudes and bodies in motion, styles that had not been attempted before. Greek style influenced the Romans, who created statues and busts that resembled real people, such as nobles, generals and emperors, rather than the gods and goddesses favored by the Greeks.

WHO: The Greek sculptor **Praxiteles** (about 400 B.C.–330 B.C.) was known for his lifelike statues of gods and goddesses.

MEDIEVAL ART

WHEN: 3rd Century to 15th Century

WHERE: Eastern Europe, Western Europe, the Middle East and North Africa

WHAT: Medieval art encompasses many genres—from stained glass to engravings and illuminated manuscripts to metalwork, sculpture and paintings of religious icons. Influenced by religion (Christianity in Europe), medieval artists turned to the lives of Jesus and the saints for inspiration. Monks in monasteries copied classical texts and Bibles by hand and decorated the pages with colorful drawings of animals and people to create "illuminated manuscripts." *The Book of Kells,* written in Ireland before the 9th century, is a beautiful example of monastic art.

A page from *The Book of Kells*

WHO: Because much medieval art was created by craftsmen—including unsigned carpets, tapestries, ceramics and metalwork—most medieval artists are not known to us.

RENAISSANCE ART

WHEN: 14th Century through 17th Century

WHERE: Italy

da Vinci's *Mona Lisa*

WHAT: Scholars say that during this period a "renaissance," or rebirth, of knowledge happened in the arts, crafts and sciences. Renaissance art is characterized by more realistic human portrayals and also the introduction of perspective. Religious themes continued to hold a prominent place in painting and sculpture.

WHO: **Leonardo da Vinci** (1452–1519), considered the greatest artist of his time, was also an inventor, scientist, architect, botanist and biologist, among other things. His *Mona Lisa* and *The Last Supper* are among the most famous paintings in the world. Another Renaissance artist, **Michelangelo Buonarroti** (1475–1564) is famous for his sculptures such as *David,* as well as his paintings on the front wall and ceiling of the Sistine Chapel in Rome. Some other famous Renaissance artists include: **Sandro Botticelli** (1445–1510), **Raffaello (Raphael) Sanzio** (1483–1520) and **Tiziano (Titian) Vecellio** (1485–1576).

BAROQUE ART

WHEN: Early 17th Century through 18th Century

WHERE: Europe

WHAT: Baroque art and architecture was very dramatic and ornate, or full of details. Baroque churches throughout Europe have ornate interiors that include gold-leafed columns and domes decorated with heavenly scenes of angels, clouds and saints.

The Church of the Invalides in Paris, France, is an example of Baroque architecture.

WHO: Rembrandt van Rijn (1606–69) and Michelangelo Merisi, better known as **Caravaggio** (1573–1610), used light to draw observers' eyes to the most important parts of their paintings. Rembrandt's *Aristotle with a Bust of Homer* and Caravaggio's *The Cardsharps* are two famous Baroque paintings. Other famous artists: **Peter Paul Rubens** (1577–1640), **Diego Velázquez** (1599–1660) and **Jan Vermeer** (1632–75).

NEOCLASSICISM

WHEN: 1780s to 1820s

WHERE: Europe

WHAT: Archeological excavations at Pompeii and Herculaneum revealed ancient art, which inspired 18th-century artists to look back to the simple, classical art of Greece and Rome. Accurately rendered figures appear in the foregrounds of many paintings, while the backgrounds reveal Roman details like columns. Many paintings from this period showed scenes from history in which heroes fought fiercely or died bravely.

WHO: Jacques-Louis David (French, 1748–1825) led the movement with his painting *The Death of Socrates*. After the French Revolution, David did several important paintings of French emperor Napoleon Bonaparte. Other famous painters: **Anton Mengs** (1728–79), **François Gérard** (1770–1837) and **John Flaxman** (1755–1826).

ROMANTICISM

WHEN: 1800–1850

WHERE: Western Europe

WHAT: After the violence of the 1789 French Revolution, some artists decided that life and nature were more unpredictable than they'd previously believed. Their brushstrokes became bigger and more swirly, and the colors used were moody. Artists started to paint what they were feeling. Nature and landscapes—touched by supernatural or divine forces—were the subject of many paintings of this era.

WHO: Eugène Delacroix (1798–1863) and **Theodore Géricault** (1791–1824) often created exotic scenes from the Middle East. Delacroix's *Abduction of*

Delacroix's *The Tiger Hunt*

Rebecca and Géricault's *The Raft of the Medusa* are two of the most well-known Romantic paintings. **J.M.W. Turner** (1775–1851) used swirling strokes to depict storms at sea. Another famous artist: **John Constable** (1771–1837).

David's *Napoleon Crossing the Alps*

IMPRESSIONISM

WHEN: 1860s to 1880s

WHERE: France and America

WHAT: This style of art gets its name from the artists' desire to capture just an impression of a person, object or landscape, rather than painting it using sharp lines or great detail. Using choppy brushstrokes and unblended colors, the Impressionists explored how to compose and contrast colors to give a sense of light, shadow, temperature and time of day.

Renoir's *Girls at the Piano*

WHO: French painters **Claude Monet** (1840–1926), **Pierre-Auguste Renoir** (1841–1919) and **Edgar Degas** (1834–1917), and American **Mary Cassatt** (1845–1926) are some of the best-known Impressionists. Monet was famous for painting the same subject, such as *Haystacks* or the *Rouen Cathedral*, at different times of the day.

POST-IMPRESSIONISM

WHEN: 1880 to 1905

WHERE: France

WHAT: The Post-Impressionists moved away from the Impressionists' natural style and gave their works more of an emotional or mystical edge with bolder, brighter colors.

WHO: Dutch painter **Vincent van Gogh's** (1853–90) painting *The Starry Night* shows how stormy and full of emotion an otherwise quiet setting can be. **Paul Gauguin** (1843–1903) painted scenes from Tahiti, an island in the South Pacific, while **Paul Cézanne** (1839–1906) favored still lifes using geometric forms. **Georges Seurat** (1959–91) used tiny dots in a style called *pointillism*.

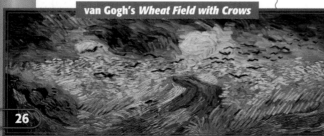

van Gogh's *Wheat Field with Crows*

EXPRESSIONISM

WHEN: 1905 to 1925

WHERE: Europe

WHAT: This style, created mostly by German artists, expresses emotion using exaggeration and distortion. Vivid colors, choppy or shaky brushstrokes and disconnected forms are part of the style. The Expressionists were not interested in portraying reality, but rather painted fantasies and dreams.

WHO: Two famous Expressionist works are *Sketch for Composition II* by **Vasily Kandinsky** (1866–1944) and *I and the Village* by **Marc Chagall** (1887–1985). **Edvard Munch** (1863–1944), famous for *The Scream*, inspired other Expressionists with his work in Berlin from 1892 to 1908.

CUBISM

WHEN: 1908 to 1914

WHERE: France

WHAT: Started by **Pablo Picasso** (Spanish, 1881–1973) and **Georges Braque** (French, 1882–1963), this movement took hold in France between 1910 and 1914. They weren't interested in showing how people and objects actually look. Instead, they imagined what might happen if those objects were broken down and flattened against the plane of the canvas. As a result, their paintings contain lots of geometric shapes and distorted images, though very little color. As the movement continued, the shapes became more and more distorted.

Braque's *The Man with a Guitar*

WHO: **Fernand Léger** (1881–1955), **Juan Gris** (1887–1927) and **Marcel Duchamp** (1887–1968) experimented with Cubism.

SURREALISM

WHEN: Late 1910s to early 1920s

WHERE: France

WHAT: Many Surrealist artists were influenced by the work of the famous psychoanalyst Sigmund Freud, who explored his patients' dreams and secret desires. Surrealists were interested in creating images that came from the subconscious mind. Their works often depicted themes of violence and destruction.

WHO: **Salvador Dali** (1904–89) was the most well-known Surrealist. Other famous artists: **René Magritte** (1898–1967), **Paul Delvaux** (1897–1994) and **Man Ray** (1890–1976).

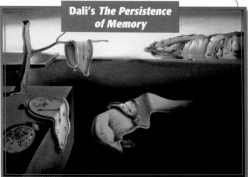

Dali's *The Persistence of Memory*

ABSTRACT EXPRESSIONISM

WHEN: 1940s

WHERE: New York City

WHAT: This movement was defined by two styles: One style showed lots of movement in the form of lines, blotches and other shapes. The other style showed large sections of color next to or on top of one another. In both, there is no central focus to the paintings. Instead, the artist works in an unplanned, spontaneous way.

WHO: **Jackson Pollock** (1912–56) dripped different colors of paint from paintbrushes onto large canvases on the floor, while **Willem de Kooning** (1904–97) used jagged lines and rough brushstrokes in his portraits of women. **Mark Rothko** (1903–70) and **Helen Frankenthaler** (1928–) worked in the color-block style.

POP ART

WHEN: 1950s to 1960s

WHERE: Britain and the U.S.

WHAT: Started in London in the 1950s, this movement quickly spread to the United States in the 1960s. Using humor, Pop artists rejected what they thought was the pretentiousness of Abstract Expressionism. Instead, they celebrated materialistic subjects from popular culture, such as advertising, movies, television and comics.

Andy Warhol

WHO: **Andy Warhol** (1928–87) often focused his attention on mass-produced objects, such as Campbell's soup cans and Coca-Cola bottles, and on celebrities, such as Elvis Presley and Marilyn Monroe. He, in turn, made mass-productions of these images onto single canvases. Pop artists closed the gap between high, or fine, art and low, or commercial, art. Other famous artists: **Jim Dine** (1935–), **Roy Lichtenstein** (1923–97) and **Robert Rauschenberg** (1925–).

MINIMALISM

WHEN: 1960–1975

WHERE: United States

WHAT: The Minimalist artist tried to remove himself or herself from the work, as well as any reference to an idea or subject. Instead, the observer is the one who takes meaning from pictures or sculptures, which have few lines or colors.

WHO: This chiefly American movement began with the work of **Frank Stella** (1936–), who painted black shapes onto other black shapes of a slightly different hue. Other famous artists: **Donald Judd** (1928–1994), **Richard Serra** (1939–) and **Anne Truitt** (1921–2004).

An exhibit of Serra sculptures

Record Breaker

One of the most expensive paintings ever sold was Jackson Pollock's *Number 5*. It cost $140 million in 2006.

TFK BODY AND HEALTH

HOW DOES YOUR BODY WORK?

Your body is an amazing thing. It's made up of different systems, which consist of organs such as your liver, kidneys or heart. Even your skin is an organ!

THE CARDIOVASCULAR SYSTEM, or circulatory system, has one main job: to pump blood throughout the body. The heart pumps blood through the arteries into all the parts of the body. Blood contains the oxygen, hormones and nutrients that cells need to grow, work and repair themselves. The cells take in these products and give off carbon dioxide and other waste materials. The blood carries this waste through the veins to the organs that remove it from the body.

The heart is the major organ of the cardiovascular system.

MUSCULAR SYSTEM Different types of muscles are located throughout the body. Skeletal muscles attach to the body's bones and move them by contracting and releasing. Smooth muscles line the digestive system and cardiac muscles pump blood through the heart to the lungs and the rest of the body.

THE SKELETAL SYSTEM is made up of bones, joints and cartilage, which is a flexible tissue that forms body parts like the nose and ears. Cartilage also helps bones and joints work together smoothly. Bones support the body and work with muscles to help it move in different ways. They also protect the body's organs from injury, produce blood cells and store important minerals such as calcium and phosphorous.

GUESS WHAT? *Bones are actually living organs!*

THE IMMUNE SYSTEM fights off disease and helps to keep you healthy in many ways. Lymph, a liquid produced by the lymph nodes, is carried in the bloodstream to the cells to clean them of harmful bacteria and waste. The center of bones, called the bone marrow, is where red and white blood cells are created. White blood cells are important because they produce antibodies, which kill toxins, bacteria and viruses. The thymus (located in the chest) produces special cells that fight disease. The spleen (under the ribs on the left side) filters out old red blood cells and other foreign bodies, such as bacteria. The adenoids (behind the nose) and tonsils (in the throat) also trap and kill bacteria and viruses.

Viruses enter the body and cause disease.

Lymph nodes are found all over the body.

THE ENDOCRINE SYSTEM'S organs are called glands. They produce hormones, which are chemicals that travel through your blood stream and tell your organs what to do. For this reason, they are often referred to as the body's "messengers." The endocrine system works to regulate mood, growth and body development, sleep, blood pressure and metabolism, which is a term for a how the body changes food into energy.

NERVOUS SYSTEM Your nervous system is made up of two parts: the central nervous system, which includes the **brain** and **spinal cord,** and the peripheral nervous system, which consists of **neurons** found all over your body. The brain helps to regulate all the other systems of the body by sending signals down the spinal cord and through the body's nerves to all the other organs. Different parts of the brain specialize in processing thoughts, memories, speech, physical coordination, balance, hunger, sleep and much more.

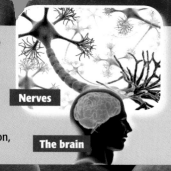

Nerves

The brain

THE DIGESTIVE SYSTEM is responsible for taking in and digesting the food and liquids you consume and making sure you get the nutrients you need from what you eat. It also gets rid of solid waste. When food enters the mouth, glands under the tongue secrete **saliva** (or "spit"), which helps moisten the food you chew. The food is swallowed into the **esophagus,** a tube that leads into the **stomach,** which produces acid that turns the food into a thick liquid. This liquid enters the **intestines,** where enzymes, bile (made by the liver and stored in the gall bladder) and insulin (made in the pancreas) digest it even further. As the food moves through the small and then large intestines, water and nutrients are absorbed into the bloodstream. Finally, the solid waste that's left is passed out of the body.

The intestines

GUESS WHAT? *At 20 feet (6 m) long, the small intestine is actually a lot larger than the large intestine. The large intestine is wider, but is only about 5 feet (1.5 m) long.*

THE RESPIRATORY SYSTEM supplies your body with oxygen. Air that enters the nose and mouth moves down the **trachea,** or windpipe, and into large bronchial tubes that enter into each lobe, or side, of the **lungs.** The tubes branch into many smaller tubes that end in tiny passageways called **alveoli.** In these teeny spaces, oxygen enters the bloodstream and carbon dioxide is removed, sent back up the trachea and breathed out through the nose and mouth.

The lungs

THE REPRODUCTIVE SYSTEM is responsible for producing **sperm cells** in men and **egg cells** in women. The sperm cell and the egg cell combine to form an embryo, which eventually becomes a human baby.

The kidneys are the major organs of the urinary system.

THE URINARY SYSTEM eliminates excess fluid from the body. The body's two **kidneys** remove toxins from the water flowing in the bloodstream. Those liquid toxins travel from the kidneys through tubes called **ureters** and into the **bladder,** where they remain until they leave the body as urine.

THE INTEGUMENTARY SYSTEM is made up of **skin, sweat glands, oil glands, nails** and **hair.** It protects the inside of the body by forming a barrier to the outside atmosphere. The skin receives feelings of touch, heat, cold and pain and sends signals to the brain. The brain then sends signals back to the appropriate body parts so they can react. Sweat glands in your skin help the body cool itself. The skin's oil glands keep the body from drying out. Nails provide defense, and hair provides protection and warmth.

WHY EXERCISE?

Exercising is one of the most important ways to keep your body healthy. When you exercise, you strengthen your bones, muscles and heart. You also burn off excess fat, improve your balance, regulate your body's metabolism (the system that turns nutrients from food into energy and heat) and improve your mood.

Today, many kids don't get enough exercise. In fact, the average kid spends about three hours each day watching television and another two and a half hours sitting down, often playing video games or surfing the Internet. Does that sound like you? If it does, it's time to get up and get moving! Whether you are playing soccer, dancing or challenging your neighbor to a game of tag, you can always find a workout that is fun for you.

THE CALORIE CONNECTION

People gain weight because they take in more calories through eating and drinking than they burn off through exercise. Calories are units of energy (see "Food and Nutrition," page 100) that you take in when you consume food. Here are a few examples of activities and how many calories they burn.

ACTIVITY	CALORIES BURNED IN 30 MINUTES
Running 2 miles (10 minutes per mile)	300
Jumping rope	300
Climbing stairs	300
Swimming laps	225
Bicycling 5 miles	150
Shooting baskets	150
Walking 2 miles (15 minutes per mile)	150

STAYING FIT

There are three aspects to fitness:

- **strength** (being able to move, lift, carry, push and pull)
- **endurance** (being able to do these things for a good amount of time)
- **flexibility** (being able to stretch, bend, turn, twist and move in all the ways your body can).

There are two kinds of exercise:

- **Aerobic** exercises, such as running, jogging or playing soccer or basketball, will make you breathe harder. When you participate in aerobic exercise, your heart beats faster and you probably get sweaty.
- **Anaerobic** exercise is high-intensity, but will not leave you breathing hard in the same way that playing soccer would. It is good for building up muscles. Lifting weights and running very fast for very short distances are forms of anaerobic exercise.

Keep Moving

Everyone knows that soccer, basketball, lacrosse and swimming are great ways to stay in shape. But there are plenty of other ways to get active. Be creative and find your own way to have fun.

- Have a relay race with your friends.
- Hop on one foot during every commercial break. Just make sure to switch legs!
- Together with an adult, create an obstacle course in your back yard.
- Play tag with a twist: The person who is "it" gets to decide how everyone will move. You could skip, walk in slow motion, crab walk or walk heel-to-toe.
- Host a dance contest. The last dancer standing wins!

Keeping Healthy and Safe Everywhere

Staying healthy is more than eating right and staying fit. You also have to pay attention to your surroundings and stay out of harm's way.

At Home

• Several times a year, practice fire drills with your family. Know the best ways to leave your house and pick a spot where you and your family can meet outside.

• Know what to do in an emergency. Role-play with your parents or guardian about how to call 911.

• Talk with your parents or guardians about the best way to use the Internet. Then tell them your computer password. Don't let anyone else—not even your best friend—know what it is. Never give out your last name, address or phone number unless you've checked with your parents.

• If a stranger calls your home while you're by yourself, never say that you're alone. Do not answer the door if a stranger knocks.

• Get plenty of sleep each night. Sleep is very important for your growth and health.

Outdoors

• Be safe when riding a bike or skateboarding. Always wear a helmet and padding, and make sure your bike has reflectors and a horn or bell. If you ride at night, ride with others and wear reflective clothing.

• Never walk or get in a car with a stranger or take any item from a stranger.

• Always swim with a buddy, and don't dive into water that is shallow.

• Ice skate at a rink, whenever possible. If you skate on a lake, make sure an adult you trust has determined that the ice is thick enough.

• On sunny days, wear sunscreen, a hat and sunglasses. Never stay in the sun long enough to burn.

• Drink plenty of water on hot days and when you're playing sports.

• Avoid places where there aren't many people, such as vacant lots, empty buildings, alleys, fields or parks.

GUESS WHAT?
Falls are the most common accidents among kids under 14. One-third of all people who go to hospital emergency rooms because of falls are kids.

At School

• Tell a teacher or other adult you trust if you see anyone at school with a weapon or drugs.

• Also tell a teacher or other trusted adult if you are being bullied or see someone else being harassed.

• Germs pass quickly from student to student. Wash your hands frequently to keep from getting a cold.

With Friends

• Don't give in to peer pressure. Part of staying safe is staying away from smoking, alcohol and drugs.

• Always let your parents or guardians know where you'll be and when you plan to return home. Know their work and cell phone numbers, as well as your home phone number.

• If anyone does something that makes you uncomfortable, tell an adult you trust.

YOUR FIVE SENSES

Information about the world around you comes to you through your five senses: sight, hearing, taste, smell and touch.

• You **SEE** light and dark, as well as color and movement, because of two kinds of eye cells on your retina, which is a membrane at the back of your eye. These two types of cells are rods and cones. Rods detect black, white and shades of gray, as well as shapes. Cones detect color. Each eye has about 120 million rods and about 6 million cones.

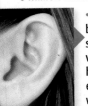

• You **HEAR** because sound vibrations hit your eardrum, which moves three little bones in your middle ear. These bones move a fluid in your inner ear that flows past tiny hairs, which send signals to your brain.

• Your tongue has about 10,000 **TASTE** buds when you're born and fewer as you get older. Different parts of your tongue can sense sourness, bitterness, sweetness and saltiness. Some scientists believe that there's a fifth kind of taste called **umami**, which essentially means "deliciousness."

• It is impossible to truly know the flavor of any food without your sense of **SMELL**. To prove this, hold your nostrils closed while you eat something.

• Your sense of **TOUCH** tells you all sorts of things about the size, shape, heat and texture of objects. Your skin is the largest organ of your body. It In the average adult, it covers 18 square feet (2 sq m). That's a little smaller than the average door of a room.

Childhood Illnesses and Disease

Diseases can occur in people of all ages. Here are some common ones found in children.

ASTHMA is a condition in which the lungs' bronchial tubes tighten and prevent the easy flow of air into or out of the lungs. A child with asthma has a hard time breathing.

ALLERGIES are a body's sensitivities to certain foods, pets, plants or tree pollen and medicines. An allergy may trigger a rash, sneezing, coughing, vomiting, headache, difficulty breathing or other reactions.

OBESITY is a major threat to the health of kids today. About 25 million American teens and children are overweight. Eating healthy foods, participating in active sports and games and avoiding stress all help prevent obesity in kids.

EAR INFECTIONS are the most common illnesses in children and babies. Usually, these infections occur in the middle ear, when tubes called the Eustachian tubes become clogged with fluid. Many ear infections will go away on their own, but those that linger require antibiotics.

STREP THROAT spreads quickly among children and is easily treated with antibiotics. A child with strep throat will have a sore, scratchy, red throat and may have a headache, fever and body pains. Sometimes, white spots will be visible on a child's tonsils.

TYPE 1 DIABETES is a disease in which the pancreas doesn't produce enough insulin to turn sugar, starch or other foods in the body into energy. Diabetic children usually have to receive (or give themselves) insulin injections.

COOL AND WACKY BODY FACTS

The two gluteus maximus muscles, which form your rear end, are the strongest muscles in your body. They pull your legs back when you walk, run and climb steps.

The blood vessels of an average human body can be 60,000 miles (96,560 km) long. That's a distance of nearly two and a half times around the Equator.

Approximately 70% of your body is made of water.

When a baby is newborn, it sees everything upside down and in black and white.

It's impossible to tickle yourself because you need to be surprised to feel tickled.

Spicy foods can give you a runny nose because of a chemical called capsaicin, usually found in hot peppers. Eating capsaicin triggers the nerves that signal the production of more mucus in the nose and stomach.

The weight of the average human brain is 3 pounds (1.36 kg).

Shivering is the body's reaction to being cold. It's caused by signals sent from the hypothalamus to the muscles in the body. The muscles start to move back and forth rapidly to produce more heat.

Fingernails usually grow faster than toenails. If you are right-handed, the nails on your right hand grow faster than those on your left. If you are left-handed, those on your left will grow more quickly.

Your teeth are the only parts of your body that can't heal or fix themselves.

People cry two different kinds of tears. One type of tears comes when you get something in your eye. The other kind appear when you are sad. Sad tears contain more protein than irritation tears. Some scientists think it's nature's way of clearing the body of toxins that are caused by stress.

A sneeze can expel air about 100 miles (166 km) an hour. If you try to hold in a sneeze, you can actually hurt yourself!

The length of an adult's intestines is about 25 to 28 feet (7.5 to 8.5 m).

Your eyes are the only parts of you that are fully grown when you are born.

GUESS WHAT?

Scurvy is a disease caused by a lack of vitamin C. It was common among sailors and pirates at one time. It also occurs in soldiers who do not get fresh fruit supplies during combat. It is not very common any more, but eating plenty of citrus fruits like oranges will make sure you are never at risk for scurvy.

WHAT IS LITERATURE?

The two biggest categories of literature are FICTION, which is made-up, and NONFICTION, which is true and has facts that can be verified. Here are the most common types of literature.

NOVEL: a piece of fiction, written in prose (which means it is written in a way that resembles the everyday language of people instead of being written in rhyming verse, for example). Novels are full-length narratives, as opposed to short stories. (*David Copperfield* by Charles Dickens)

SHORT STORY: a prose narrative that is about the length of one chapter in a novel (*The Gift of the Magi* by O. Henry)

BIOGRAPHY: the factual account of a person's life, told by another person (*Sally Ride: A Space Biography* by Barbara Kramer)

AUTOBIOGRAPHY: the factual account of a person's life, told by that person (*The Autobiography of Benjamin Franklin* by Benjamin Franklin)

HISTORY: the factual recording of past events (*A Little History of the World* by E.H. Gombrich)

SCIENCE FICTION: a novel in which science and technology play important roles; science fiction (or sci-fi) often takes place in the future or portrays time travel or life on other planets (*The Martian Chronicles* by Ray Bradbury)

FANTASY: an imaginative story with bizarre characters that takes place in an unnatural setting (*Harry Potter and the Sorcerer's Stone* by J.K. Rowling)

MYSTERY: a novel in which a crime, usually a murder, is solved (*Murder on the Orient Express* by Agatha Christie)

POEM: a reflection or narrative written in lines of verse that may or may not rhyme ("Stopping by Woods on a Snowy Evening" by Robert Frost)

DRAMA: dialogue and action among characters that is meant to be acted out onstage (*Death of a Salesman* by Arthur Miller)

ESSAY: a discussion of a particular topic from a personal perspective (*Civil Disobedience* by Henry David Thoreau)

JOURNAL/DIARY: a collection of day-to-day recordings of a person's thoughts, feelings, actions and relationships (*The Diary of Anne Frank*)

FABLE: a moral tale whose central characters are animals that speak and act like humans ("The Fox and the Grapes" by Aesop)

LEGEND: a popular story about the past that may or may not have actually happened (*Robin Hood*)

TALL TALE: a story featuring a larger-than-life hero or heroine whose characteristics and actions are exaggerated (*Paul Bunyan*)

MYTH: an ancient spiritual or religious story which is not considered true (*The Fall of Prometheus*)

FAIRY TALE: a story set in an imaginative place in the distant past in which magic drives the action (*Cinderella*)

FOLKTALE: an ethnic story, often humorous, whose characters are simple people (*Stone Soup*)

Record Breaker

The Bible (Old and New Testaments) is the best-selling book of all time. More than 6 billion copies have been printed in over 2,000 languages and dialects.

RECOMMENDED BOOKS

These are some books recommended for children of middle-school age by the Association of Library Service to Children.

Millicent Min: Girl Genius by Lisa Yee. What's so great about being an ultra-smart, underage high school student if everyone thinks you're weird? In this funny book, readers follow Millicent, 11, as she desperately tries to fit in, despite her awkward, embarrassing attempts to be "normal."

No Laughter Here by Rita Williams-Garcia. After her friend Victoria's return from a visit to Nigeria, Akilah tries to understand the sad emotional changes in her friend, only to find out about an often-taboo coming-of-age custom that permanently affects many African girls.

Run, Boy, Run by Uri Orlev, translated from the Hebrew by Hillel Halkin. The true story of a young Jewish boy in Poland during the Holocaust who struggles to survive and escape capture by Nazi soldiers.

The Heart of a Chief by Joseph Bruchac. A Native American boy on a reservation learns how to be a leader while dealing with issues that can affect the future of his people.

This Land was Made for You and Me: The Life and Songs of Woody Guthrie by Elizabeth Partridge. Readers follow the adventures of one of this country's greatest folksingers from his youth to his travels across America during the Depression and finally to his challenges coping with a serious disease.

AWARD-WINNING BOOKS

2008 NEWBERY AWARD
Good Masters! Sweet Ladies! Voices from a Medieval Village
by Laura Amy Schlitz

2008 CALDECOTT AWARD
The Invention of Hugo Cabret by Brian Selznick

2007 BOOK SENSE BOOK OF THE YEAR FOR CHILDREN'S LITERATURE
The Book Thief by Markus Zusak

2007 NATIONAL BOOK AWARD FOR YOUNG PEOPLE'S LITERATURE
The Absolutely True Diary of a Part-Time Indian by Sherman Alexie

TYPES OF POETRY

Poetry comes in many forms. Most poetry today is written in free verse, in which there are few or no rhymes, the length of the lines vary and the lines have no predictable rhythm. In the past, several other kinds of poetry were popular. Here are three of the most famous forms.

THE LYRIC: The term *lyric* comes from the word *lyre*, which was a hand-held harp in ancient Greece. It is believed that ancient Greek poets would recite words while playing the lyre. A lyric is a kind of song in which the speaker (who may or may not be the poet) shares his or her feelings on a subject. There have been many lyric poets throughout history. Some famous ones are **John Keats** (English, 1795–1821), **William Butler Yeats** (Irish, 1865–1939), **Walt Whitman** (American, 1819–92), **Emily Dickinson** (American, 1830–86), **Seamus Heaney** (Irish, 1939–) and **Sharon Olds** (American, 1942–).

THE SONNET: This is a rhyming lyric poem that has 14 lines. The Italian poet **Francesco Petrarca (Petrarch)** (1304–74) was known for his sonnets in which the first eight lines form one thought and the last six lines form another. The most famous sonnet writer was **William Shakespeare** (English, 1564–1616). English poets **Edmund Spenser** (1552–99) and **John Milton** (1608–74) were also known for their sonnets.

Shakespeare

Whitman

A Shakespearean sonnet is divided into four parts: three sections of four lines each and the final two lines, called a couplet, which draw a conclusion.

Yeats

SONNET XVIII
by William Shakespeare

Shall I compare thee to a summer's day?
Thou art more lovely and more temperate:
Rough winds do shake the darling buds of May,
And summer's lease hath all too short a date:

Sometime too hot the eye of heaven shines,
And often is his gold complexion dimm'd;
And every fair from fair sometime declines,
By chance, or nature's changing course untrimm'd;

But thy eternal summer shall not fade,
Nor lose possession of that fair thou ow'st,
Nor shall death brag thou wander'st in his shade,
When in eternal lines to time thou grow'st;

So long as men can breathe, or eyes can see,
So long lives this, and this gives life to thee.

GUESS WHAT?

Harry Potter and the Deathly Hallows, the seventh and final book in J.K. Rowling's series, sold a total of 11 million copies in Britain and the United States in its first 24 hours on bookstore shelves.

THE HAIKU (HY-KOO):
This form of Japanese poetry began in the 16th century with the poet **Matsuo Basho** (1644–94) and spread around the world. There are many forms of haiku, but the most popular and traditional consists of 17 syllables broken up into three lines of five, seven and five syllables per line. Because it is such a short poem, a haiku relies on intense observation of nature or a single action.

Basho

TWO POEMS BY BASHO

All along this road
not a single soul—only
autumn evening comes

Wrapping dumplings in
bamboo leaves, with one finger
she tidies her hair

CAN YOU WRITE A HAIKU?

_____
_____ (5 syllables)
_____
_____ (7 syllables)
_____
_____ (5 syllables)

Famous Pseudonyms

A pseudonym, or pen name, is a name a writer may use to disguise his or her identity. Here are some real names of famous authors, along with their pseudonyms.

Currer Bell ▼
   Charlotte Brontë
Dr. Seuss ▼
   Theodore Seuss Geisel
George Eliot ▼
   Mary Ann Evans
Lewis Carroll ▼
   Charles Lutwidge Dodgson
Mark Twain ▼
   Samuel Langhorne Clemens

Brontë

By the Book

It's Larry the Librarian's first day on the job. He is up to his ears in books! Help him put each book in its place. Read each title. Decide if it belongs in Fiction, Science or Biography. Then draw a line from the book to the shelf where it belongs.

ANSWERS ON PAGE 244

TFK GAME

Mystery Person ?

CLUE 1: I was born in Britain in 1917.

CLUE 2: I am a British author who has penned dozens of science-fiction novels, including *2001: A Space Odyssey*. I also cowrote the film version of the story with director Stanley Kubrick.

CLUE 3: An asteroid and a species of ceratopsian dinosaur are named in my honor.

WHO AM I? _____

ANSWERS ON PAGE 244

AQUARIUM ARCHITECT

FROM TFK MAGAZINE

A scientist prepares a new aquarium exhibit to match animals' natural environments.

Architect Bobby Poole's career is second nature to him—and wow, does he love nature! Poole spent part of his childhood on a wildlife preserve in North Carolina. His dad was a wildlife protection officer on the preserve. They loved to fish together. Today, Poole travels the world designing aquariums.

Many architects design houses, office buildings and other structures. But Poole and his partners, Peter Chermayeff and Peter Sollogub, specialize in bright, roomy homes for underwater creatures. The three architects own a firm in Boston, Massachusetts. They have built some of the largest aquariums in the world and are working on even more aquarium projects. Two of their most famous creations are the Baltimore Aquarium in Maryland and the Osaka Ring of Fire Aquarium in Japan. About 3 million people visit the Osaka aquarium each year. They have also recently worked on the Lisbon Oceanarium and the Genoa Aquarium.

Poole and his partners put together a team of scientists, writers and artists to create each space. The architects design the building and giant fish tanks. The goal: to make sea creatures feel at home while making humans feel as if they are part of the environment. "The life-support system [in each tank] is related to specific types of marine life," Poole explains. Sea mammals such as whales need very clean water. Jellyfish are less fussy.

It's not cheap to create a terrific place for sea creatures. Building the new Marine Mammal Pavilion for the Virginia Marine Science Museum will cost $40 million! The exhibit will feature a 1.5-million–gallon aquarium for dolphins and seals. But for Poole, who recently had his "heart stolen away by a baby dolphin," bringing the wonder of the sea to millions of visitors is truly priceless.

—By Laura Weiss

Visitors check out the shark tank at the Baltimore Aquarium.

How Does That Work?

**Skyscrapers, bridges and tunnels are engineering wonders of the modern world.
Read below to learn more about them.**

SKYSCRAPERS

The base of a skyscraper is set very deeply into the ground. The taller the building, the deeper its foundation is buried. Upright steel columns are set into the base. Each floor of the skyscraper is made by attaching horizontal steel beams, called girders, to these columns. The outside of the skyscraper, usually made of glass and concrete, is attached to the girders.
EXAMPLES: Sears Tower (Chicago, IL), Empire State Building (New York, NY), Petronas Towers (Kuala Lumpur, Malaysia), Eiffel Tower (Paris, France)

Empire State Building

TUNNELS are

horizontal pathways that go underground or through water or mountains. All kinds of things can travel through tunnels: ore from mines, water and sewage from cities and people traveling by car, bus or train. Tunnels are dug using human labor, explosives, huge machines and other techniques. Some tunnels may appear to be circular, but they are really long arches that push against the weight of the rock or water all around it. Tunnels are usually dug from both ends at the same time. If the dirt around the tunnel is soft, a round shield of metal is placed inside as each section is dug. In the case of an underwater tunnel, a long trench is dug at the bottom of the body of water. Long tubes are placed in the trench and connected to one another. Then the tubes are completely covered with dirt or other material. Finally, the water in the tubes is pumped out.

The Chunnel

GUESS WHAT? The *Channel Tunnel*, or *Chunnel*, is 32 miles (9.8 km) long and connects Britain to France. Some of the boring machines used to dig the Chunnel were as long as two football fields. They could bore through 250 feet (76.2 m) of stone, mud and muck each day.

BRIDGES
There are three basic kinds of bridges: beam, arch and suspension. A **BEAM BRIDGE** consists of a horizontal structure supported by two vertical structures called piers. Beam bridges are used to span short distances. **EXAMPLES:** Belle Isle Central Avenue Bridge (Detroit, MI); Plymouth Avenue Bridge (Minneapolis, MN). Several beam bridges can be linked together to make a continuous span bridge. The Chesapeake Bay Bridge-Tunnel is one of these.

An **ARCH BRIDGE** can span a larger distance. That is because the arch is a semicircle. The arch is supported by two structures called abutments. When something passes over the arch, its weight is transferred down the arch's curve and into the abutments. **EXAMPLES:** Sydney Harbor Bridge (Sydney, Australia), Natchez Trace Bridge (Franklin, TN), New River Gorge Bridge (Fayetteville, WV)

A **SUSPENSION BRIDGE** can span the greatest distance because it uses cables, which are long chains or ropes. The cables attach to the bridge's two towers as well as to each end of the bridge. Underneath the roadway of the bridge is a strong metal frame that gives the bridge added support.
EXAMPLES: Golden Gate Bridge (San Francisco, CA), Brooklyn Bridge (New York, NY), Akashi Kaikyo Bridge (Kobe, Japan)

Eight Cool Constructions

THE GREAT PYRAMID in Giza, Egypt, is a tomb built for the pharaoh Khufu. The Great Pyramid is about 4,500 years old. It took 20,000 workers about 20 years to set more than 2 million stones in place. The average stone weighed 2.5 tons (2.3 t). At 481 feet (147 m) high, it was the tallest structure in the world for more than 3,000 years.

THE TAJ MAHAL Built in Agra, India, around 1648, it was the tomb of Mumtaz Mahal, the wife of the Muslim emperor Shah Jahan, and later the tomb of the emperor himself. It is noted for its detailed stone carvings, colorful tiles and the four tall minarets, or towers, that flank its corners. The Taj's majestic surroundings consist of a reflecting pool and a garden lined with trees and fountains.

THE EIFFEL TOWER This 1,063-foot (324-m) iron tower built by Gustave Eiffel in 1889 is the tallest structure in Paris, France. It was built to be the entrance arch to an exhibition marking the 100th anniversary of the French Revolution. Today, millions of people visit it each year, climbing it and riding its elevator to the top to get a stunning view of the city.

TAIPEI 101 This structure in Taipei, Taiwan, is currently considered the world's tallest building (1670.6 ft/509.2 m). Built to survive typhoons and earthquakes, it rises 101 stories high and has five stories below the ground. Its elevator is the fastest in the world, rising 37.7 miles per hour (60.6 km per hour).

PYRAMIDE DU LOUVRE In 1985, a plan was announced to build a glass pyramid as the entrance to the Louvre Museum in Paris. Critics immediately complained that such a modern structure would not work with the classical architecture of the Louvre. According to the architect I.M. Pei (who also designed the Rock and Roll Hall of Fame in Cleveland, Ohio, and the National Center for Atmospheric Research in Boulder, Colorado), there are 698 panes of glass in the pyramid.

GUGGENHEIM MUSEUM Museums are usually designed so that there are many rectangular rooms connected to one another. Visitors pass through room and after room and often need to retrace their steps to exit. Architect Frank Lloyd Wright wanted to try something new. At the Guggenheim Museum, which opened in New York City in 1959, visitors can take an elevator to the top of the building then walk down a continuous ramp in a spiral pattern, viewing exhibits as they go.

SYDNEY OPERA HOUSE Located in the Sydney harbor, this might be the best-known building in Australia. Danish architect Jorn Utzon won a design competition for his idea, which featured a unique roof made from interlocking "shells." The Sydney Opera House opened its doors in 1973.

SWISS RE TOWER Known throughout England as "the Gherkin" (a gherkin is a small cucumber), this commercial office building is said to be London's first environmentally sustainable skyscraper. Designed by Foster and Partners, the building was the winner of the 2004 RIBA Stirling Prize for Architecture.

Record Breaker

An office, retail and residential tower called the Burj Dubai is being built in the city of Dubai in the United Arab Emirates. Its builders are planning to make it at least 2,625 feet (800 m) high. When it is completed around June 2009, it may well be the tallest building in the world.

A Monument Matchup

STATUE OF LIBERTY

RAINBOW BRIDGE

Some of these national monuments were built by humans. Others are natural wonders. But all are exciting sights to see. Match each monument with the facts about it.

1. This natural bridge is 275 feet (84 m) long and 290 feet (88 m) high. It is the largest natural bridge in the world. You can find it in Utah. _____

2. This South Dakota sight shows four U.S. presidents. Their faces are carved into the side of a mountain. _____

3. This 151-foot (46-m) tall gift from France stands for our nation's freedom. It is located in New York City. _____

4. Sequoias are the tallest trees in the world. They touch the sky at this California hot spot. _____

5. This Washington, D.C., attraction is 555 feet (169 m) tall. It is the tallest structure in our nation's capital. _____

WASHINGTON MONUMENT

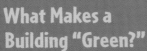

MOUNT RUSHMORE

MUIR WOODS NATIONAL MONUMENT

ANSWERS ON PAGE 244

What Makes a Building "Green?"

At a time when the earth's environment is being threatened by pollution and waste of its resources, an increasing number of architects around the world are creating "green" buildings. These buildings are designed to save energy and money by using natural materials in the most efficient way. Here are some possible characteristics of a green building:

LOCATION: Positioning the building to take advantage of sunlight and breezes

BUILDING MATERIALS: Floors and frames made from bamboo, adobe or recycled wood

PLUMBING: Toilets that use a small amount of water to flush; rainwater that is saved, filtered and used for bathing or showering and for washing clothes or cars; faucets that push a little water out at a greater pressure

HEATING: Solar panels on the roof; electricity made from wind or water power; walls and windows that keep heat inside in the winter and let heat out in the summer

New York City's first green office building is 7 World Trade Center.

TFK CALENDARS AND HOLIDAYS

2009 Calendar

JANUARY

S	M	T	W	T	F	S
				1	2	3
4	5	6	7	8	9	10
11	12	13	14	15	16	17
18	19	20	21	22	23	24
25	26	27	28	29	30	31

FEBRUARY

S	M	T	W	T	F	S
						1
2	3	4	5	6	7	8
9	10	11	12	13	14	15
16	17	18	19	20	21	22
23	24	25	26	27	28	

MARCH

S	M	T	W	T	F	S
						1
2	3	4	5	6	7	8
9	10	11	12	13	14	15
16	17	18	19	20	21	22
23	24	25	26	27	28	29
30	31					

APRIL

S	M	T	W	T	F	S
			1	2	3	4
5	6	7	8	9	10	11
12	13	14	15	16	17	18
19	20	21	22	23	24	25
26	27	28	29	30		

MAY

S	M	T	W	T	F	S
					1	2
3	4	5	6	7	8	9
10	11	12	13	14	15	16
17	18	19	20	21	22	23
24	25	26	27	28	29	30
31						

JUNE

S	M	T	W	T	F	S
	1	2	3	4	5	6
7	8	9	10	11	12	13
14	15	16	17	18	19	20
21	22	23	24	25	26	27
28	29	30				

JULY

S	M	T	W	T	F	S
			1	2	3	4
5	6	7	8	9	10	11
12	13	14	15	16	17	18
19	20	21	22	23	24	25
26	27	28	29	30	31	

AUGUST

S	M	T	W	T	F	S
						1
2	3	4	5	6	7	8
9	10	11	12	13	14	15
16	17	18	19	20	21	22
23	24	25	26	27	28	29
30	31					

SEPTEMBER

S	M	T	W	T	F	S
		1	2	3	4	5
6	7	8	9	10	11	12
13	14	15	16	17	18	19
20	21	22	23	24	25	26
27	28	29	30			

OCTOBER

S	M	T	W	T	F	S
				1	2	3
4	5	6	7	8	9	10
11	12	13	14	15	16	17
18	19	20	21	22	23	24
25	26	27	28	29	30	31

NOVEMBER

S	M	T	W	T	F	S
1	2	3	4	5	6	7
8	9	10	11	12	13	14
15	16	17	18	19	20	21
22	23	24	25	26	27	28
29	30					

DECEMBER

S	M	T	W	T	F	S
		1	2	3	4	5
6	7	8	9	10	11	12
13	14	15	16	17	18	19
20	21	22	23	24	25	26
27	28	29	30	31		

HOLIDAYS 2009

JANUARY 1: New Year's Day

JANUARY 19: Martin Luther King Day commemorates the birthday of the civil rights leader, who was born January 15, 1929.

FEBRUARY 2: Every Groundhog Day, people gather in Pennsylvania to watch a groundhog named Punxsutawney Phil emerges from his burrow. According to the story, if he sees his shadow, there will be six more weeks of winter. If he doesn't, spring is on the way.

FEBRUARY 12: Lincoln's Birthday. This holiday celebrates the life and leadership of our 16th president, Abraham Lincoln, who was born in 1809.

FEBRUARY 14: Valentine's Day

FEBRUARY 16: President's Day, a federal holiday, falls on the third Monday of the month. It honors both Abraham Lincoln and George Washington.

FEBRUARY 24: Mardi Gras, which means "Fat Tuesday" in French, is the last day of festivities before Lent begins. During Mardi Gras parades, beads are tossed into the crowd from spectacular floats. Participants wear colorful costumes and outrageous masks.

MARCH 8: Daylight Saving Time begins.

MARCH 17: St. Patrick's Day

APRIL 1: April Fool's Day

APRIL 9–16: Passover is an eight-day holiday during which Jews celebrate the Israelites being freed from slavery in Egypt.

APRIL 12: Easter. On Easter, Christians celebrate the resurrection of Jesus Christ. In addition to attending church services, many children dye Easter eggs, participate in Easter egg hunts and receive baskets of goodies from the Easter Bunny.

APRIL 22: Earth Day

MAY 5: *Cinco de Mayo* means the "fifth of May" in Spanish. It commemorates a Mexican victory over the French during a battle in 1862. It is celebrated in Mexico and within Hispanic communities in the United States.

MAY 10: Mother's Day

MAY 25: Memorial Day. This day is reserved to remember those in the armed forces who were killed during wars.

JUNE 21: Father's Day

JULY 4: Independence Day

SEPTEMBER 7: Labor Day, which honors working people, has been on the calendar since 1882.

SEPTEMBER 19: Rosh Hashanah is the first day of the Jewish new year.

SEPTEMBER 29: Yom Kippur is the Jewish day of atonement.

OCTOBER 12: Columbus Day remembers Columbus' arrival in the New World in 1492.

OCTOBER 31: Halloween

NOVEMBER 1: Daylight Saving Time ends.

NOVEMBER 11: Veteran's Day

NOVEMBER 26: Thanksgiving

DECEMBER 12–19: Hanukkah is an eight-day Jewish holiday often referred to as the "Festival of Lights."

DECEMBER 25: Christmas

A Merry Christmas

TFK TOP 5 Kids' New Year's Resolutions

Did you make a New Year's resolution? Almost 8,000 kids voted in a New Year's poll at timeforkids.com. Here are the resolutions that got the most votes. Is yours on the list?

Get better grades:	2,121 votes
Be nicer to my brother/sister:	877 votes
Eat less junk food:	869 votes
Get more sleep:	828 votes
Get more exercise:	811 votes

HOLIDAYS FROM AROUND THE WORLD

Every November 5th, people in the United Kingdom celebrate **GUY FAWKES DAY** with bonfires and fireworks. To protest the prejudice against Catholics, Guy Fawkes and other angry Catholics planned to blow up the Parliament building on November 5, 1605. The night before, Fawkes was caught in a cellar under the Parliament building with 36 barrels of gunpowder. He later confessed and was executed for treason along with others involved in the "gunpowder plot." The British throw straw dummies representing Fawkes into the bonfires to celebrate the failure of his plans.

SHICHI-GO-SAN, or "Seven-Five-Three," is a holiday in Japan that celebrates children ages 7, 5 or 3. On November 15, they dress in their best clothes and carry long, narrow paper bags decorated with symbols of youth and long life, such as pine trees, tortoises and cranes. The children and their families go to a temple or shrine to give thanks and ask for blessings for the child's future. Afterwards, the parents buy candy and toys to fill the child's bag. Once they are home, the children can exchange these for gifts from relatives.

SANTA LUCIA'S DAY marks the beginning of the holiday season for Swedes. Celebrated on December 13, it commemorates an Italian girl who lived in the fourth century and was martyred for her Christian beliefs. On the morning of Santa Lucia day, the oldest daughter of each household dresses in a long white nightgown with a red sash and wears a wreath with candles around her head. She wakes her family and brings her parents saffron buns, coffee and ginger cookies. Other girls and boys act as Lucia's helpers, walking with her in local processions. The girls dress as *tärnor*, or handmaidens, wearing long white gowns and holding candles. The boys can either be *stjärngossar* (starboys) or *tomtar* (brownies). The *stjärngossar* carry stars on poles and wear cone-shaped hats, while the *tomtar* walk at the back of the procession and carry lanterns.

During **DÍA DE LOS MUERTOS** (October 31–November 2), Mexicans believe that the souls of dead loved ones visit them. They construct colorful *ofrendas*, or altars, topped with incense, flowers, skull decorations and food. Participants make special food such as *calaveras*, which are sugary treats in the shapes of skulls, and *pan de muerto*, which is sweet bread covered in sugar. Sometimes *pan de muerto* is made in the shape of skeletons, skulls or animals. After the spirits have helped themselves, participants will eat the food from the *ofrendas*. The origins of *Día de los Muertos*, which means "Day of the Dead" in Spanish, lie in Aztec rituals that were performed for thousands of years.

HOLI marks the beginning of spring in India and is known as the "Festival of Colors." It begins with the lighting of bonfires on the full moon of the lunar month Phalunga (which falls in late February or early March). The fires often contain a dummy of Holika, a female demon whom the gods made immune to fire. According to the story, Holika tried to kill her nephew in a fire for being more faithful to the god Vishnu than to his father Hiranyakashyap, the demon king. Because she used her powers for evil, she lost her supernatural abilities and died, while her nephew lived. For Hindus, this story is a reminder that good conquers evil. The day after the bonfires, people celebrate in the street. They wear white clothing, smear paint on each other's faces and throw *gulal* (colored powder) into the air. Some people even fill squirt guns and water balloons with paint to spray on both their friends and strangers. The normally strict rules of class and gender are set aside, and there are contests between men and women.

CHINESE NEW YEAR

Chinese New Year starts on the first day of the lunar year, usually between January 21 and February 19. Before the new year starts, families clean their houses to prepare for the year ahead and to "sweep out" any bad luck from the old year. On New Year's Eve, families have a large traditional meal. Children get red packets of money from their relatives, and fireworks are set off to frighten away evil spirits. Fifteen days later, there is a festival featuring lantern processions and a dragon dance.

The Chinese Calendar

Each year on the Chinese calendar corresponds to one of twelve animals in the Chinese zodiac. This chart shows you a list of years from 1924 to 2019. In what year were you born? How about your brothers and sisters?

rat	1924	1936	1948	1960	1972	1984	1996	2008
ox	1925	1937	1949	1961	1973	1985	1997	2009
tiger	1926	1938	1950	1962	1974	1986	1998	2010
rabbit (or hare)	1927	1939	1951	1963	1975	1987	1999	2011
dragon	1928	1940	1952	1964	1976	1988	2000	2012
snake	1929	1941	1953	1965	1977	1989	2001	2013
horse	1930	1942	1954	1966	1978	1990	2002	2014
ram (or sheep)	1931	1943	1955	1967	1979	1991	2003	2015
monkey	1932	1944	1956	1968	1980	1992	2004	2016
rooster	1933	1945	1957	1969	1981	1993	2005	2017
dog	1934	1946	1958	1970	1982	1994	2006	2018
boar (or pig)	1935	1947	1959	1971	1983	1995	2007	2019

Favorite Halloween Costumes

TFK TOP 5

They're creepy and they're kooky, mysterious and spooky. Halloween costumes make the autumn holiday extra-fun for everyone. Here are the most popular dress-up choices for 2007.

1. Princess 4,168,472

2. Spider-Man 1,882,536

3. Pirate 1,848,919

4. Witch 1,647,219

5. Fairy 1,109,351

Creepy Counting

TFK GAME

What makes Halloween scary? Let's add up the spooky sights!

1. Count the stars in the sky. Is the number even or odd? _____

2. Bats outnumber cats by how many? _____

3. True or false: There are more bats than ghosts. _____

4. Two ghosts leave for a haunted-house party. How many ghosts are left? _____

ANSWERS ON PAGE 244

PROTECT YOUR SPACE

FROM TFK MAGAZINE

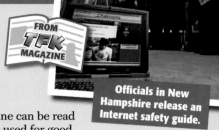

Officials in New Hampshire release an Internet safety guide.

Bridget M., 15, had a lot of fun at a party thrown by her cousin. At the gathering, she and nine other girls hung out, played games and gossiped. They ended up taking crazy photographs of each other posing as fashion models. But the fun ended days later, when Bridget's cousin e-mailed the pictures to one of the girls at the party. The girl posted them on her MySpace page.

The photos were meant to be seen only by the partygoers. But with the click of a computer mouse, they ended up on several more profiles and began to attract attention online. "We didn't think anyone else would see them," Bridget told TFK. Luckily, the images also caught the eye of Bridget's uncle. He immediately contacted the girls' parents, and the photos were removed from the pages that could be accessed by strangers.

A GROWING WORRY

Bridget's experience is not unique. As the use of social-networking sites like MySpace and Facebook has soared, so has the number of kids who reveal too much about themselves online. The sites allow users to create profiles and display personal information to build networks of friends.

According to the Pew Research Center, 29% of teens online have posted their full name and e-mail address in their profiles. Some 79% have included photos of themselves. And 21% of those who have been contacted by a stranger online have responded to that person.

The Internet has transformed life for this generation of kids in an overwhelmingly positive way. But sharing personal information, including social plans and passwords, can make networking sites dangerous places for kids. Anything that is posted online can be read and used for good or bad by friends, enemies and even strangers. Amber Casselman, 11, told TFK Kid Reporter Machaela Jensen that she e-mailed her Webkinz password to a friend. The friend passed it on to another girl, who changed the password. "Now, when I log in, it doesn't work," said Amber.

A NETWORK FOR SAFETY

Internet companies are working to protect kids from such online risks. After hearing such concerns, MySpace agreed with legal authorities in 49 states to take steps to shield kids from online threats. The new measures include blocking users over 18 from contacting kids they don't know, and searching for ways to involve parents. Kid-friendly social-networking sites, like Imbee and i-Safe, have created secure places for kids to hang out online. The kids-only chat rooms on i-Safe encourage users to "keep it cool, clean and positive." Imbee requires parents to set up an account.

Some states are working on laws to require schools to teach cybersafety. Virginia has had such a law since 2006. But parents, teachers, Internet companies and the law can only do so much to keep you safe. They can't be there every time you click "send."

BEWARE AND AWARE

Katie Canton, of the education site Web Wise Kids, says kids need to protect themselves. How? By being aware of what they are revealing and whom they are talking to. "It's easy to think that you're safe online because you're in your bedroom," Katie told TFK. "But it's your job to protect yourself and your friends."

—By Joe McGowan

STAYING SAFE WHILE YOU SURF

Protect yourself from being a cyber-victim by following these simple tips:

• Talk with your parents about when and how you will use the Internet and send e-mails and instant messages. Together, create a "pledge" all of you can sign, and review this pledge from time to time to see if any changes are needed.

• Never give out personal information—such as your name, address, phone number, school, a photo, where you like to hang out or whether or not you are home alone—to anyone who contacts you unless your parents say it's okay.

• If you ever receive a message that frightens you or makes you uncomfortable, tell your parents or your teacher. Also tell your parents if anyone you don't know wants to send you a gift or tells you to keep your communication with them private.

• Don't make plans to meet in person anyone you've met online unless your parents give you permission and accompany you.

• Never share your passwords with anyone except your parents.

• Treat everyone on the Internet the same way you would want to be treated. Don't be a bully.

• Don't open any e-mails from senders you don't recognize. To see if it's from a sender who is safe, learn how to view the message's source without opening up the message itself.

GUESS WHAT?
More than 50 million U.S. students between the ages of 5 and 17 use computers regularly.

IM Dictionary

Chatting online takes more time than chatting aloud, so clever computer users have come up with a shorthand to speed up IM conversations.

KIT LOL! YW

BTW 143!

!	I have a comment
?	I have a question
121	one to one
143	I love you
2moro	tomorrow
2nite	tonight
AEAP	as early as possible
ALAP	as late as possible
BRB	be right back
BTW	by the way
CBB	can't be bothered
CTO	check this out
DETI	don't even think it
EML	e-mail me later
FSR	for some reason
FYI	for your information
GAS	got a second
GTG	got to go
IDK	I don't know
J/C	just checking
KIT	keep in touch
LOL	laughing out loud
NTW	not to worry
OTP	on the phone
RUT	Are you there?
SOT	short on time
SUP	What's up?
T@YL	talk to you later
TTFN	ta ta for now
U Up	Are you up?
WDYT	What do you think?
YW	you're welcome

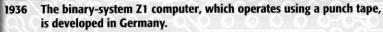

COMPUTER TIMELINE

The modern computer is a pretty new device. It came about in the 20th century. Check out this timeline of some computer milestones.

ENIAC

A computer in 1953

A 1973 NASA computer

An early cell phone

1936	The binary-system Z1 computer, which operates using a punch tape, is developed in Germany.
1945	Programmer Grace Hopper coins the term computer "bug." The first electronic computer, ENIAC (Electronic Numerical Integrator and Computer), is completed.
1950	The first chess-playing machine is built at the Massachusetts Institute of Technology.
1952	The first game of tic-tac-toe is played on a computer.
1955	The term "artificial intelligence" is coined by mathematics professor John McCarthy of Dartmouth College.
1958	The first microchip is demonstrated.
1961	General Motors Company starts up the first industrial robot, named Unimate, in its factory in New Jersey. It weighs 4,000 pounds (1,800 kg).
1962	"SpaceWar!," the first game specifically intended for computers, is released.
1963	The computer mouse is invented and patented.
1967	The first floppy disc is created by IBM.
1969	Four American universities are linked by an electronic communications network called ARPANET. This event is considered the beginning of the Internet.
1970	The first computer language for guided missile systems is created. The microprocessor is invented.
1972	Network e-mail is introduced, and the compact disc is invented. Atari's Pong is the first commercial videogame.
1973	The first cellular phone call is made.
1974	The term "Internet" is coined.
1975	Bill Gates and Paul Allen start Microsoft.
1976	The 5¼-inch floppy disc is introduced. Steve Jobs and Steve Wozniak found Apple Computers.
1977	Apple, Radio Shack and Commodore begin selling computers on a widespread scale.

Steve Jobs, John Scully and Steve Wozniak with the Apple IIc computer

GUESS WHAT?
According to the International Telecommunications Union, 1,131,000,000 people used the Internet in 2006. That's about one-sixth of the world's population.

1981 The IBM PC enters the market.

1982 The WordPerfect word-processing program is introduced.

1983 Microsoft Windows is introduced.

1984 The first Apple Macintosh is sold.

1985 The Nintendo Entertainment System is released.

1991 Tim Berners-Lee launches the World Wide Web as a research tool.

1993 A White House Web page is created, as well as e-mail addresses for the President, Vice President and First Lady.

1994 Yahoo.com is launched.
In a speech, Vice President Al Gore coins the phrase "information superhighway."

1995 Amazon.com and eBay are launched.
Hotmail is announced.
An open-editing database, called a "wiki," is created.

1998 The first Internet Web logs, or "blogs" appear.
Sergey Brin and Larry Page found Google.
Apple launches the iMac.

2000 The Y2K scare concerning computers' ability to switch from years beginning with the numbers "19" to years beginning with "20" proves to be unfounded. No major glitches occur.

2001 Apple launches the iPod.

2003 MySpace.com is founded.

2004 Google launches Gmail. Facebook.com is created.

2005 YouTube.com goes live.

2006 High-definition (HD) DVDs are introduced.

2007 Microsoft Windows Vista and Apple's iPhone are available to the public.

Berners-Lee

Amazon.com's first gateway page

Google founders

MySpace.com

Japanese girls surf the Web.

Top 10 Countries with the Most Personal Computers

COUNTRY	NUMBER IN MILLIONS	PERCENTAGE OF TOTAL COMPUTERS WORLDWIDE
1. U.S.	240.5	24.15
2. Japan	77.95	7.83
3. China	74.11	7.44
4. Germany	54.48	5.47
5. U.K.	41.53	4.17
6. France	35.99	3.61
7. South Korea	30.62	3.07
8. Italy	29.31	2.94
9. Russia	26.97	2.71
10. Brazil	25.99	2.61

Source: Computer Industry Almanac, www.c-i-a.com

HELPFUL INTERNET RESOURCES

GENERAL

TIME FOR KIDS www.timeforkids.com

4Kids.org 4kids.org

Smithsonian Education
www.smithsonianeducation.org/students

Brain Pop www.brainpop.com

Homework Help Yahoo! Kids
kids.yahoo.com/learn

Internet Public Library www.ipl.org/div/kidspace;
www.ipl.org/div/teen

ART

The Artist's Toolkit
www.artsconnected.
org/toolkit

Museum Kids
www.metmuseum.
org/explore/museumkids.htm

NGA (National Gallery of Art) Kids
www.nga.gov/kids

WebMuseum, Paris www.ibiblio.org/wm/

BIOGRAPHY

Biography.com www.biography.com

Academy of Achievement www.achievement.org/
galleryachieve.html

ECOLOGY & THE ENVIRONMENT

EPA Environmental Kids Club www.epa.gov/kids

Illinois EPA Envirofun
www.epa.state.il.us/
kids/index.html

**National Institute of
Environmental Health
Sciences (NIEHS)
Kids' Pages** kids.
niehs.nih.gov/

GEOGRAPHY

National Geographic Kids kids.nationalgeographic.
com/; magma.nationalgeographic.com/
ngexplorer/

Central Intelligence Agency–The World Factbook
www.cia.gov/library/publications/the-world-
factbook/

50states.com
www.50states.com

GOVERNMENT & POLITICS

Kids.gov www.kids.gov

Congress for Kids
www.congressforkids.net

White House Kids www.
whitehouse.gov/kids

HEALTH

KidsHealth www.kidshealth.org/kid;
www.kidshealth.org/teen

BAM! Body and Mind www.bam.gov

Kidnetic.com www.kidnetic.com

HISTORY

History.com This Day in History www.history.
com/this-day-in-history.do

Women in World History www.
womeninworldhistory.com/

America's Library www.americaslibrary.gov

PBS African American World www.pbs.org/wnet/
aaworld

NativeWeb www.nativeweb.org/resources/history

LITERATURE, LANGUAGE & COMMUNICATION

FCC Kids Zone www.fcc.gov/cgb/kidszone

Aaron Shepard's Home Page www.aaronshep.
com/index.html

Sylvan Book Adventure bookadventure.org/ki/bs/
ki_bs_helpfind.asp

ABC's of the Writing Process www.angelfire.com/
wi/writingprocess/index.html

RIF Reading Planet www.rif.org/readingplanet

The Blue Book of Grammar and Punctuation
www.grammarbook.com

MUSIC, GAMES & ENTERTAINMENT

Zoom: By Kids for Kids pbskids.org/zoom/games/
index.html

**Dallas Symphony
Orchestra (DSO)
Kids** www.dsokids.
com/2001/rooms/
musicroom.asp

**San Francisco
Symphony
(SFS) Kids** www.sfskids.org

A Game a Day www.agameaday.com

PBS Kids Games pbskids.org/games/index.html

FunBrain.com www.funbrain.com/kidscenter.html

Club Penguin www.clubpenguin.com/

GUESS WHAT?

The first emoticons ever used were the "smiley" and "frownie" on September 19, 1982, by Scott Fahlman of Carnegie Mellon University. In an e-mail bulletin-board message, he suggested these symbols be added to messages to clarify the sender's meaning and avoid misunderstandings.

NATURE

Animal Corner **www.animalcorner.co.uk**
Kids' Planet **www.kidsplanet.org/**
National Wildlife Federation **www.nwf.org/kids/**

NEWS & CURRENT EVENTS

Yahoo! Kids News **kids.**
  yahoo.com/news
TIME FOR KIDS News
  www.timeforkids.com

SCIENCE, TECHNOLOGY & MATHEMATICS

The Exploratorium, San Francisco
  www.exploratorium.edu/
Ask Dr. Universe **www.**
  wsu.edu/DrUniverse
The Yuckiest Site on
  the Internet **yucky.**
  discovery.com/flash/
Discovery Kids **kids.**
  discovery.com/
CoolMath.com **www.coolmath.com**
Webmath.com **www.webmath.com**
Ask Dr. Math **www.mathforum.org/dr.math**

SPORTS

Sports Illustrated Kids
  www.sikids.com
Major League
  Baseball
  www.mlb.com
Major League Soccer **www.mlsnet.com**
National Basketball Association **www.nba.com**
Women's National Basketball Association
  www.wnba.com
National Football League **www.nfl.com**
National Hockey League **www.nhl.com**

Is the Web Site You Are Reading Reliable?

- **Look at the Web site address, or URL. What letters does it end with? The suffixes** .edu, .gov **and** .org **stand for educational, governmental and (nonprofit) organizational institutions. The information on these pages is often trustworthy.**

- **Click on links labeled "About Us" or "About the Author" to identify the writer(s). Look for the author's credentials, such as educational degrees, experience and other published material that relates to the content of the Web page. If the site is written by an organization, check to see that it is a legitimate group.**

- **How current is the information on the page? Check out the publication date, copyright date or "last update" line (usually at the bottom of the page) to see how up-to-date the information is.**

- **Consider the quality of the site. Is the page cluttered and confusing? Are there spelling and grammatical errors? Do the links work? A reliable Web site often includes footnotes and/or a bibliography.**

Online Searching Tips

Try these tips when searching online:

1. Putting an "AND" between two words will reveal sites in which both words appear (ecology AND environment).

2. Putting an "OR" between two words will reveal sites where at least one word will appear (ecology OR environment).

3. Separating words or phrases with "NOT" will reduce the search to only those words you want (George Washington NOT Carver).

4. Using * or ? to stand for missing letters will reveal sites in which variations of that word appear (ecolog* will reveal sites containing ecology and ecological; wom?n will reveal sites containing woman and women).

5. Putting quotation marks around a phrase ("artificial intelligence") will reveal sites with that exact phrase.

Video Games By the Numbers

VIDEO GAME HARDWARE	UNITS SOLD IN 2007	TOTAL UNITS SOLD BY JAN. 1, 2008
Nintendo DS	8.50 million	17.65 million
Wii	6.29 million	7.38 million
Xbox 360	4.62 million	9.15 million
PlayStation 2	3.97 million	41.12 million
PlayStation Portable	3.82 million	10.47 million
PlayStation 3	2.56 million	3.25 million

Source: The NDP Group

Best-Selling Video Games of 2007

GAME	MILLIONS SOLD
1. Halo 3 (Xbox 360)	4.82
2. Wii Play w/remote (Wii)	4.12
3. Call of Duty 4: Modern Warfare (Xbox 360)	3.04
4. Guitar Hero III: Legends of Rock (PlayStation 2)	2.72
5. Super Mario Galaxy (Wii)	2.52

Source: The NDP Group

Best-Selling Games for PCs in 2007

GAME	NUMBER SOLD
1. World of Warcraft: The Burning Crusade	2.25 million
2. World of Warcraft	914,000
3. The Sims 2	534,000
4. The Sims 2 Seasons Expansion Pack	433,000
5. Call of Duty 4: Modern Warfare	383,000

Source: The NDP Group

2007 Webby Awards

Activism: Green my Apple
www.greenpeace.org/apple

Art: Electrolux Design Lab
www.electrolux.com/designlab/

Education: HowStuffWorks
www.howstuffworks.com

Fashion: ZOOZOOM "The Original Online Glossy"
www.zoozoom.com

Games: Samorost2
www.samorost.net/samorost2/

Magazine: MediaStorm
mediastorm.org

Movie & Film: Pan's Labyrinth
www.panslabyrinth.com

Music: Last.fm
www.last.fm

News: BBC News
www.bbc.co.uk/news

Science: HubbleSite
hubblesite.org

Sports: The Reggie Bush Project
www.thereggiebushproject.com

Television: Current TV
www.current.tv

Youth: OwnYourC
www.ownyourc.com

YouTube founders Steve Chen and Chad Hurley won a Webby for being "Person of the Year."

File-Sharing Sites

File-sharing sites are on the rise. They allow users to download, copy or change information on a site. This application takes many forms, from music and video downloads (iTunes, YouTube, Napster, iMesh) to social networking (MySpace, Facebook, Kazaa).

CELLULAR TECHNOLOGY

CELL PHONES are much more than voice-communication devices. They can send and receive e-mail and text messages, surf the Internet, take pictures, keep track of appointments, transmit TV programs, navigate using global positioning, download music and more. How can a small hand-held device do so much? Here are the basics:

CELL PHONES: These are sophisticated radios that tune in to frequencies transmitted by towers located all over. Each tower covers a range of about 10 square miles (26 sq km).

TOWERS: These are usually made of steel and are hundreds of feet tall. Sometimes they are disguised to look like other structures, such as flagpoles or even trees. The towers have antennae and transmitters that are often shared by several different phone companies. As a cell phone user moves from place to place, a different tower picks up the signal and transmits to it.

TECHNOLOGY: Unlike on a walkie-talkie or CB radio where only one person can speak at a time, cell phones have a dual-frequency capacity. They can send and receive signals at the same time. This allows the speaker and the listener to talk at the same time, as on a regular telephone. Inside the phone is a microprocessor that is similar to one inside a computer. It enables the phone to act like a computer and do such a wide variety of tasks.

SATELLITE PHONES use a different technology. They bypass landlines and cellular networks by relying on "low Earth orbiting" satellites to receive and relay phone messages. This technology is valuable especially during weather disasters, which can break land wires and topple cellular towers. The signal of a satellite call is sent to the satellites of the caller's phone company. These satellites receive the call and send it back to Earth using a ground station, or gateway. The gateway then sends the call to the recipient using regular landlines or cellular networks.

WIRELESS FIDELITY (WiFi) or **BROADBAND SERVICE** uses low-power microwave radio signals to connect computers to the Internet using wireless network cards and hubs. The advantage of this system is that a computer need not be connected to an electrical or telephone outlet or cable line.

Wireless router

Some cities and towns have outfitted parks and open spaces with wireless connections.

GUESS WHAT? A December 2007, Nielsen report on kids ages 8 to 12 estimated that 35% of tweens own a mobile phone, 20% have used text messaging and 21% have used ringtones and answer tones.

GUESS WHAT? By August 2007, more than 3 billion people subscribed to a cell-phone plan. That's nearly half the world's population.

COMPUTERS AND COMMUNICATION

53

TOUGH LESSONS

Girls at Zarghona High School in Kabul study under a tent.

Principal Surava Sarwary loves the sound of her second-grade girls reciting a new lesson. Prior to 2001 that sound would have put her life in danger. Back then, Afghanistan was controlled by the Taliban (tah-*lee*-bahn). Its members enforce an extremely strict version of Islam. The Taliban outlawed education for girls. A few brave teachers taught them in secret. Sarwary, 36, recalls gathering students in her home and whispering lessons, for fear that neighbors might report her. These days, as the principal of a school with 1,500 students in Herat province, she worries that the girls' voices may drown out the math lesson next door.

"Our students have talent and a passion for learning," she says. "But we still have problems." Girls are so eager to go to school that the building cannot possibly hold all of them. The second graders huddle in a ragged tent, where torn canvas blocks many girls' view of the blackboard. The fierce desert wind threatens to tear the one textbook from students' hands. There is no playground, no running water, only a hole in the ground for a bathroom. Yet the school is one of the most successful in Herat, and Herat has the top schools in the nation.

A NEW CHANCE TO LEARN

After the Taliban was toppled by U.S.-led forces in 2001, the rest of the world cheered Afghan women's newfound chance at equal rights and an education. "If women are educated, that means their children will be too," says Ghulam Hazrat Tanha, Herat's director of education.

Since 2001, 3,500 new schools have opened. But more than half of these are in tents or outside, under shade trees. Funds for education are not a top priority. Of the 40,000 teachers needed this year, the government has budgeted for only 10,000.

AFGHANISTAN'S TRADITION OF SEPARATION

The Taliban policy of keeping girls out of school was based on a strong cultural belief that women should not mix with unrelated men. "My family says that they would rather I be illiterate than taught by a man," says Yasamin Rezzaie, 18.

A recent report by the international aid group Oxfam shows that boys outnumber girls in primary school by a ratio of two to one. But by high school, there are four boys for every girl. Overall, only 10% of girls in school actually graduate. The same report identifies another factor holding girls back: Only 28% of the country's accredited teachers are women. If so few girls graduate, where will the next generation of women teachers come from?

AGAINST THE ODDS

Afghanistan's leaders face another harsh reality: The Taliban is making a strong comeback in some places. In little over a year, 130 schools have been burned, 105 students and teachers killed and 307 schools closed down due to security concerns. On June 12, two gunmen fired on a crowd of female students in Logar province. Lida Ahmadyar, a 12-year-old whose sister was killed in the shooting, went back to school last month. She clings to her dream of becoming a doctor. "I am afraid," she says. "But I like school because I am learning something, and that will make me important. With education, I can save my country." If enough Afghan girls get the chance to finish school, they will do just that.

THE WORLD'S NATIONS FROM A TO Z

On the following pages you will find information about the world's nations. Here's an example.

If you divide the population by the area, you can find out the population density—how many people there are per square mile.

This tells the main languages and the official languages (if any) spoken in a nation. In this case, most people in the nation speak Icelandic.

This is the type of money used in the nation.

Life expectancy is the number of years a person can expect to live. It's affected by heredity, a person's health and nutrition, the health care and wealth of a nation and a person's occupation.

This tells the percentage of people who can read and write.

This is an interesting fact about the country.

ICELAND

LOCATION: Europe
CAPITAL: Reykjavik
AREA: 39,768 sq mi (103,000 sq km)
POPULATION ESTIMATE (2007): 301,931
GOVERNMENT: Constitutional republic
LANGUAGES: Icelandic, English
MONEY: Icelandic krona
LIFE EXPECTANCY: 80.4
LITERACY RATE: 99%
GUESS WHAT? *Iceland's legislative body, the Althing, was established in 930 A.D. It is the oldest active parliament in the world.*

AFGHANISTAN

LOCATION: Asia
CAPITAL: Kabul
AREA: 251,737 sq mi (647,500 sq km)
POPULATION ESTIMATE (2007): 31,889,923
GOVERNMENT: Islamic republic
LANGUAGES: Pushtu and Dari Persian (both official), others
MONEY: Afghani
LIFE EXPECTANCY: 43.7
LITERACY RATE: 28%
GUESS WHAT?
Afghanistan was occupied by the Soviet Union for nine years. The troop withdrawal began in 1988 and ended in February 1989.

Background: Algeria

ALGERIA

LOCATION: Africa
CAPITAL: Algiers
AREA: 919,590 sq mi (2,381,740 sq km)
POPULATION ESTIMATE (2007): 33,333,216
GOVERNMENT: Republic
LANGUAGES: Arabic (official), French, Berber dialects
MONEY: Dinar
LIFE EXPECTANCY: 73.5
LITERACY RATE: 70%
GUESS WHAT? *The rock art found at Tassili-n-Ajjer dates back to 6000 B.C. The paintings show the area as green and lush rather than the dry sandy desert it is today.*

ALBANIA

LOCATION: Europe
CAPITAL: Tirana
AREA: 11,100 sq mi (28,750 sq km)
POPULATION ESTIMATE (2007): 3,600,523
GOVERNMENT: Emerging democracy
LANGUAGES: Albanian (Tosk is the official dialect), Greek
MONEY: Lek
LIFE EXPECTANCY: 77.6
LITERACY RATE: 98%
GUESS WHAT? *The ancient town of Butrint is one of Albania's most important archeological sites.*

ANDORRA

LOCATION: Europe
CAPITAL: Andorra la Vella
AREA: 181 sq mi (468 sq km)
POPULATION ESTIMATE (2007): 71,822
GOVERNMENT: Parliamentary democracy
LANGUAGES: Catalán (official), French, Spanish, Portuguese
MONEY: Euro (formerly French franc and Spanish peseta)
LIFE EXPECTANCY: 83.5
LITERACY RATE: 100%
GUESS WHAT? *Even though tourism is the backbone of the economy, there are no airports in Andorra.*

ANGOLA

LOCATION: Africa
CAPITAL: Luanda
AREA: 481,350 sq mi (1,246,700 sq km)
POPULATION ESTIMATE (2007): 12,263,596
GOVERNMENT: Republic
LANGUAGES: Bantu, Portuguese (official)
MONEY: Kwanza
LIFE EXPECTANCY: 37.6
LITERACY RATE: 67%
GUESS WHAT? *After 14 years of guerilla fighting, Angola won independence from Portugal in 1975.*

ANTIGUA AND BARBUDA

LOCATION: North America
CAPITAL: St. John's
AREA: 171 sq mi (443 sq km)
POPULATION ESTIMATE (2007): 69,481
GOVERNMENT: Constitutional monarchy
LANGUAGE: English
MONEY: East Caribbean dollar
LIFE EXPECTANCY: 72.4
LITERACY RATE: 86%
GUESS WHAT? *Antigua, pronounced an-TEE-guh, is only 14 miles (23 km) long and 11 miles (18 km) wide.*

ARGENTINA

LOCATION: South America
CAPITAL: Buenos Aires
AREA: 1,068,296 sq mi (2,766,890 sq km)
POPULATION ESTIMATE (2007): 40,301,927
GOVERNMENT: Republic
LANGUAGES: Spanish (official), English, Italian, German, French
MONEY: Argentine peso
LIFE EXPECTANCY: 76.3
LITERACY RATE: 97%
GUESS WHAT? *Some of the oldest dinosaur fossils ever found have been located in Argentina.*

ARMENIA

LOCATION: Asia
CAPITAL: Yerevan
AREA: 11,500 sq mi (29,800 sq km)
POPULATION ESTIMATE (2007): 2,971,650
GOVERNMENT: Republic
LANGUAGE: Armenian
MONEY: Dram
LIFE EXPECTANCY: 72.1
LITERACY RATE: 99%
GUESS WHAT? *Although Mount Ararat is located in Turkey, it is one of Armenia's national symbols.*

Background: Argentina

AUSTRALIA

LOCATION: Pacific Ocean
CAPITAL: Canberra
AREA: 2,967,893 sq mi (7,686,850 sq km)
POPULATION ESTIMATE (2007): 20,434,176
GOVERNMENT: Democracy
LANGUAGE: English
MONEY: Australian dollar
LIFE EXPECTANCY: 80.6
LITERACY RATE: 99%
GUESS WHAT?
Koala bears are protected by law in Australia. They are not related to bears, but are marsupials like kangaroos, possums and wombats.

AUSTRIA

LOCATION: Europe
CAPITAL: Vienna
AREA: 32,375 sq mi (83,850 sq km)
POPULATION ESTIMATE (2007): 8,199,783
GOVERNMENT: Federal Republic
LANGUAGE: German
MONEY: Euro (formerly schilling)
LIFE EXPECTANCY: 79.2
LITERACY RATE: 98%
GUESS WHAT?
Artist Gustav Klimt and composers Wolfgang Amadeus Mozart and Franz Schubert were all born in Austria.

AZERBAIJAN

LOCATION: Asia
CAPITAL: Baku
AREA: 33,400 sq mi (86,600 sq km)
POPULATION ESTIMATE (2007): 8,120,247
GOVERNMENT: Republic
LANGUAGES: Azerbaijani, Lezgi, Russian, Armenian
MONEY: Manat
LIFE EXPECTANCY: 66
LITERACY RATE: 99%
GUESS WHAT? *The Nagorno-Karabakh section of Azerbaijan has a heavily Armenian population. The two countries have been fighting over this area off and on since 1918.*

BAHAMAS

LOCATION: North America
CAPITAL: Nassau
AREA: 5,380 sq mi (13,940 sq km)
POPULATION ESTIMATE (2007): 305,655
GOVERNMENT: Parliamentary democracy
LANGUAGES: English, Creole
MONEY: Bahamian dollar
LIFE EXPECTANCY: 65.7
LITERACY RATE: 96%
GUESS WHAT? *The 700 islands that make up the Bahamas are spread over 100,000 square miles (259,000 sq km) of ocean.*

BAHRAIN

LOCATION: Asia
CAPITAL: Manama
AREA: 257 sq mi (665 sq km)
POPULATION ESTIMATE (2007): 708,573
GOVERNMENT: Constitutional monarchy
LANGUAGES: Arabic (official), English, Farsi, Urdu
MONEY: Bahraini dinar
LIFE EXPECTANCY: 74.7
LITERACY RATE: 87%
GUESS WHAT? *There is a Formula One race track in Bahrain.*

Background: Barbados

BANGLADESH

LOCATION: Asia
CAPITAL: Dhaka
AREA: 55,598 sq mi (144,000 sq km)
POPULATION ESTIMATE (2007): 150,448,339
GOVERNMENT: Parliamentary democracy
LANGUAGES: Bangla (official), English
MONEY: Taka
LIFE EXPECTANCY: 62.8
LITERACY RATE: 43%
GUESS WHAT? *Bangladesh is a flat country. Roughly 90% of the land is less than 33 feet (10 m) above sea level.*

BARBADOS

LOCATION: North America
CAPITAL: Bridgetown
AREA: 166 sq mi (431 sq km)
POPULATION ESTIMATE (2007): 280,946
GOVERNMENT: Parliamentary democracy
LANGUAGE: English
MONEY: Barbadian dollar
LIFE EXPECTANCY: 73
LITERACY RATE: 100%
GUESS WHAT? *Of the Caribbean Islands, Barbados is the farthest east, putting it first in line for hurricanes.*

BELARUS

LOCATION: Europe
CAPITAL: Minsk
AREA: 80,154 sq mi (207,600 sq km)
POPULATION ESTIMATE (2007): 9,724,723
GOVERNMENT: Republic
LANGUAGES: Belarusian, Russian
MONEY: Belarusian ruble
LIFE EXPECTANCY: 70
LITERACY RATE: 100%
GUESS WHAT? *The 730-year old Belaya Vezha, or White Tower, is the symbol of Belarus.*

BELGIUM

LOCATION: Europe
CAPITAL: Brussels
AREA: 11,781 sq mi (30,510 sq km)
POPULATION ESTIMATE (2007): 10,392,226
GOVERNMENT: Parliamentary democracy under a constitutional monarchy
LANGUAGES: Dutch (Flemish), French, German (all official)
MONEY: Euro (formerly Belgian franc)
LIFE EXPECTANCY: 78.4
LITERACY RATE: 98%
GUESS WHAT? *Since the Renaissance, Belgium has been famous for its handmade lace.*

BELIZE

LOCATION: Central America
CAPITAL: Belmopan
AREA: 8,865 sq mi (22,960 sq km)
POPULATION ESTIMATE (2007): 294,385
GOVERNMENT: Parliamentary democracy
LANGUAGES: English (official), Creole, Spanish, Garifuna, Mayan
MONEY: Belizean dollar
LIFE EXPECTANCY: 67.4
LITERACY RATE: 94%
GUESS WHAT? *Much of Belize is made up of tropical rainforests, which are home to many species of exotic plants, including 250 types of orchids.*

BENIN

LOCATION: Africa
CAPITAL: Porto-Novo
AREA: 43,483 sq mi (112,620 sq km)
POPULATION ESTIMATE (2007): 8,078,314
GOVERNMENT: Republic
LANGUAGES: French (official), Fon, Yoruba, other African languages
MONEY: CFA franc
LIFE EXPECTANCY: 53.4
LITERACY RATE: 35%
GUESS WHAT? *Benin was known as the Kingdom of Dahomey until 1974.*

BHUTAN

LOCATION: Asia
CAPITAL: Thimphu
AREA: 18,147 sq mi (47,000 sq km)
POPULATION ESTIMATE (2007): 2,327,849
GOVERNMENT: Monarchy
LANGUAGE: Dzongkha
MONEY: Ngultrum
LIFE EXPECTANCY: 55.2
LITERACY RATE: 47%
GUESS WHAT? *The national dish of Bhutan is called* emadatse *and is made with spicy chilies and cheese.* Emadatse *is often served with rice.*

BOLIVIA

LOCATION: South America
CAPITAL: La Paz (seat of government), Sucre (legal capital)
AREA: 424,162 sq mi (1,098,580 sq km)
POPULATION ESTIMATE (2007): 9,119,152
GOVERNMENT: Republic
LANGUAGES: Spanish, Quechua, Aymara (all official)
MONEY: Boliviano
LIFE EXPECTANCY: 66.2
LITERACY RATE: 87%
GUESS WHAT? *Some traditional Bolivian music is played on the* charango, *a type of guitar made from the shell of an armadillo.*

BOSNIA AND HERZEGOVINA

LOCATION: Europe
CAPITAL: Sarajevo
AREA: 19,741 sq mi (51,129 sq km)
POPULATION ESTIMATE (2007): 4,552,198
GOVERNMENT: Emerging democracy
LANGUAGES: The language is called Serbian, Croatian or Bosnian depending on the speaker.
MONEY: Convertible mark
LIFE EXPECTANCY: 72.6
LITERACY RATE: 94.6%
GUESS WHAT? *Much of Bosnia and Herzegovina is mountainous. The country's highest peak, Mt. Maglic, is 7,831 feet (2,387 m) tall.*

BOTSWANA

LOCATION: Africa
CAPITAL: Gaborone
AREA: 231,800 sq mi (600,370 sq km)
POPULATION ESTIMATE (2007): 1,815,508
GOVERNMENT: Parliamentary republic
LANGUAGES: English (official), Setswana, Kalanga
MONEY: Pula
LIFE EXPECTANCY: 50.6
LITERACY RATE: 81%
GUESS WHAT?
Botswana's Tsodilo Hills may have been inhabited for as many as 100,000 years. Located in the Kalahari desert, the Tsodilo Hills are home to more than 4,000 rock paintings.

BRAZIL

LOCATION: South America
CAPITAL: Brasília
AREA: 3,286,470 sq mi (8,511,965 sq km)
POPULATION ESTIMATE (2007): 190,010,647
GOVERNMENT: Federal republic
LANGUAGES: Portuguese (official), Spanish, English, French
MONEY: Real
LIFE EXPECTANCY: 72.2
LITERACY RATE: 89%
GUESS WHAT? Brazil has won the FIFA World Cup five times—that's more than any other country.

Background: Brazil

BRUNEI

LOCATION: Asia
CAPITAL: Bandar Seri Begawan
AREA: 2,228 sq mi (5,770 sq km)
POPULATION ESTIMATE (2007): 374,577
GOVERNMENT: Constitutional sultanate
LANGUAGES: Malay (official), Chinese, English
MONEY: Bruneian dollar
LIFE EXPECTANCY: 75.3
LITERACY RATE: 93%
GUESS WHAT? Brunei is similar in size to the state of Delaware.

BULGARIA

LOCATION: Europe
CAPITAL: Sofia
AREA: 48,822 sq mi (110,910 sq km)
POPULATION ESTIMATE (2007): 7,322,858
GOVERNMENT: Parliamentary democracy
LANGUAGE: Bulgarian, Turkish
MONEY: Lev
LIFE EXPECTANCY: 72.6
LITERACY RATE: 98%
GUESS WHAT?
Bulgaria joined the European Union in 2007.

BURKINA FASO

LOCATION: Africa
CAPITAL: Ouagadougou
AREA: 105,870 sq mi (274,200 sq km)
POPULATION ESTIMATE (2007): 14,326,203
GOVERNMENT: Parliamentary republic
LANGUAGES: French (official), tribal languages
MONEY: CFA franc
LIFE EXPECTANCY: 49.2
LITERACY RATE: 22%
GUESS WHAT? Burkina Faso has the largest population of *elephants* in West Africa.

BURUNDI

LOCATION: Africa
CAPITAL: Bujumbura
AREA: 10,745 sq mi (27,830 sq km)
POPULATION ESTIMATE (2007): 8,390,505
GOVERNMENT: Republic
LANGUAGES: Kirundi and French (both official), Swahili
MONEY: Burundi franc
LIFE EXPECTANCY: 51.3
LITERACY RATE: 59%
GUESS WHAT? Burundi is a land-locked country, but its southwest border falls on Lake Tanganyika, which is one of the largest lakes in the world.

CAMBODIA

LOCATION: Asia
CAPITAL: Phnom Penh
AREA: 69,900 sq mi (181,040 sq km)
POPULATION ESTIMATE (2007): 13,995,904
GOVERNMENT: Multiparty democracy under a constitutional monarchy
LANGUAGES: Khmer (official), French, English
MONEY: Riel
LIFE EXPECTANCY: 61.3
LITERACY RATE: 74%

GUESS WHAT? *Construction on Angkor Wat, Cambodia's famous temple, began in 1113 A.D. It took 37 years to build.*

CAMEROON

LOCATION: Africa
CAPITAL: Yaoundé
AREA: 183,567 sq mi (475,440 sq km)
POPULATION ESTIMATE (2007): 18,060,382
GOVERNMENT: Republic
LANGUAGES: French and English (both official), African languages
MONEY: CFA franc
LIFE EXPECTANCY: 52.9
LITERACY RATE: 68%

GUESS WHAT? *Mount Cameroon is an active volcano. It erupted nine times between 1900 and 2000. Locals call it Mount Faka or the "Chariot of the Gods."*

CANADA

LOCATION: North America
CAPITAL: Ottawa, Ontario
AREA: 3,855,081 sq mi (9,984,670 sq km)
POPULATION ESTIMATE (2007): 33,390,141
GOVERNMENT: Parliamentary democracy
LANGUAGES: English and French (both official)
MONEY: Canadian dollar
LIFE EXPECTANCY: 80.3
LITERACY RATE: 99%

GUESS WHAT? *The beaver and the maple tree are official symbols of Canada.*

Background: Canada

CAPE VERDE

LOCATION: Africa
CAPITAL: Praia
AREA: 1,557 sq mi (4,033 sq km)
POPULATION ESTIMATE (2007): 423,613
GOVERNMENT: Republic
LANGUAGES: Portuguese, Crioulo
MONEY: Cape Verdean escudo
LIFE EXPECTANCY: 71
LITERACY RATE: 77%

GUESS WHAT? *Portuguese explorers discovered Cape Verde around 1460. The islands gained independence in 1975.*

CENTRAL AFRICAN REPUBLIC

LOCATION: Africa
CAPITAL: Bangui
AREA: 240,534 sq mi (622,984 sq km)
POPULATION ESTIMATE (2007): 4,369,038
GOVERNMENT: Republic
LANGUAGES: French (official), Sangho, Arabic, Hansa, Swahili
MONEY: CFA franc
LIFE EXPECTANCY: 43.7
LITERACY RATE: 51%

GUESS WHAT? *The Central African Republic is home to western lowland gorillas, which are an endangered species.*

CHAD

LOCATION: Africa
CAPITAL: N'Djamena
AREA: 495,752 sq mi (1,284,000 sq km)
POPULATION ESTIMATE (2007): 9,885,661
GOVERNMENT: Republic
LANGUAGES: French and Arabic (both official), Sara, others
MONEY: CFA franc
LIFE EXPECTANCY: 47.2
LITERACY RATE: 48%

GUESS WHAT? *The population of northern Chad is mostly Arab-Muslim, whereas the people in the south are mainly Christian.*

CHILE

LOCATION: South America
CAPITAL: Santiago
AREA: 292,258 sq mi (756,950 sq km)
POPULATION ESTIMATE (2007): 16,284,741
GOVERNMENT: Republic
LANGUAGE: Spanish
MONEY: Chilean peso
LIFE EXPECTANCY: 77
LITERACY RATE: 96%

GUESS WHAT? *Easter Island, located off the coast of Chile, is home to 887 impressive statues called moai. The largest one, known as "El Gigante," is 71.9 feet tall (21.6 m) and weighs 145–160 tons.*

CHINA

LOCATION: Asia
CAPITAL: Beijing
AREA: 3,705,386 sq mi (9,596,960 sq km)
POPULATION ESTIMATE (2007): 1,321,851,888
GOVERNMENT: Communist state
LANGUAGES: Chinese (Mandarin), Yue (Cantonese), local dialects
MONEY: Yuan Renminbi
LIFE EXPECTANCY: 72.9
LITERACY RATE: 91%

GUESS WHAT? *In 2003, China became the third nation to launch a manned spaceflight.*

COLOMBIA

LOCATION: South America
CAPITAL: Bogotá
AREA: 439,733 sq mi (1,138,910 sq km)
POPULATION ESTIMATE (2007): 44,379,598
GOVERNMENT: Republic
LANGUAGE: Spanish
MONEY: Colombian peso
LIFE EXPECTANCY: 72.3
LITERACY RATE: 93%

GUESS WHAT? *Colombia is the only South American country with coastlines on both the Pacific Ocean and Caribbean Sea.*

Background: China

COMOROS

LOCATION: Africa
CAPITAL: Moroni
AREA: 838 sq mi (2,170 sq km)
POPULATION ESTIMATE (2007): 711,417
GOVERNMENT: Republic
LANGUAGES: French and Arabic (both official), Shikomoro
MONEY: Comoran franc
LIFE EXPECTANCY: 62.7
LITERACY RATE: 57%

GUESS WHAT? *Comoros is one of the largest producers of vanilla.*

CONGO, DEMOCRATIC REPUBLIC OF THE

LOCATION: Africa
CAPITAL: Kinshasa
AREA: 905,562 sq mi (2,345,410 sq km)
POPULATION ESTIMATE (2007): 65,751,512
GOVERNMENT: Republic
LANGUAGES: French (official), Swahili, Lingala, Tshiluba, Kikongo, others
MONEY: Congolese franc
LIFE EXPECTANCY: 57.2
LITERACY RATE: 66%

GUESS WHAT? *Most of the Democratic Republic of the Congo is situated farther inland than the Republic of Congo, but it does have 23 miles (37 km) of coastline on the Atlantic Ocean.*

CONGO, REPUBLIC OF THE

LOCATION: Africa
CAPITAL: Brazzaville
AREA: 132,046 sq mi (342,000 sq km)
POPULATION ESTIMATE (2007): 3,800,610
GOVERNMENT: Republic
LANGUAGES: French (official), Lingala, Kikongo, others
MONEY: CFA franc
LIFE EXPECTANCY: 53.3
LITERACY RATE: 84%

GUESS WHAT? *The Republic of the Congo became independent from France in 1960.*

COSTA RICA

LOCATION: Central America
CAPITAL: San José
AREA: 19,730 sq mi (51,100 sq km)
POPULATION ESTIMATE (2007): 4,133,884
GOVERNMENT: Democratic republic
LANGUAGES: Spanish, English
MONEY: Colón
LIFE EXPECTANCY: 77.2
LITERACY RATE: 96%

GUESS WHAT? *Nature lovers can find 1,000 species of butterflies in Costa Rica.*

CÔTE D'IVOIRE

LOCATION: Africa
CAPITAL: Yamoussoukro
AREA: 124,502 sq mi (322,460 sq km)
POPULATION ESTIMATE (2007): 18,013,409
GOVERNMENT: Republic
LANGUAGES: French (official), African languages
MONEY: CFA franc
LIFE EXPECTANCY: 49
LITERACY RATE: 51%

GUESS WHAT? *The elephant is a national symbol of Côte D'Ivoire, or the Ivory Coast.*

CROATIA

LOCATION: Europe
CAPITAL: Zagreb
AREA: 21,831 sq mi (56,542 sq km)
POPULATION ESTIMATE (2007): 4,493,312
GOVERNMENT: Parliamentary democracy
LANGUAGE: Croatian
MONEY: Kuna
LIFE EXPECTANCY: 74.9
LITERACY RATE: 98%

GUESS WHAT? *Famous inventor Nikola Tesla was born in the village of Smiljan, located in Croatia.*

CUBA

LOCATION: North America
CAPITAL: Havana
AREA: 42,803 sq mi (110,860 sq km)
POPULATION ESTIMATE (2007): 11,394,043
GOVERNMENT: Communist state
LANGUAGE: Spanish
MONEY: Cuban peso
LIFE EXPECTANCY: 77
LITERACY RATE: 98%

GUESS WHAT? *The Tocororo or Cuban trogon is the national bird of Cuba. Its feathers are the colors of the Cuban flag.*

CYPRUS

LOCATION: Europe
CAPITAL: Nicosia
AREA: 3,571 sq mi (9,250 sq km)
POPULATION ESTIMATE (2007): 788,457
GOVERNMENT: Republic
LANGUAGES: Greek, Turkish
MONEY: Euro (formerly Cypriot pound), Turkish new lira
LIFE EXPECTANCY: 78
LITERACY RATE: 99%

GUESS WHAT? *Copper has been mined in Cyprus for thousands of years.*

CZECH REPUBLIC

LOCATION: Europe
CAPITAL: Prague
AREA: 30,450 sq mi (78,866 sq km)
POPULATION ESTIMATE (2007): 10,228,744
GOVERNMENT: Parliamentary democracy
LANGUAGE: Czech
MONEY: Koruna
LIFE EXPECTANCY: 76.4
LITERACY RATE: 99%

GUESS WHAT? *Czech playwright Karel Capek introduced the word "robot" to the English language with his play R.U.R., which stands for "Rossum's Universal Robots."*

Background: Croatia

DENMARK

LOCATION: Europe
CAPITAL: Copenhagen
AREA: 16,639 sq mi (43,094 sq km)
POPULATION ESTIMATE (2007): 5,468,120
GOVERNMENT: Constitutional monarchy
LANGUAGES: Danish, Faroese, Greenlandic, German
MONEY: Krone
LIFE EXPECTANCY: 78
LITERACY RATE: 99%

GUESS WHAT? *Windmills have been a part of Denmark's landscape for centuries.*

Wind power is a great source of renewable energy and windmills are becoming an important export.

DJIBOUTI

LOCATION: Africa
CAPITAL: Djibouti
AREA: 8,800 sq mi (23,000 sq km)
POPULATION ESTIMATE (2007): 496,374
GOVERNMENT: Republic
LANGUAGES: Arabic and French (both official), Somali, Afar
MONEY: Djiboutian franc
LIFE EXPECTANCY: 43.3
LITERACY RATE: 68%

GUESS WHAT? *Once known as French Somaliland, this country became the French Territory of the Afars and the Issas in 1967. Ten years later, it was renamed Djibouti.*

Background: Denmark

DOMINICA

LOCATION: North America
CAPITAL: Roseau
AREA: 291 sq mi (754 sq km)
POPULATION ESTIMATE (2007): 72,386
GOVERNMENT: Parliamentary democracy
LANGUAGES: English (official), French patois
MONEY: East Caribbean dollar
LIFE EXPECTANCY: 75.1
LITERACY RATE: 94%

GUESS WHAT? *Unlike many Caribbean islands, Dominica has few sandy beaches. Much of the country is covered with mountains and dense rainforests.*

DOMINICAN REPUBLIC

LOCATION: North America
CAPITAL: Santo Domingo
AREA: 18,815 sq mi (48,730 sq km)
POPULATION ESTIMATE (2007): 9,365,818
GOVERNMENT: Democratic republic
LANGUAGE: Spanish
MONEY: Dominican peso
LIFE EXPECTANCY: 73
LITERACY RATE: 87%

GUESS WHAT? *Founded in 1496, Santo Domingo is the oldest European settlement in the Western Hemisphere.*

EAST TIMOR

LOCATION: Asia
CAPITAL: Dili
AREA: 5,794 sq mi (15,007 sq km)
POPULATION ESTIMATE (2007): 1,084,971
GOVERNMENT: Republic
LANGUAGES: Tetum and Portuguese (both official), Bahasa Indonesian, English
MONEY: U.S. dollar
LIFE EXPECTANCY: 66.6
LITERACY RATE: 59%

GUESS WHAT? *East Timor declared its independence from Portugal in 1975, but was invaded by Indonesia nine days later. The country finally achieved independence in 2002.*

ECUADOR

LOCATION: South America
CAPITAL: Quito
AREA: 109,483 sq mi (283,560 sq km)
POPULATION ESTIMATE (2007): 13,755,680
GOVERNMENT: Republic
LANGUAGES: Spanish (official), Quechua
MONEY: U.S. dollar
LIFE EXPECTANCY: 76.6
LITERACY RATE: 91%

GUESS WHAT? *Ecuador's Galapagos Islands are known for the unique animals that live there, like blue-footed boobies and flightless cormorants.*

EGYPT

LOCATION: Africa
CAPITAL: Cairo

AREA: 386,660 sq mi (1,001,450 sq km)
POPULATION ESTIMATE (2007): 80,335,036
GOVERNMENT: Republic
LANGUAGE: Arabic
MONEY: Egyptian pound
LIFE EXPECTANCY: 71.6
LITERACY RATE: 71%
GUESS WHAT? *Egypt controls the Suez Canal, which links the Indian Ocean to the Mediterranean Sea. Before the opening of the Suez Canal, boats going from Asia to Europe had to travel around the southern tip of Africa.*

EL SALVADOR

LOCATION: Central America
CAPITAL: San Salvador

AREA: 8,124 sq mi (21,040 sq km)
POPULATION ESTIMATE (2007): 6,948,073
GOVERNMENT: Republic
LANGUAGE: Spanish
MONEY: U.S. dollar
LIFE EXPECTANCY: 71.8
LITERACY RATE: 80%
GUESS WHAT? *During 12 years of Civil War, approximately 75,000 Salvadorans lost their lives. A peace treaty was finally signed in 1992.*

EQUATORIAL GUINEA

LOCATION: Africa
CAPITAL: Malabo
AREA: 10,830 sq mi (28,051 sq km)
POPULATION ESTIMATE (2007): 551,201
GOVERNMENT: Republic
LANGUAGES: Spanish (official), French (second official), Fang, Bubi
MONEY: CFA franc
LIFE EXPECTANCY: 49.5
LITERACY RATE: 86%
GUESS WHAT? *Equatorial Guinea has one of the highest incomes per person in the world.*

ERITREA

LOCATION: Africa
CAPITAL: Asmara
AREA: 46,842 sq mi (121,320 sq km)
POPULATION ESTIMATE (2007): 4,906,585
GOVERNMENT: Transitional
LANGUAGES: Afar, Arabic, Tigre, Kunama, Tigrinya, others
MONEY: Nakfa
LIFE EXPECTANCY: 59.6
LITERACY RATE: 59%
GUESS WHAT? *Eritrea is a desperately poor country faced with natural disasters such as drought and plagues of locusts.*

ESTONIA

LOCATION: Europe
CAPITAL: Tallinn
AREA: 17,462 sq mi (45,226 sq km)
POPULATION ESTIMATE (2007): 1,315,912
GOVERNMENT: Parliamentary republic
LANGUAGES: Estonian (official), Russian
MONEY: Kroon
LIFE EXPECTANCY: 72.3
LITERACY RATE: 100%
GUESS WHAT? *Tallinn's Old Town is one of the best-preserved medieval towns in Europe. Buildings from the 11th through the 16th centuries still stand.*

ETHIOPIA

LOCATION: Africa
CAPITAL: Addis Ababa
AREA: 435,184 sq mi (1,127,127 sq km)
POPULATION ESTIMATE (2007): 76,511,887
GOVERNMENT: Federal republic
LANGUAGES: Amharic (official), Oromigna, Tigrigna, Somaligna, others
MONEY: Birr
LIFE EXPECTANCY: 49.2
LITERACY RATE: 43%
GUESS WHAT? *Ethiopians eat with their hands, using injera to pick up hunks of meat or vegetable dishes. Injera is a flat spongy bread made from teff flour.*

FIJI

LOCATION: Pacific Ocean
CAPITAL: Suva
AREA: 7,054 sq mi (18,270 sq km)
POPULATION ESTIMATE (2007): 918,675
GOVERNMENT: Republic
LANGUAGES: Fijian and English (both official), Hindustani
MONEY: Fijian dollar
LIFE EXPECTANCY: 70.1
LITERACY RATE: 94%
GUESS WHAT? *Fiji is made up of approximately 330 islands. A few more than 100 of them are inhabited. Two islands, Viti Levu and Vanua Levu, make up 85% of the land mass of Fiji.*

FINLAND

LOCATION: Europe
CAPITAL: Helsinki
AREA: 130,127 sq mi (337,030 sq km)
POPULATION ESTIMATE (2007): 5,238,460
GOVERNMENT: Republic
LANGUAGES: Finnish and Swedish (both official)
MONEY: Euro (formerly markka)
LIFE EXPECTANCY: 78.7
LITERACY RATE: 100%
GUESS WHAT? *Finland is home to 1.7 million saunas. Traditionally, a sauna is a wooden building heated by hot stones. Bathers sit in the rooms, sweating and sometimes tossing water on the stones to make steam. Finns go from the sauna to a cool bath and back again.*

FRANCE

LOCATION: Europe
CAPITAL: Paris
AREA: 211,208 sq mi (547,030 sq km)
POPULATION ESTIMATE (2007): 60,876,136
GOVERNMENT: Republic
LANGUAGE: French
MONEY: Euro (formerly French franc)
LIFE EXPECTANCY: 80.6
LITERACY RATE: 99%
GUESS WHAT? *The Loire Valley in France is home to more than 1,000 châteaux, or castles.*

GABON

LOCATION: Africa
CAPITAL: Libreville
AREA: 103,346 sq mi (267,667 sq km)
POPULATION ESTIMATE (2007): 1,454,867
GOVERNMENT: Republic
LANGUAGES: French (official), Fang, Myene, Nzebi, Bapounou/Eschira, Bandjabi
MONEY: CFA franc
LIFE EXPECTANCY: 54
LITERACY RATE: 63%
GUESS WHAT? *Libreville, which is French for "freetown," was established in 1849 as a landing site for freed slaves.*

THE GAMBIA

LOCATION: Africa
CAPITAL: Banjul
AREA: 4,363 sq mi (11,300 sq km)
POPULATION ESTIMATE (2007): 1,688,359
GOVERNMENT: Republic
LANGUAGES: English (official), Mandinka, Wolof, others
MONEY: Dalasi
LIFE EXPECTANCY: 54.5
LITERACY RATE: 40%
GUESS WHAT? *The Gambia is bordered by Senegal on three sides and the Atlantic Ocean to the west. The Gambia River runs through the center of the country and is central to many Gambians' lives.*

GEORGIA

LOCATION: Asia
CAPITAL: T'bilisi
AREA: 26,911 sq mi (69,700 sq km)
POPULATION ESTIMATE (2007): 4,646,003
GOVERNMENT: Republic
LANGUAGES: Georgian (official), Russian, Armenian, Azerbaijani
MONEY: Lari
LIFE EXPECTANCY: 76.3
LITERACY RATE: 100%
GUESS WHAT? *A human skull found in the village of Dmanisi is thought to be more than 1.7 million years old.*

GERMANY

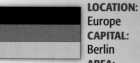

LOCATION: Europe
CAPITAL: Berlin
AREA: 137,846 sq mi (357,021 sq km)
POPULATION ESTIMATE (2007): 82,400,996
GOVERNMENT: Federal republic
LANGUAGE: German
MONEY: Euro (formerly deutsche mark)
LIFE EXPECTANCY: 79
LITERACY RATE: 99%

GUESS WHAT? *Some famous Germans include artist Max Ernst, composer Johann Sebastian Bach, writer Thomas Mann and scientist Albert Einstein.*

GHANA

LOCATION: Africa
CAPITAL: Accra
AREA: 92,456 sq mi (239,460 sq km)
POPULATION ESTIMATE (2007): 22,931,299
GOVERNMENT: Constitutional democracy
LANGUAGES: English (official), Asante, Ewe, Fante, others
MONEY: Cedi
LIFE EXPECTANCY: 59.1
LITERACY RATE: 60%

GUESS WHAT? *Soups play a large part in Ghanaian cuisine. In soups and other dishes, Ghanaians also eat a lot of plantains, yams and cassava.*

GREECE

LOCATION: Europe
CAPITAL: Athens
AREA: 50,942 sq mi (131,940 sq km)
POPULATION ESTIMATE (2007): 10,706,290
GOVERNMENT: Parliamentary republic
LANGUAGE: Greek
MONEY: Euro (formerly drachma)
LIFE EXPECTANCY: 79.4
LITERACY RATE: 96%

GUESS WHAT? *Greece is home to many ancient temples and sites, such as the Acropolis in Athens, the ruins of the original Olympic games at Olympia, the sanctuaries at Delphi and the medieval city of Rhodes.*

GRENADA

LOCATION: North America
CAPITAL: Saint George's
AREA: 133 sq mi (344 sq km)
POPULATION ESTIMATE (2007): 89,971
GOVERNMENT: Parliamentary democracy
LANGUAGES: English (official), French patois
MONEY: East Caribbean dollar
LIFE EXPECTANCY: 65.2
LITERACY RATE: 96%

GUESS WHAT? *Grenada was struck by Hurricane Ivan in 2004, causing extreme damage.*

GUATEMALA

LOCATION: Central America
CAPITAL: Guatemala City
AREA: 42,042 sq mi (108,890 sq km)
POPULATION ESTIMATE (2007): 12,728,111
GOVERNMENT: Republic
LANGUAGES: Spanish (official), Amerindian languages
MONEY: Quetzal
LIFE EXPECTANCY: 69.7
LITERACY RATE: 69%

GUESS WHAT? *Guatemala was ruled by Spain until 1821.*

GUINEA

LOCATION: Africa
CAPITAL: Conakry
AREA: 94,925 sq mi (245,860 sq km)
POPULATION ESTIMATE (2007): 9,947,814
GOVERNMENT: Republic
LANGUAGES: French (official), native tongues
MONEY: Guinean franc
LIFE EXPECTANCY: 49.7
LITERACY RATE: 30%

GUESS WHAT? *Guinea is the second-largest producer of bauxite. Aluminum, which is lightweight and does not rust easily, is extracted from bauxite ore.*

GUINEA-BISSAU

LOCATION: Africa
CAPITAL: Bissau
AREA: 13,946 sq mi (36,120 sq km)
POPULATION ESTIMATE (2007): 1,472,780
GOVERNMENT: Republic
LANGUAGES: Portuguese (official), Crioulo African languages
MONEY: CFA franc
LIFE EXPECTANCY: 47.2
LITERACY RATE: 42%
GUESS WHAT? Guinea-Bissau is one of the world's poorest countries. It is one of the world's biggest exporters of **cashew nuts**.

GUYANA

LOCATION: South America
CAPITAL: Georgetown
AREA: 83,000 sq mi (214,970 sq km)
POPULATION ESTIMATE (2007): 769,095
GOVERNMENT: Republic
LANGUAGES: English (official), Amerindian dialects
MONEY: Guyanese dollar
LIFE EXPECTANCY: 66.1
LITERACY RATE: 99%
GUESS WHAT? Kaieteur Falls, a waterfall on the Potaro River in Guyana, is 741 feet (226 m) tall—that is more than four times as tall as Niagara Falls.

HAITI

LOCATION: North America
CAPITAL: Port-au-Prince
AREA: 10,714 sq mi (27,750 sq km)
POPULATION ESTIMATE (2007): 8,706,497
GOVERNMENT: Republic
LANGUAGES: Creole and French (both official)
MONEY: Gourde
LIFE EXPECTANCY: 57
LITERACY RATE: 53%
GUESS WHAT? During the week before Easter Sunday, many Haitians celebrate Rara, a festival of music, dancing, parades and performances.

HONDURAS

LOCATION: Central America
CAPITAL: Tegucigalpa
AREA: 43,278 sq mi (112,090 sq km)
POPULATION ESTIMATE (2007): 7,483,763
GOVERNMENT: Republic
LANGUAGES: Spanish, Amerindian dialects
MONEY: Lempira
LIFE EXPECTANCY: 69.4
LITERACY RATE: 80%
GUESS WHAT? The ancient Mayan city of Copán was abandoned mysteriously around 900 A.D. Tourists can visit the impressive stone sculptures at the site.

HUNGARY

LOCATION: Europe
CAPITAL: Budapest
AREA: 35,919 sq mi (93,030 sq km)
POPULATION ESTIMATE (2007): 9,956,108
GOVERNMENT: Parliamentary democracy
LANGUAGE: Magyar (Hungarian)
MONEY: Forint
LIFE EXPECTANCY: 72.9
LITERACY RATE: 99%
GUESS WHAT? Food in Hungary can often be very spicy, using flavors like black pepper, **paprika,** garlic and onion. A hearty soup called goulash is a traditional dish.

ICELAND

LOCATION: Europe
CAPITAL: Reykjavik
AREA: 39,768 sq mi (103,000 sq km)
POPULATION ESTIMATE (2007): 301,931
GOVERNMENT: Constitutional republic
LANGUAGES: Icelandic, English
MONEY: Icelandic krona
LIFE EXPECTANCY: 80.4
LITERACY RATE: 99%
GUESS WHAT? Most of the energy in Iceland comes from renewable sources, such as hydroelectric and geothermal power.

INDIA

LOCATION: Asia
CAPITAL: New Delhi

AREA: 1,269,338 sq mi (3,287,590 sq km)
POPULATION ESTIMATE (2007): 1,129,866,154
GOVERNMENT: Republic
LANGUAGES: Hindi (national), English; 24 major languages plus more than 1,600 dialects
MONEY: Rupee
LIFE EXPECTANCY: 68.6
LITERACY RATE: 61%
GUESS WHAT? *Just over 80% of Indians are Hindu, but with more than 120 million Indian Muslims, the country also has one of the largest Islamic populations in the world.*

INDONESIA

LOCATION: Asia
CAPITAL: Jakarta

AREA: 741,096 sq mi (1,919,440 sq km)
POPULATION ESTIMATE (2007): 234,693,997
GOVERNMENT: Republic
LANGUAGES: Bahasa Indonesia (official), Dutch, English; more than 500 languages and dialects
MONEY: Rupiah
LIFE EXPECTANCY: 70.1
LITERACY RATE: 90%
GUESS WHAT? *Made up of approximately 17,000 islands, Indonesia boasts more than 33,990 miles (54,700 km) of coastline.*

IRAN

LOCATION: Middle East
CAPITAL: Tehran

AREA: 636,293 sq mi (1,648,000 sq km)
POPULATION ESTIMATE (2007): 65,397,521
GOVERNMENT: Islamic Republic
LANGUAGES: Farsi (Persian), Turkic, Kurdish
MONEY: Rial
LIFE EXPECTANCY: 70.6
LITERACY RATE: 77%
GUESS WHAT? *Iran became an Islamic state after a revolution in 1979.*

IRAQ

LOCATION: Middle East
CAPITAL: Baghdad
AREA: 168,753 sq mi (437,072 sq km)
POPULATION ESTIMATE (2007): 27,499,638
GOVERNMENT: Parliamentary democracy
LANGUAGES: Arabic, Kurdish
MONEY: New Iraqi dinar
LIFE EXPECTANCY: 69.3
LITERACY RATE: 74%
GUESS WHAT? *The British occupied Iraq during World*

IRELAND

LOCATION: Europe
CAPITAL: Dublin
AREA: 27,136 sq mi (70,280 sq km)
POPULATION ESTIMATE (2007): 4,109,086
GOVERNMENT: Republic
LANGUAGES: English, Irish (Gaelic)
MONEY: Euro (formerly Irish pound, or punt)
LIFE EXPECTANCY: 77.9
LITERACY RATE: 99%
GUESS WHAT? *Some famous Irishmen are actors Richard Harris and Gabriel Byrne, singer Bono and writers George Bernard Shaw, Oscar Wilde and William*

ISRAEL

LOCATION: Middle East
CAPITAL: Jerusalem
AREA: 8,020 sq mi (20,770 sq km)
POPULATION ESTIMATE (2007): 6,426,679
GOVERNMENT: Parliamentary democracy
LANGUAGES: Hebrew (official), Arabic, English
MONEY: Shekel
LIFE EXPECTANCY: 79.6
LITERACY RATE: 97%
GUESS WHAT? *The kidnapping of two Israeli soldiers sparked a conflict between Israel and Lebanon in the summer of 2006.*

ITALY

LOCATION: Europe
CAPITAL: Rome
AREA: 116,305 sq mi (301,230 sq km)
POPULATION ESTIMATE (2007): 58,147,733
GOVERNMENT: Republic
LANGUAGE: Roman
MONEY: Euro (formerly lira)
LIFE EXPECTANCY: 79.9
LITERACY RATE: 98%

GUESS WHAT? *The ancient Italian city of Pompeii was destroyed by a volcano in 79 A.D. when Mount Vesuvius erupted and buried the city and its people under volcanic rock and ash.*

JAMAICA

LOCATION: North America
CAPITAL: Kingston
AREA: 4,244 sq mi (10,991 sq km)
POPULATION ESTIMATE (2007): 2,780,132
GOVERNMENT: Parliamentary democracy
LANGUAGES: English, English patois
MONEY: Jamaican dollar
LIFE EXPECTANCY: 73.1
LITERACY RATE: 88%

GUESS WHAT? *Jamaica is a bit smaller than the state of Connecticut.*

JAPAN

LOCATION: Asia
CAPITAL: Tokyo
AREA: 145,882 sq mi (377,835 sq km)
POPULATION ESTIMATE (2007): 127,433,494
GOVERNMENT: Constitutional monarchy
LANGUAGE: Japanese
MONEY: Yen
LIFE EXPECTANCY: 82
LITERACY RATE: 99%

GUESS WHAT? *Two traditions in Japanese culture are ikebana, the art of flower arranging, and sado or chado, an age-old tea ceremony.*

JORDAN

LOCATION: Middle East
CAPITAL: Amman
AREA: 35,637 sq mi (92,300 sq km)
POPULATION ESTIMATE (2007): 6,053,193
GOVERNMENT: Constitutional monarchy
LANGUAGES: Arabic (official), English
MONEY: Jordanian dinar
LIFE EXPECTANCY: 78.6
LITERACY RATE: 90%

GUESS WHAT? *One of the most visited sites in Jordan is the spectacular city of Petra, which was carved into rock more than two thousand years ago.*

KAZAKHSTAN

LOCATION: Asia
CAPITAL: Astana
AREA: 1,049,150 sq mi (2,717,300 sq km)
POPULATION ESTIMATE (2007): 15,284,929
GOVERNMENT: Republic
LANGUAGES: Kazak (Qazaq) and Russian (both official)
MONEY: Tenge
LIFE EXPECTANCY: 67.2
LITERACY RATE: 99%

GUESS WHAT?
Kazakhstan is one of the ten largest countries in the world.

Background: Jordan

KENYA

LOCATION: Africa
CAPITAL: Nairobi
AREA: 224,960 sq mi (582,650 sq km)
POPULATION ESTIMATE (2007): 36,913,721
GOVERNMENT: Republic
LANGUAGES: English (official), Swahili, others
MONEY: Kenyan shilling
LIFE EXPECTANCY: 55.3
LITERACY RATE: 85%

GUESS WHAT? *In 2004, Kenyan Wangari Maathai won the Nobel Peace Prize for her work helping the environment and contributing to peace and democracy. She was the first African woman to win the prize.*

KIRIBATI

LOCATION: Pacific Islands
CAPITAL: Tarawa
AREA: 313 sq mi (811 sq km)
POPULATION ESTIMATE (2007): 107,817
GOVERNMENT: Republic
LANGUAGES: English (official), I-Kiribati (Gilbertese)
MONEY: Australian dollar
LIFE EXPECTANCY: 62.5
LITERACY RATE: Not available
GUESS WHAT? *The Republic of Kiribati consists of thirty-three atolls in the Pacific Ocean. An atoll is a coral island usually made up of a reef surrounding a lagoon.*

KOREA, NORTH

LOCATION: Asia
CAPITAL: Pyongyang
AREA: 46,540 sq mi (120,540 sq km)
POPULATION ESTIMATE (2007): 23,301,725
GOVERNMENT: Communist dictatorship
LANGUAGE: Korean
MONEY: Won
LIFE EXPECTANCY: 71.9
LITERACY RATE: 99%
GUESS WHAT? *North Korea maintains one of the world's largest armies.*

KOREA, SOUTH

LOCATION: Asia
CAPITAL: Seoul
AREA: 38,023 sq mi (98,480 sq km)
POPULATION ESTIMATE (2007): 49,044,790
GOVERNMENT: Republic
LANGUAGE: Korean
MONEY: Won
LIFE EXPECTANCY: 77.2
LITERACY RATE: 98%
GUESS WHAT? *In 2000, South Korean President Kim Dae-jung won the Nobel Peace Prize for his work for democracy and human rights in Asia and his efforts for peace with North Korea.*

Background: South Korea

KOSOVO

LOCATION: Europe
CAPITAL: Pristina
AREA: 4,203 sq mi (10,887 sq km)
POPULATION ESTIMATE (2007): 2,126,708
GOVERNMENT: Republic
LANGUAGES: Albanian and Serbian (both official), Bosnian, Turkish, Roma
MONETARY UNIT: Euro (also Serbian dinar)
LIFE EXPECTANCY: 75.1
LITERACY RATE: 96.4%
GUESS WHAT? *Kosovo declared its independence from Serbia on February 17, 2008. It was recognized as an independent country by the U.S. and several European countries the next day.*

KUWAIT

LOCATION: Middle East
CAPITAL: Kuwait
AREA: 6,880 sq mi (17,820 sq km)
POPULATION ESTIMATE (2007): 2,505,559
GOVERNMENT: Constitutional monarchy (emirate)
LANGUAGES: Arabic (official), English
MONEY: Kuwaiti dinar
LIFE EXPECTANCY: 77.4
LITERACY RATE: 94%
GUESS WHAT? *The Liberation Tower in Kuwait was completed in 1996. One of the tallest telecommunications towers in the world, the Liberation Tower is taller than Paris's Eiffel Tower.*

KYRGYZSTAN

LOCATION: Asia
CAPITAL: Bishkek
AREA: 76,641 sq mi (198,500 sq km)
POPULATION ESTIMATE (2007): 5,284,149
GOVERNMENT: Republic
LANGUAGES: Kyrgyz and Russian (official)
MONEY: Som
LIFE EXPECTANCY: 68.8
LITERACY RATE: 99%
GUESS WHAT? *Many Kyrgyzstanis are nomadic, which means that they do not live in one place, but travel depending on the seasons and availability of food for livestock. Many still live in yurts, traditional round nomadic tents.*

LAOS

LOCATION: Asia
CAPITAL: Vientiane
AREA: 91,429 sq mi (236,800 sq km)
POPULATION ESTIMATE (2007): 6,521,998
GOVERNMENT: Communist state
LANGUAGES: Lao (official), French, English
MONEY: Kip
LIFE EXPECTANCY: 55.9
LITERACY RATE: 69%
GUESS WHAT? *Modern-day Laos was once part of the ancient kingdom of Lan Xang, which also included part of what is now Thailand. Lan Xang means "land of a million elephants."*

LATVIA

LOCATION: Europe
CAPITAL: Riga
AREA: 24,938 sq mi (64,589 sq km)
POPULATION ESTIMATE (2007): 2,259,810
GOVERNMENT: Parliamentary democracy
LANGUAGES: Latvian, Russian
MONEY: Lat
LIFE EXPECTANCY: 71.6
LITERACY RATE: 100%
GUESS WHAT? *Standing atop the Freedom Monument in Riga is the Liberty Statue of a woman holding stars that represent the three regions of Latvia. It was completed in 1935 during the period when Latvia was independent between World War I and World War II. Locally, the monument is known as Milda.*

LEBANON

LOCATION: Middle East
CAPITAL: Beirut
AREA: 4,015 sq mi (10,400 sq km)
POPULATION ESTIMATE (2007): 3,925,502
GOVERNMENT: Republic
LANGUAGES: Arabic (official), French, English
MONEY: Lebanese pound
LIFE EXPECTANCY: 73.1
LITERACY RATE: 87%
GUESS WHAT?

A typical Lebanese meal features meze, or several appetizers or small dishes. Some popular meze are hummus (pureed chickpeas), olives and baba ghanoush (an eggplant dish).

Background: Lebanon

LESOTHO

LOCATION: Africa
CAPITAL: Maseru
AREA: 11,720 sq mi (30,350 sq km)
POPULATION ESTIMATE (2007): 2,125,262
GOVERNMENT: Constitutional monarchy
LANGUAGES: English and Sesotho (both official), Zulu, Xhosa
MONEY: Loti
LIFE EXPECTANCY: 40
LITERACY RATE: 85%
GUESS WHAT? *The Lesothosaurus is a small, plant-eating dinosaur named after this small African nation. Fossils of this 3-foot-long (1-m) dinosaur have been found in Lesotho.*

LIBERIA

LOCATION: Africa
CAPITAL: Monrovia
AREA: 43,000 sq mi (111,370 sq km)
POPULATION ESTIMATE (2007): 3,195,931
GOVERNMENT: Republic
LANGUAGES: English (official), tribal dialects
MONEY: Liberian dollar
LIFE EXPECTANCY: 40.4
LITERACY RATE: 58%
GUESS WHAT? *Ellen Johnson-Sirleaf became Liberia's President in 2006. She is the first female President in Africa.*

LIBYA

LOCATION: Africa
CAPITAL: Tripoli
AREA: 679,358 sq mi (1,759,540 sq km)
POPULATION ESTIMATE (2007): 6,036,914
GOVERNMENT: Military dictatorship
LANGUAGES: Arabic, Italian, English
MONEY: Libyan dinar
LIFE EXPECTANCY: 76.8
LITERACY RATE: 83%
GUESS WHAT? *The ancient city of Leptis Magna in Libya has been a trading port since around 1000 B.C.*

LIECHTENSTEIN

LOCATION: Europe
CAPITAL: Vaduz
AREA: 62 sq mi (160 sq km)
POPULATION ESTIMATE (2007): 34,247
GOVERNMENT: Constitutional monarchy
LANGUAGES: German (official), Alemannic dialect
MONEY: Swiss franc
LIFE EXPECTANCY: 79.8
LITERACY RATE: 100%

GUESS WHAT? More than 30% of Liechtenstein's population comes from other countries, mainly Switzerland, Austria and Germany.

LITHUANIA

LOCATION: Europe
CAPITAL: Vilnius
AREA: 25,174 sq mi (65,200 sq km)
POPULATION ESTIMATE (2007): 3,575,439
GOVERNMENT: Parliamentary democracy
LANGUAGES: Lithuanian (official), Polish, Russian
MONEY: Litas
LIFE EXPECTANCY: 74.4
LITERACY RATE: 100%

GUESS WHAT? The current Lithuanian flag was created in 1918. The yellow in the flag represents the Sun, freedom and prosperity. The green stands for the country's forests and the people's hope and joy. Red was chosen as the color of earth, courage and blood.

LUXEMBOURG

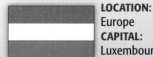

LOCATION: Europe
CAPITAL: Luxembourg
AREA: 998 sq mi (2,586 sq km)
POPULATION ESTIMATE (2007): 480,222
GOVERNMENT: Constitutional monarchy
LANGUAGES: Luxembourgish, French, German
MONEY: Euro (formerly Luxembourg franc)
LIFE EXPECTANCY: 79
LITERACY RATE: 100%

GUESS WHAT? There are more than 14 miles (23 km) of tunnels underneath the fortress of Luxembourg.

MACEDONIA

LOCATION: Europe
CAPITAL: Skopje
AREA: 9,928 sq mi (25,713 sq km)
POPULATION ESTIMATE (2007): 2,055,915
GOVERNMENT: Parliamentary democracy
LANGUAGES: Macedonian, Albanian
MONEY: Denar
LIFE EXPECTANCY: 74.2
LITERACY RATE: 96%

GUESS WHAT? Some early Christians built places of worship in caves. Many of these cave churches still exist near Lake Ohrid in Macedonia. One of the oldest, the church of the Archangel Michael, includes frescoes, or wall paintings, from the 13th century.

MADAGASCAR

LOCATION: Africa
CAPITAL: Antananarivo
AREA: 226,656 sq mi (587,040 sq km)
POPULATION ESTIMATE (2007): 19,448,815
GOVERNMENT: Republic
LANGUAGES: Malagasy, French, English (all official)
MONEY: Malagasy ariary
LIFE EXPECTANCY: 62.1
LITERACY RATE: 69%

GUESS WHAT? Lemurs can only be found on the island of Madagascar.

MALAWI

LOCATION: Africa
CAPITAL: Lilongwe
AREA: 45,745 sq mi (118,480 sq km)
POPULATION ESTIMATE (2007): 13,603,181
GOVERNMENT: Multiparty democracy
LANGUAGE: Chichewa
MONEY: Kwacha
LIFE EXPECTANCY: 43
LITERACY RATE: 63%

GUESS WHAT? Malawi shares the shores of Lake Malawi with Tanzania and Mozambique.

MALAYSIA

LOCATION: Asia
CAPITAL: Kuala Lumpur
AREA: 127,316 sq mi (329,750 sq km)
POPULATION ESTIMATE (2007): 24,821,286
GOVERNMENT: Constitutional monarchy
LANGUAGES: Malay (official), Chinese, Tamil, English, others
MONEY: Ringgit
LIFE EXPECTANCY: 72.8
LITERACY RATE: 89%
GUESS WHAT? *At 88 stories tall, the Petronas towers in Kuala Lumpur are two of the tallest buildings in the world. They are 1,483 feet (452 m) tall.*

MALDIVES

LOCATION: Asia
CAPITAL: Male
AREA: 116 sq mi (300 sq km)
POPULATION ESTIMATE (2007): 369,031
GOVERNMENT: Republic
LANGUAGES: Dhivehi (official), English
MONEY: Rufiyaa
LIFE EXPECTANCY: 64.8
LITERACY RATE: 96%
GUESS WHAT? *The coconut palm is the national tree of Maldives. Throughout its history, coconuts have played a part in the country's economy.*

MALI

LOCATION: Africa
CAPITAL: Bamako
AREA: 478,764 sq mi (1,240,000 sq km)
POPULATION ESTIMATE (2007): 11,995,402
GOVERNMENT: Republic
LANGUAGES: French (official), Bambara, African languages
MONEY: CFA franc
LIFE EXPECTANCY: 49.5
LITERACY RATE: 46%
GUESS WHAT? *The Djenné mosque in Mali is made entirely of mud.*

MALTA

LOCATION: Europe
CAPITAL: Valletta
AREA: 122 sq mi (316 sq km)
POPULATION ESTIMATE (2007): 401,880
GOVERNMENT: Republic
LANGUAGES: Maltese and English (both official)
MONEY: Maltese lira
LIFE EXPECTANCY: 79
LITERACY RATE: 93%
GUESS WHAT? *Malta is an archipelago, or group of islands, located in the Mediterranean Sea just south of Sicily. Malta is the name of the largest island in the group. Gozo and Camino are the other two major islands in the group.*

MARSHALL ISLANDS

LOCATION: Pacific Islands
CAPITAL: Majuro
AREA: 70 sq mi (181.3 sq km)
POPULATION ESTIMATE (2007): 61,815
GOVERNMENT: Constitutional government
LANGUAGES: Marshallese and English (both official)
MONEY: U.S. dollar
LIFE EXPECTANCY: 70.6
LITERACY RATE: 94%
GUESS WHAT? *Bikini Atoll in the Marshall Islands was the site of the U.S. atomic bomb testing in the 1940s and 1950s.*

MAURITANIA

LOCATION: Africa
CAPITAL: Nouakchott
AREA: 397,953 sq mi (1,030,700 sq km)
POPULATION ESTIMATE (2007): 3,270,065
GOVERNMENT: Democratic Republic
LANGUAGES: Arabic (official), French, Pulaar, Soninke, others
MONEY: Ouguiya
LIFE EXPECTANCY: 53.5
LITERACY RATE: 51%
GUESS WHAT? *Much of Mauritania is part of the Sahara Desert.*

Background: Malta

MAURITIUS

LOCATION: Africa
CAPITAL: Port Louis
AREA: 788 sq mi (2,040 sq km)
POPULATION ESTIMATE (2007): 1,250,882
GOVERNMENT: Parliamentary democracy
LANGUAGES: English (official), Creole, Bhojpuri, French
MONEY: Mauritian rupee
LIFE EXPECTANCY: 72.9
LITERACY RATE: 84%
GUESS WHAT? *The dodo, a flightless bird extinct since the 1680s, was only found on the island of Mauritius in the Indian Ocean.*

MEXICO

LOCATION: North America
CAPITAL: Mexico City
AREA: 761,602 sq mi (1,972,550 sq km)
POPULATION ESTIMATE (2007): 108,700,891
GOVERNMENT: Republic
LANGUAGES: Spanish, Indian languages
MONEY: Peso
LIFE EXPECTANCY: 75.6
LITERACY RATE: 91%
GUESS WHAT? *Ruins of Mayan temples can be found throughout Mexico. The most-visited ruins are located at the ancient city of Chichen Itza.*

MICRONESIA

LOCATION: Pacific Islands
CAPITAL: Palikir
AREA: 271 sq mi (702 sq km)
POPULATION ESTIMATE (2007): 107,862
GOVERNMENT: Constitutional government
LANGUAGES: English (official), native languages
MONEY: U.S. dollar
LIFE EXPECTANCY: 70.4
LITERACY RATE: 89%
GUESS WHAT? *In 1899, Spain sold the island of Micronesia to Germany.*

MOLDOVA

LOCATION: Europe
CAPITAL: Chisinau
AREA: 13,067 sq mi (33,843 sq km)
POPULATION ESTIMATE (2007): 4,320,490
GOVERNMENT: Republic
LANGUAGES: Moldovan (official), Russian, Gagauz
MONEY: Leu
LIFE EXPECTANCY: 70
LITERACY RATE: 99%
GUESS WHAT? *Most of Moldova was part of Romania until World War II.*

MONACO

LOCATION: Europe
CAPITAL: Monaco
AREA: 0.75 sq mi (1.95 sq km)
POPULATION ESTIMATE (2007): 32,671
GOVERNMENT: Constitutional monarchy
LANGUAGES: French (official), English, Italian, Monégasque
MONEY: Euro (formerly French franc)
LIFE EXPECTANCY: 79.8
LITERACY RATE: 99%
GUESS WHAT? *With a few exceptions, there is no income tax in Monaco.*

MONGOLIA

LOCATION: Asia
CAPITAL: Ulaanbaatar
AREA: 604,247 sq mi (1,565,000 sq km)
POPULATION ESTIMATE (2007): 2,951,786
GOVERNMENT: Parliamentary republic
LANGUAGES: Mongol (official), Turkic, Russian, Chinese
MONEY: Tugrik/togrog
LIFE EXPECTANCY: 67
LITERACY RATE: 98%
GUESS WHAT? *With its many mountains and plateaus, Mongolia is one of the highest countries in the world.*

MONTENEGRO

LOCATION: Europe
CAPITAL: Podgorica
AREA: 5,333 sq mi (13,812 sq km)
POPULATION ESTIMATE (2007): 684,736
GOVERNMENT: Republic
LANGUAGES: Serbian/ Montenegrin, Ijekavian dialect (official)
MONEY: Euro
LIFE EXPECTANCY: 72.8
LITERACY RATE: 94%
GUESS WHAT? *The gusle, a single-stringed instrument, is a traditional Montenegrin musical instrument.*

MOROCCO

LOCATION: Africa
CAPITAL: Rabat
AREA: 172,413 sq mi (446,550 sq km)
POPULATION ESTIMATE (2007): 33,757,175
GOVERNMENT: Constitutional monarchy
LANGUAGES: Arabic (official), French, Berber dialects, Spanish
MONEY: *Dirham*
LIFE EXPECTANCY: 71.2
LITERACY RATE: 52%
GUESS WHAT? *While Rabat is the country's capital, Casablanca is the largest city in Morocco. It is also the commercial center and the country's leading port.*

MOZAMBIQUE

LOCATION: Africa
CAPITAL: Maputo
AREA: 309,494 sq mi (801,590 sq km)
POPULATION ESTIMATE (2007): 20,905,585
GOVERNMENT: Republic
LANGUAGES: Portuguese (official), Emakhuwa, Xichangana, others
MONEY: Metical
LIFE EXPECTANCY: 40.9
LITERACY RATE: 48%
GUESS WHAT? *In 2000, Mozambique experienced catastrophic flooding.*

MYANMAR (BURMA)

LOCATION: Asia
CAPITAL: Rangoon
AREA: 261,969 sq mi (678,500 sq km)
POPULATION ESTIMATE (2007): 47,373,958
GOVERNMENT: Military regime
LANGUAGES: Burmese, minority languages
MONEY: Kyat
LIFE EXPECTANCY: 62.5
LITERACY RATE: 90%
GUESS WHAT? *The Shwezigon temple is a sacred site in Bagan, Myanmar. Every year, pilgrims travel to the temple for a great festival.*

NAMIBIA

LOCATION: Africa
CAPITAL: Windhoek
AREA: 318,694 sq mi (825,418 sq km)
POPULATION ESTIMATE (2007): 2,055,080
GOVERNMENT: Republic
LANGUAGES: Afrikaans, German, English (official), native languages
MONEY: Namibian dollar
LIFE EXPECTANCY: 43.1
LITERACY RATE: 84%
GUESS WHAT? *Namibia is the "Cheetah Capital of the World."*

NAURU

LOCATION: Pacific Islands
CAPITAL: Yaren District (unofficial)
AREA: 8.11 sq mi (21 sq km)
POPULATION ESTIMATE (2007): 13,528
GOVERNMENT: Republic
LANGUAGES: Nauruan (official), English
MONEY: Australian dollar
LIFE EXPECTANCY: 63.4
LITERACY RATE: Not available
GUESS WHAT? *Phosphate mining has caused environmental damage to the island of Nauru. Phosphates are used as fertilizer around the world.*

Background: Namibia

NEPAL

LOCATION: Asia
CAPITAL: Kathmandu
AREA: 54,363 sq mi (140,800 sq km)
POPULATION ESTIMATE (2007): 28,901,790
GOVERNMENT: Constitutional monarchy
LANGUAGES: Nepali (official), Maithali, Bhojpuri
MONEY: Nepalese rupee
LIFE EXPECTANCY: 60.6
LITERACY RATE: 49%
GUESS WHAT? *At 29,035 feet (8,850 m) tall, Mount Everest in Nepal is the highest mountain on Earth. It is called Sagarmatha in Nepali and Chomolungma in Tibetan.*

THE NETHERLANDS

LOCATION: Europe
CAPITAL: Amsterdam
AREA: 16,036 sq mi (41,532 sq km)
POPULATION ESTIMATE (2007): 16,570,613
GOVERNMENT: Constitutional monarchy
LANGUAGES: Dutch and Frisian (both official)
MONEY: Euro (formerly guilder)
LIFE EXPECTANCY: 79.1
LITERACY RATE: 99%
GUESS WHAT? *During World War II, Anne Frank and her family hid from the Nazis in a home in Amsterdam.*

NEW ZEALAND

LOCATION: Pacific Islands
CAPITAL: Wellington
AREA: 103,737 sq mi (268,680 sq km)
POPULATION ESTIMATE (2007): 4,115,771
GOVERNMENT: Parliamentary democracy
LANGUAGES: English, Maori, sign language (all official)
MONEY: New Zealand dollar
LIFE EXPECTANCY: 78.5
LITERACY RATE: 99%
GUESS WHAT? *In 1893, New Zealand became the first country to grant women the right to vote.*

Background: The Netherlands

NICARAGUA

LOCATION: Central America
CAPITAL: Managua
AREA: 49,998 sq mi (129,494 sq km)
POPULATION ESTIMATE (2007): 5,675,356
GOVERNMENT: Republic
LANGUAGE: Spanish
MONEY: gold cordoba
LIFE EXPECTANCY: 70.9
LITERACY RATE: 68%
GUESS WHAT? *The Miskito Cays, off the east coast of Nicaragua, were often used by pirates as safe places to hide out. Now, the white sand beaches welcome tourists.*

NIGER

LOCATION: Africa
CAPITAL: Niamey
AREA: 489,189 sq mi (1,267,000 sq km)
POPULATION ESTIMATE (2007): 12,894,865
GOVERNMENT: Republic
LANGUAGES: French (official), Hausa, Djerma
MONEY: CFA franc
LIFE EXPECTANCY: 44
LITERACY RATE: 29%
GUESS WHAT? *The correct pronunciation of Niger is nee-jair.*

NIGERIA

LOCATION: Africa
CAPITAL: Abuja
AREA: 356,667 sq mi (923,768 sq km)
POPULATION ESTIMATE (2007): 135,031,164
GOVERNMENT: Republic
LANGUAGES: English (official), Hausa, Yoruba, Igbo, more than 200 others
MONEY: Naira
LIFE EXPECTANCY: 47.4
LITERACY RATE: 68%
GUESS WHAT? *Nigeria's capital city moved from Lagos to Abuja in 1991.*

NORWAY

LOCATION: Europe
CAPITAL: Oslo
AREA: 125,181 sq mi (324,220 sq km)
POPULATION ESTIMATE (2007): 4,627,926
GOVERNMENT: Constitutional monarchy
LANGUAGES: Two official forms of Norwegian, Bokmal and Nynorsk
MONEY: Krone
LIFE EXPECTANCY: 79.7
LITERACY RATE: 100%
GUESS WHAT? *The Sami people, often called Lapps, are some of the original, nomadic people of northern Europe, known as Arctic reindeer herders. Today, Norway is the home to the largest population of Lapps.*

OMAN

LOCATION: Middle East
CAPITAL: Muscat
AREA: 82,031 sq mi (212,460 sq km)
POPULATION ESTIMATE (2007): 3,204,897
GOVERNMENT: Monarchy
LANGUAGES: Arabic (official), English, Indian languages
MONEY: Omani rial
LIFE EXPECTANCY: 73.6
LITERACY RATE: 81%
GUESS WHAT? *Some women in Oman wear a particular type of heavy silver necklace called a hirz. The necklaces have compartments that hold verses from the Koran and are considered protection against evil.*

Background: Panama

PAKISTAN

LOCATION: Asia
CAPITAL: Islamabad
AREA: 310,401 sq mi (803,940 sq km)
POPULATION ESTIMATE (2007): 164,741,924
GOVERNMENT: Republic
LANGUAGES: Punjabi, Sindhi, Siraiki, Pashtu, Urdu (official), others
MONEY: Pakistan rupee
LIFE EXPECTANCY: 63.8
LITERACY RATE: 50%
GUESS WHAT? *Jasmine is the official flower of Pakistan. The deodar, a type of cedar tree, is the national tree and the markhor, a member of the goat family with huge spiraling horns, is the Pakistani national animal.*

PANAMA

LOCATION: Central America
CAPITAL: Panama City
AREA: 30,193 sq mi (78,200 sq km)
POPULATION ESTIMATE (2007): 3,242,173
GOVERNMENT: Constitutional democracy
LANGUAGES: Spanish (official), English
MONEY: Balboa, U.S. dollar
LIFE EXPECTANCY: 75.2
LITERACY RATE: 92%
GUESS WHAT? *Panama took over control of the Panama Canal on December 31, 1999. Opened in 1914, the Panama Canal connects the Atlantic and Pacific Oceans.*

PALAU

LOCATION: Pacific Islands
CAPITAL: Melekeok
AREA: 177 sq mi (458 sq km)
POPULATION ESTIMATE (2007): 20,842
GOVERNMENT: Constitutional government
LANGUAGES: Palauan and English (official), others
MONEY: U.S. dollar
LIFE EXPECTANCY: 70.7
LITERACY RATE: 92%
GUESS WHAT? *Palau is a favorite destination of scuba divers.*

PAPUA NEW GUINEA

LOCATION: Pacific Islands
CAPITAL: Port Moresby
AREA: 178,703 sq mi (462,840 sq km)
POPULATION ESTIMATE (2007): 5,795,887
GOVERNMENT: Constitutional monarchy
LANGUAGES: Melanesian pidgin, more than 820 native languages
MONEY: Kina
LIFE EXPECTANCY: 65.6
LITERACY RATE: 57%
GUESS WHAT? *Papua New Guinea is the only place to find the Queen Alexandra birdwing, the largest butterfly in the world.*

PARAGUAY

LOCATION: South America
CAPITAL: Asunción
AREA: 157,046 sq mi (406,750 sq km)
POPULATION ESTIMATE (2007): 6,669,086
GOVERNMENT: Republic
LANGUAGES: Spanish and Guaraní (both official)
MONEY: Guaraní
LIFE EXPECTANCY: 75.3
LITERACY RATE: 94%
GUESS WHAT? *Guaraní is the name of the indigenous people of Paraguay. They lived on the land before the arrival of the Europeans.*

Background: Poland

PERU

LOCATION: South America
CAPITAL: Lima
AREA: 496,223 sq mi (1,285,220 sq km)
POPULATION ESTIMATE (2007): 28,674,757
GOVERNMENT: Republic
LANGUAGES: Spanish and Quechua (both official), Aymara, other native languages
MONEY: Nuevo sol
LIFE EXPECTANCY: 70.1
LITERACY RATE: 88%
GUESS WHAT?
Used for producing wool, carrying items, guarding smaller animals, pulling carts or even as pets, llamas were an important part of the ancient Incan Empire and are still found in Peru today.

THE PHILIPPINES

LOCATION: Asia
CAPITAL: Manila
AREA: 115,830 sq mi (300,000 sq km)
POPULATION ESTIMATE (2007): 91,077,287
GOVERNMENT: Republic
LANGUAGES: Filipino (based on Tagalog) and English (both official), regional languages
MONEY: Philippine peso
LIFE EXPECTANCY: 70.5
LITERACY RATE: 93%
GUESS WHAT? *More than 7,000 islands make up the Philippines. Luzon is the largest.*

POLAND

LOCATION: Europe
CAPITAL: Warsaw
AREA: 120,728 sq mi (312,685 sq km)
POPULATION ESTIMATE (2007): 38,518,241
GOVERNMENT: Republic
LANGUAGE: Polish
MONEY: Zloty
LIFE EXPECTANCY: 75.1
LITERACY RATE: 100%
GUESS WHAT? *Poland is known for its sausage, called kielbasa, and its dumplings, called pierogi, which are stuffed with cheese, potatoes, onion, meat, cabbage or other vegetables and boiled.*

PORTUGAL

LOCATION: Europe
CAPITAL: Lisbon
AREA: 35,672 sq mi (92,391 sq km)
POPULATION ESTIMATE (2007): 10,642,836
GOVERNMENT: Parliamentary democracy
LANGUAGES: Portuguese and Mirandese (both official)
MONEY: Euro (formerly escudo)
LIFE EXPECTANCY: 77.8
LITERACY RATE: 93%
GUESS WHAT? *Bacalhau is the Portuguese word for cod. It generally refers to the dried and salted version, which is a favorite food of the Portuguese.*

QATAR

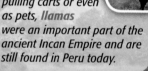

LOCATION: Middle East
CAPITAL: Doha
AREA: 4,416 sq mi (11,437 sq km)
POPULATION ESTIMATE (2007): 907,229
GOVERNMENT: Traditional monarchy (emirate)
LANGUAGES: Arabic (official), English
MONEY: Qatari rial
LIFE EXPECTANCY: 74.1
LITERACY RATE: 89%
GUESS WHAT? *Qatar is surrounded by many salty marshes known as sbakhat.*

ROMANIA

LOCATION: Europe
CAPITAL: Bucharest
AREA: 91,699 sq mi (237,500 sq km)
POPULATION ESTIMATE (2007): 22,276,056
GOVERNMENT: Republic
LANGUAGES: Romanian (official), Hungarian, Romany
MONEY: Lu
LIFE EXPECTANCY: 71.9
LITERACY RATE: 98%
GUESS WHAT? *Bram Stoker based his novel Dracula on* Vlad Tepes, *a cruel fifteenth-century Wallachian prince. Wallachia merged with Moldavia in 1859 to become Romania.*

RUSSIA

LOCATION: Europe and Asia
CAPITAL: Moscow
AREA: 6,592,735 sq mi (17,075,200 sq km)
POPULATION ESTIMATE (2007): 141,377,752
GOVERNMENT: Federation
LANGUAGES: Russian, others
MONEY: Ruble
LIFE EXPECTANCY: 65.9
LITERACY RATE: 99%
GUESS WHAT? *Russia is such a large country that it spans eleven time zones.*

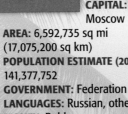

Background: Saint Lucia

RWANDA

LOCATION: Africa
CAPITAL: Kigali
AREA: 10,169 sq mi (26,338 sq km)
POPULATION ESTIMATE (2007): 9,907,509
GOVERNMENT: Republic
LANGUAGES: Kinyarwanda, French, English (all official)
MONEY: Rwandan franc
LIFE EXPECTANCY: 49
LITERACY RATE: 70%
GUESS WHAT? *In April 1994, the presidents of both Rwanda and Burundi were flying over Rwanda when their plane was shot down. The assassinations led to instability, conflict and genocide.*

SAINT KITTS AND NEVIS

LOCATION: North America
CAPITAL: Basseterre
AREA: 101 sq mi (261 sq km)
POPULATION ESTIMATE (2007): 39,349
GOVERNMENT: Parliamentary democracy
LANGUAGE: English
MONEY: East Caribbean dollar
LIFE EXPECTANCY: 72.7
LITERACY RATE: 98%
GUESS WHAT? *The island of Nevis held a vote in 1998 on the subject of separating from Saint Kitts. Nevis did not get the two-thirds majority it needed to split from Saint Kitts, and many still campaign for independence.*

SAINT LUCIA

LOCATION: North America
CAPITAL: Castries
AREA: 238 sq mi (616 sq km)
POPULATION ESTIMATE (2007): 170,649
GOVERNMENT: Parliamentary democracy
LANGUAGES: English (official), French patois
MONEY: East Caribbean dollar
LIFE EXPECTANCY: 74.1
LITERACY RATE: 90%
GUESS WHAT? *Saint Lucia is known for the* Pitons, *Gros Piton and Petit Piton, which are twin peaks that dominate the island's landscape.*

SAINT VINCENT AND THE GRENADINES

LOCATION: North America
CAPITAL: Kingstown
AREA: 150 sq mi (389 sq km)
POPULATION ESTIMATE (2007): 118,149
GOVERNMENT: Parliamentary democracy
LANGUAGES: English (official), French patois
MONEY: East Caribbean dollar
LIFE EXPECTANCY: 74.1
LITERACY RATE: 96%
GUESS WHAT? *The growth and export of* bananas *is the backbone of the Vincentian economy.*

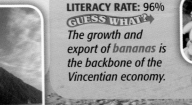

SAMOA

LOCATION: Pacific Islands
CAPITAL: Apia
AREA: 1,137 sq mi (2,944 sq km)
POPULATION ESTIMATE (2007): 214,265
GOVERNMENT: Parliamentary Democracy
LANGUAGES: Samoan, English
MONEY: Tala
LIFE EXPECTANCY: 71.3
LITERACY RATE: 100%

GUESS WHAT? *Between 1962 and 1997, Samoa was known as "Western Samoa."*

Background: Saudi Arabia

SAN MARINO

LOCATION: Europe
CAPITAL: San Marino
AREA: 24 sq mi (61 sq km)
POPULATION ESTIMATE (2007): 29,615
GOVERNMENT: Republic
LANGUAGE: Italian
MONEY: Euro (formerly Italian lira)
LIFE EXPECTANCY: 81.8
LITERACY RATE: 96%

GUESS WHAT? *The white in the San Marino flag stands for the snow on Monte Titano, which is the country's highest peak. The blue stands for the sky. This flag has been used since 1862.*

SÃO TOMÉ AND PRÍNCIPE

LOCATION: Africa
CAPITAL: São Tomé
AREA: 386 sq mi (1,001 sq km)
POPULATION ESTIMATE (2007): 199,579
GOVERNMENT: Republic
LANGUAGE: Portuguese
MONEY: Dobra
LIFE EXPECTANCY: 67.6
LITERACY RATE: 85%

GUESS WHAT? *São Tomé's economy has been largely dependent on cocoa production. The recent discovery of oil may change that.*

SAUDI ARABIA

LOCATION: Middle East
CAPITAL: Riyadh
AREA: 830,000 sq mi (2,149,690 sq km)
POPULATION ESTIMATE (2007): 27,601,038
GOVERNMENT: Monarchy
LANGUAGE: Arabic
MONEY: Saudi Riyal
LIFE EXPECTANCY: 75.9
LITERACY RATE: 79%

GUESS WHAT? *About 95% of Saudi Arabia is desert.*

SENEGAL

LOCATION: Africa
CAPITAL: Dakar
AREA: 75,749 sq mi (196,190 sq km)
POPULATION ESTIMATE (2007): 12,521,851
GOVERNMENT: Republic
LANGUAGES: French (official), Wolof, Pulaar, Jola, Mandinka
MONEY: CFA franc
LIFE EXPECTANCY: 56.7
LITERACY RATE: 39%

GUESS WHAT? *Peanuts are an important export for Senegal.*

SERBIA

LOCATION: Europe
CAPITAL: Belgrade
AREA: 29,913 sq mi (77,474 sq km)
POPULATION ESTIMATE (2007): 8,023,557
GOVERNMENT: Republic
LANGUAGES: Serbian, Hungarian, other
MONEY: Serbian dinar
LIFE EXPECTANCY: 75.1
LITERACY RATE: 96.4%

GUESS WHAT? *Belgrade, the capital of Serbia, is situated where the Danube and Sava Rivers come together.*

SEYCHELLES

LOCATION: Africa
CAPITAL: Victoria
AREA: 176 sq mi (455 sq km)
POPULATION ESTIMATE (2007): 81,895
GOVERNMENT: Republic
LANGUAGES: Creole, English (official), other
MONEY: Seychelles rupee
LIFE EXPECTANCY: 72.3
LITERACY RATE: 91%
GUESS WHAT? *Seychelles is made up of more than 100 islands in the Indian Ocean.*

SIERRA LEONE

LOCATION: Africa
CAPITAL: Freetown
AREA: 27,699 sq mi (71,740 sq km)
POPULATION ESTIMATE (2007): 6,144,562
GOVERNMENT: Constitutional democracy
LANGUAGES: English (official), Mende, Temne, Krio
MONEY: Leone
LIFE EXPECTANCY: 40.6
LITERACY RATE: 35%
GUESS WHAT? *The coast of Sierra Leone is flat and swampy and prone to flooding. The rivers and swamps are home to many types of fish—including sharks.*

SINGAPORE

LOCATION: Asia
CAPITAL: Singapore
AREA: 267 sq mi (692.7 sq km)
POPULATION ESTIMATE (2007): 4,553,009
GOVERNMENT: Parliamentary republic
LANGUAGES: Chinese (Mandarin), English, Malay, Hokkien, others
MONEY: Singapore dollar
LIFE EXPECTANCY: 81.8
LITERACY RATE: 93%
GUESS WHAT? *The national flower of Singapore is the Vanda Miss Joaquim, a type of orchid. It was discovered in the garden of Miss Agnes Joaquim in 1893.*

SLOVAKIA

LOCATION: Europe
CAPITAL: Bratislava
AREA: 18,859 sq mi (48,845 sq km)
POPULATION ESTIMATE (2007): 5,447,502
GOVERNMENT: Parliamentary democracy
LANGUAGES: Slovak (official), Hungarian
MONEY: Koruna
LIFE EXPECTANCY: 74.9
LITERACY RATE: 99%
GUESS WHAT? *Slovakia is famous for its caves. Of the thousands located around the country, fewer than 20 are open to the public.*

SLOVENIA

LOCATION: Europe
CAPITAL: Ljubljana
AREA: 7,827 sq mi (20,273 sq km)
POPULATION ESTIMATE (2007): 2,009,245
GOVERNMENT: Parliamentary republic
LANGUAGES: Slovenian, Serbo-Croatian
MONEY: Euro (formerly Slovenian tolar)
LIFE EXPECTANCY: 76.5
LITERACY RATE: 100%
GUESS WHAT? *Slovenia became independent from Yugoslavia in 1991 and joined the European Union in 2004.*

SOLOMON ISLANDS

LOCATION: Pacific Islands
CAPITAL: Honiara
AREA: 10,985 sq mi (28,450 sq km)
POPULATION ESTIMATE (2007): 566,842
GOVERNMENT: Parliamentary democracy
LANGUAGES: Melanesian pidgin, English, more than 120 local languages
MONEY: Solomon Islands dollar
LIFE EXPECTANCY: 73.2
LITERACY RATE: Not available
GUESS WHAT? *Fierce battles took place on the Solomon Islands during World War II.*

SOMALIA

LOCATION: Africa
CAPITAL: Mogadishu
AREA: 246,199 sq mi (637,657 sq km)
POPULATION ESTIMATE (2007): 9,118,773
GOVERNMENT: Transitional government
LANGUAGES: Somali (official), Arabic, English, Italian
MONEY: Somali shilling
LIFE EXPECTANCY: 48.8
LITERACY RATE: 38%

GUESS WHAT? *The "Republic of Somaliland" is the northwest section of Somalia. It seceded from Somalia in 1991, but its independence has not been recognized internationally.*

SOUTH AFRICA

LOCATION: Africa
CAPITAL: Pretoria (administrative), Cape Town (legislative)
AREA: 471,008 sq mi (1,219,912 sq km)
POPULATION ESTIMATE (2007): 43,997,828
GOVERNMENT: Republic
LANGUAGES: Zulu, Xhosa, Afrikaans, English, Sesotho, Sesotho sa Leboa, Setswana, Sepedi, Swati, Tshivenda, Tsonga, Tswana, Ndebele (all official)
MONEY: Rand
LIFE EXPECTANCY: 42.5
LITERACY RATE: 86%

GUESS WHAT? *In 2010, South Africa will host the World Cup soccer championship. It will be the first time the competition will be held in Africa.*

SPAIN

LOCATION: Europe
CAPITAL: Madrid
AREA: 194,896 sq mi (504,782 sq km)
POPULATION ESTIMATE (2007): 40,448,191
GOVERNMENT: Parliamentary monarchy
LANGUAGES: Castilian Spanish (official), Catalan, Galician, Basque
MONEY: Euro (formerly peseta)
LIFE EXPECTANCY: 79.8
LITERACY RATE: 98%

GUESS WHAT? *Spain produces more olive oil than anywhere else in the world.*

SRI LANKA

LOCATION: Asia
CAPITAL: Colombo
AREA: 25,332 sq mi (65,610 sq km)
POPULATION ESTIMATE (2007): 20,926,315
GOVERNMENT: Republic
LANGUAGES: Sinhala (official), Tamil, English
MONEY: Sri Lankan rupee
LIFE EXPECTANCY: 74.8
LITERACY RATE: 91%

GUESS WHAT? *"Hoppers" are a favorite dish in Sri Lanka. Similar to a crisp pancake, they are cup-shaped and often topped with an egg, some curry or honey and yogurt.*

SUDAN

LOCATION: Africa
CAPITAL: Khartoum
AREA: 967,493 sq mi (2,505,810 sq km)
POPULATION ESTIMATE (2007): 39,379,358
GOVERNMENT: Authoritarian regime
LANGUAGES: Arabic (official), Nubian, Ta Bedawie, others
MONEY: Sudanese dinar
LIFE EXPECTANCY: 49.1
LITERACY RATE: 61%

GUESS WHAT? *Sudan became independent from Britain in 1956. It has been plagued by conflict between the Arab Muslims in the north of the country and black Christians in the South ever since.*

SURINAME

LOCATION: South America
CAPITAL: Paramaribo
AREA: 63,039 sq mi (163,270 sq km)
POPULATION ESTIMATE (2007): 470,784
GOVERNMENT: Constitutional democracy
LANGUAGES: Dutch (official), Surinamese, English
MONEY: Suriname dollar
LIFE EXPECTANCY: 73.2
LITERACY RATE: 90%

GUESS WHAT? *Rainforests cover 80% of Suriname.*

Background: South Africa

SWAZILAND

LOCATION: Africa
CAPITAL: Mbabane
AREA: 6,704 sq mi (17,360 sq km)
POPULATION ESTIMATE (2007): 1,133,066
GOVERNMENT: Monarchy
LANGUAGES: Swati and English (both official)
MONEY: Lilangeni
LIFE EXPECTANCY: 32.2
LITERACY RATE: 82%

GUESS WHAT? *The average life expectancy of a Swazi is only 32.2 years. That is the lowest in the world.*

Background: Sweden

SWEDEN

LOCATION: Europe
CAPITAL: Stockholm
AREA: 173,731 sq mi (449,964 sq km)
POPULATION ESTIMATE (2007): 9,031,088
GOVERNMENT: Constitutional monarchy
LANGUAGE: Swedish
MONEY: Krona
LIFE EXPECTANCY: 80.6
LITERACY RATE: 99%

GUESS WHAT? *Some famous Swedes include film director Ingmar Bergman, playwright August Strindberg, actor Stellan Skarsgard and diplomat Dag Hammarskjold, who was the Secretary General of the United Nations.*

SWITZERLAND

LOCATION: Europe
CAPITAL: Bern
AREA: 15,942 sq mi (41,290 sq km)
POPULATION ESTIMATE (2007): 7,554,661
GOVERNMENT: Federal republic
LANGUAGES: German, French, Italian, Romansch (all official)
MONEY: Swiss franc
LIFE EXPECTANCY: 80.6
LITERACY RATE: 99%

GUESS WHAT? *The Matterhorn, in the Alps mountain range, is 14,700 feet (4,480 m) high and was first scaled in 1865.*

SYRIA

LOCATION: Middle East
CAPITAL: Damascus
AREA: 71,498 sq mi (185,180 sq km)
POPULATION ESTIMATE (2007): 19,314,747
GOVERNMENT: Republic under an authoritarian regime
LANGUAGES: Arabic (official), Kurdish, Armenian, Aramaic, Circassian, French
MONEY: Syrian pound
LIFE EXPECTANCY: 70.6
LITERACY RATE: 80%

GUESS WHAT? *Damascus is one of the oldest cities in the world.*

TAIWAN

LOCATION: Asia
CAPITAL: Taipei
AREA: 13,892 sq ,mi (35,980 sq km)
POPULATION ESTIMATE (2007): 22,858,872
GOVERNMENT: Multiparty democracy
LANGUAGE: Chinese (Mandarin), Taiwanese, Hakka dialects
MONEY: New Taiwan dollar
LIFE EXPECTANCY: 77.6
LITERACY RATE: 96%

GUESS WHAT? *Taiwan is subject to dangerous tropical cyclones that are known in Asia as typhoons. They begin out in the oceans and then reach land, causing great damage.*

TAJIKISTAN

LOCATION: Asia
CAPITAL: Dushanbe
AREA: 55,251 sq mi (143,100 sq km)
POPULATION ESTIMATE (2007): 7,076,598
GOVERNMENT: Republic
LANGUAGE: Tajik (official), Russian
MONEY: Somoni
LIFE EXPECTANCY: 64.6
LITERACY RATE: 99%

GUESS WHAT? *Tajikistan is largely mountainous. The majority of the population lives in the valleys between the mountains.*

TANZANIA

LOCATION: Africa
CAPITAL: Dar es Salaam
AREA: 364,898 sq mi (945,087 sq km)
POPULATION ESTIMATE (2007): 39,384,223
GOVERNMENT: Republic
LANGUAGES: Swahili and English (both official), Arabic, local languages
MONEY: Tanzanian shilling
LIFE EXPECTANCY: 50.7
LITERACY RATE: 69%

GUESS WHAT? The green in the Tanzanian flag stands for the country's agriculture and forests. The gold refers to Tanzania's mineral wealth and the blue represents the sea.

Background: Tanzania

THAILAND

LOCATION: Asia
CAPITAL: Bangkok
AREA: 198,455 sq mi (514,000 sq km)
POPULATION ESTIMATE (2007): 65,068,149
GOVERNMENT: Constitutional monarchy
LANGUAGES: Thai (Siamese), English, regional dialects
MONEY: Baht
LIFE EXPECTANCY: 72.6
LITERACY RATE: 93%

GUESS WHAT? Small motorized vehicles called tuk-tuks are found all over Thailand. They are very popular in Bangkok and are often used as taxis.

TOGO

LOCATION: Africa
CAPITAL: Lomé
AREA: 21,925 sq mi (56,790 sq km)
POPULATION ESTIMATE (2007): 5,701,579
GOVERNMENT: Republic
LANGUAGES: French (official), Ewe, Mina, Kabye, Dagomba
MONEY: CFA franc
LIFE EXPECTANCY: 57.9
LITERACY RATE: 61%

GUESS WHAT? Togo was called French Togoland until it gained independence in 1960.

TONGA

LOCATION: Pacific Islands
CAPITAL: Nuku'alofa
AREA: 289 sq mi (748 sq km)
POPULATION ESTIMATE (2007): 116,921
GOVERNMENT: Constitutional monarchy
LANGUAGES: Tongan, English
MONEY: Pa'anga
LIFE EXPECTANCY: 70.1
LITERACY RATE: 99%

GUESS WHAT? Tonga's main crops are squash, coconuts, bananas and vanilla beans.

TRINIDAD AND TOBAGO

LOCATION: North America
CAPITAL: Port-of-Spain
AREA: 1,980 sq mi (5,138 sq km)
POPULATION ESTIMATE (2007): 1,056,608
GOVERNMENT: Parliamentary democracy
LANGUAGES: English (official), Hindi, French, Spanish, Chinese
MONEY: Trinidad and Tobago dollar
LIFE EXPECTANCY: 66.9
LITERACY RATE: 99%

GUESS WHAT? The national motto of Trinidad and Tobago is "Together we aspire, together we achieve."

TUNISIA

LOCATION: Africa
CAPITAL: Tunis
AREA: 63,170 sq mi (163,610 sq km)
POPULATION ESTIMATE (2007): 10,276,158
GOVERNMENT: Republic
LANGUAGES: Arabic (official), French
MONEY: Tunisian dinar
LIFE EXPECTANCY: 75.3
LITERACY RATE: 74%

GUESS WHAT? Harissa is a spicy chili paste or sauce used in North African cooking, especially in Tunisian cuisine.

TFK

TURKEY

LOCATION: Europe and Asia
CAPITAL: Ankara
AREA: 301,382 sq mi (780,580 sq km)
POPULATION ESTIMATE (2007): 71,158,647
GOVERNMENT: Parliamentary democracy
LANGUAGES: Turkish, Kurdish
MONEY: New Turkish lira
LIFE EXPECTANCY: 72.9
LITERACY RATE: 87%

GUESS WHAT? *The Hagia Sofia in Istanbul, Turkey, was built between 532 and 537 A.D. It is one of the finest examples of Byzantine architecture.*

TURKMENISTAN

LOCATION: Asia
CAPITAL: Ashgabat (Ashkhabad)
AREA: 188,455 sq mi (488,100 sq km)
POPULATION ESTIMATE (2007): 5,136,262
GOVERNMENT: Republic
LANGUAGES: Turkmen, Russian, Uzbek, others
MONEY: Manat
LIFE EXPECTANCY: 68.3
LITERACY RATE: 98%

GUESS WHAT? *Turkmenistan is world-renowned for horse-breeding.*

TUVALU

LOCATION: Pacific Islands
CAPITAL: Funafuti
AREA: 10 sq mi (26 sq km)
POPULATION ESTIMATE (2007): 11,992
GOVERNMENT: Constitutional monarchy
LANGUAGES: Tuvaluan, English, Samoan, Kiribati
MONEY: Australian dollar, Tuvaluan dollar
LIFE EXPECTANCY: 68.6
LITERACY RATE: Not available

GUESS WHAT? *The name "Tuvalu" means "eight standing together," referring to eight of the atolls, or coral islands, that make up the tiny country. The country is actually made up of nine atolls, but the smallest one, Niulakita, remained uninhabited until 1949.*

UKRAINE

LOCATION: Europe
CAPITAL: Kyiv (Kiev)
AREA: 233,089 sq mi (603,700 sq km)
POPULATION ESTIMATE (2007): 46,299,862
GOVERNMENT: Republic
LANGUAGES: Ukrainian, Russian
MONEY: Hryvnia
LIFE EXPECTANCY: 66.9
LITERACY RATE: 99%

GUESS WHAT? *Ukraine is considered "the bread basket" of Europe because of its rich soil and abundance of agriculture.*

UGANDA

LOCATION: Africa
CAPITAL: Kampala
AREA: 91,135 sq mi (236,040 sq km)
POPULATION ESTIMATE (2007): 30,262,610
GOVERNMENT: Republic
LANGUAGES: English (official), Luganda, Swahili, others
MONEY: Ugandan shilling
LIFE EXPECTANCY: 51.7
LITERACY RATE: 67%

GUESS WHAT? *On the Ugandan flag, the red color represents the brotherhood of man. Black represents the African people and the yellow stands for the Sun.*

UNITED ARAB EMIRATES

LOCATION: Middle East
CAPITAL: Abu Dhabi
AREA: 32,000 sq mi (82,880 sq km)
POPULATION ESTIMATE (2007): 4,444,011
GOVERNMENT: Federation
LANGUAGES: Arabic (official), Persian, English, Hindi, Urdu
MONEY: U.A.E. dirham
LIFE EXPECTANCY: 75.7
LITERACY RATE: 78%

GUESS WHAT? *Oil was discovered in the United Arab Emirates in 1958.*

UNITED KINGDOM

LOCATION: Europe
CAPITAL: London
AREA: 94,525 sq mi (244,820 sq km)
POPULATION ESTIMATE (2007): 60,776,238
GOVERNMENT: Constitutional monarchy
LANGUAGES: English, Welsh, Scottish Gaelic
MONEY: British pound
LIFE EXPECTANCY: 78.7
LITERACY RATE: 99%

GUESS WHAT? *Big Ben is the nickname for the clock tower of the Tower of Westminster in London. "Big Ben" actually refers to the largest of five bells in the tower, which weighs more than 13 tons.*

UNITED STATES

LOCATION: North America
CAPITAL: Washington, D.C.
AREA: 3,717,792 sq mi (9,629,091 sq km)
POPULATION ESTIMATE (2007): 301,139,947
GOVERNMENT: Republic
LANGUAGES: English, Spanish (spoken by a sizable minority)
MONEY: U.S. dollar
LIFE EXPECTANCY: 78
LITERACY RATE: 99%

GUESS WHAT? *In 1987, President Reagan declared the rose the national flower of the United States.*

URUGUAY

LOCATION: South America
CAPITAL: Montevideo
AREA: 68,039 sq mi (176,220 sq km)
POPULATION ESTIMATE (2007): 3,460,607
GOVERNMENT: Republic
LANGUAGES: Spanish, Portunal
MONEY: Uruguayan peso
LIFE EXPECTANCY: 75.9
LITERACY RATE: 98%

GUESS WHAT? *Uruguay is slightly smaller than the state of Washington.*

Background: United Kingdom

UZBEKISTAN

LOCATION: Asia
CAPITAL: Tashkent
AREA: 172,741 sq mi (447,400 sq km)
POPULATION ESTIMATE (2007): 27,780,059
GOVERNMENT: Republic
LANGUAGES: Uzbek, Russian, Tajik, others
MONEY: Uzbekistani som
LIFE EXPECTANCY: 65
LITERACY RATE: 99%

GUESS WHAT? *Samarkand is Uzbekistan's second-largest city. Located on the Silk Road, which was the trade route connecting Asia to Europe, the ancient city is 2,750 years old.*

VANUATU

LOCATION: Pacific Islands
CAPITAL: Port-Vila
AREA: 4,710 sq mi (12,200 sq km)
POPULATION ESTIMATE (2007): 211,971
GOVERNMENT: Republic
LANGUAGES: Most people speak one of more than 100 local languages; Bislama, English
MONEY: Vatu
LIFE EXPECTANCY: 63.2
LITERACY RATE: 74%

GUESS WHAT? *When France and Great Britain controlled the 83 islands of Vanuatu, they were known as the New Hebrides.*

VATICAN CITY (HOLY SEE)

LOCATION: Europe
CAPITAL: Vatican City
AREA: 0.17 sq mi (0.44 sq km)
POPULATION ESTIMATE (2007): 821
GOVERNMENT: Ecclesiastical
LANGUAGES: Italian, Latin, French
MONEY: Euro
LIFE EXPECTANCY: 77.5
LITERACY RATE: 100%

GUESS WHAT? *Though it is the smallest independent nation in the world, Vatican City has its own radio station.*

VENEZUELA

LOCATION: South America
CAPITAL: Caracas
AREA: 352,143 sq mi (912,050 sq km)
POPULATION ESTIMATE (2007): 26,023,528
GOVERNMENT: Republic
LANGUAGES: Spanish (official), native languages
MONEY: Bolivar
LIFE EXPECTANCY: 73.3
LITERACY RATE: 93%
GUESS WHAT? *The capybara is an animal found in Venezuela and some other South American countries. The largest rodent in the world, an adult capybara can weigh 120 pounds!*

VIETNAM

LOCATION: Asia
CAPITAL: Hanoi
AREA: 127,243 sq mi (329,560 sq km)
POPULATION ESTIMATE (2007): 85,262,356
GOVERNMENT: Communist state
LANGUAGES: Vietnamese (official), French, English, Khmer, Chinese
MONEY: Dong
LIFE EXPECTANCY: 71.1
LITERACY RATE: 90%

GUESS WHAT? *In 1954, the Geneva Accords divided Vietnam into two parts: North Vietnam and South Vietnam. After much bloodshed, the country was reunited in 1975.*

YEMEN

LOCATION: Middle East
CAPITAL: Sanaa
AREA: 203,849 sq mi (527,970 sq km)
POPULATION ESTIMATE (2007): 22,230,531
GOVERNMENT: Republic
LANGUAGE: Arabic
MONEY: Yemeni Rial
LIFE EXPECTANCY: 62.5
LITERACY RATE: 50%
GUESS WHAT? Saltah, *which means soup, is the national dish of Yemen. It is a spicy mixture of meat (usually lamb) and vegetables (often potatoes, onions and tomatoes).*

ZAMBIA

LOCATION: Africa
CAPITAL: Lusaka
AREA: 290,584 sq mi (752,614 sq km)
POPULATION ESTIMATE (2007): 11,477,447
GOVERNMENT: Republic
LANGUAGES: English (official), local dialects
MONEY: Kwacha
LIFE EXPECTANCY: 38.4
LITERACY RATE: 81%
GUESS WHAT? *Zambia is a major producer of emeralds.*

ZIMBABWE

LOCATION: Africa
CAPITAL: Harare
AREA: 150,803 sq mi (390,580 sq km)
POPULATION ESTIMATE (2007): 12,311,143
GOVERNMENT: Parliamentary democracy
LANGUAGES: English (official), Shona, Ndebele (Sindebele)
MONEY: Zimbabwean dollar
LIFE EXPECTANCY: 39.5
LITERACY RATE: 91%
GUESS WHAT? *Victoria Falls, an enormous waterfall on Zimbabwe's Zambezi River, is more than a mile (1.6 km) wide. Mist coming off the falls can be seen more than 12 miles (19 km) away.*

New Countries

Fifteen countries became independent when the Soviet Union broke up in 1991. They are:

1. Armenia
2. Azerbaijan
3. Belarus
4. Estonia
5. Georgia
6. Kazakhstan
7. Kyrgyzstan
8. Latvia
9. Lithuania
10. Moldova
11. Russia
12. Tajikistan
13. Turkmenistan
14. Ukraine
15. Uzbekistan

The land that once made up Yugoslavia now belongs to seven different countries.

1. Bosnia and Herzegovina
2. Croatia
3. Kosovo
4. Macedonia
5. Montenegro
6. Serbia
7. Slovenia

SOME TOP TOURIST DESTINATIONS
AROUND THE WORLD

Neuschwanstein Castle, Germany

The Alhambra, Spain

Stonehenge, United Kingdom

Chichen Itza, Mexico

Machu Picchu, Peru

The Colosseum, Italy

Christ Redeemer, Brazil

Top 10 Places Most-Visited by Tourists

Tourists have weighed in on their favorite destinations. What's yours?

1. France
2. Spain
3. United States
4. China
5. Italy
6. United Kingdom
7. Hong Kong
8. Mexico
9. Germany
10. Austria

Source: World Tourism Organization, 2005

Kiyomizu Temple, Japan

The Great Wall of China

Petra, Jordan

The Eiffel Tower, France

The Kremlin, Russia

The Acropolis, Greece

89

RACE TO THE TOP OF THE WORLD

FROM TFK MAGAZINE

The great race to the Arctic is on! But the goal isn't to plant a flag on top of the frozen North Pole. This time, the rush is on to find ways to tap the valuable natural resources lying deep below the Arctic sea floor.

CLAIMING ARCTIC RESOURCES

In the summer of 2007, five nations staked their claims to Arctic wealth. Norwegians celebrated the production of natural gas from a well drilled 300 miles (483 km) north of the Arctic Circle in the Barents Sea. The well is expected to deliver $1.4 billion worth of natural gas yearly for the next 25 years.

Denmark governs Greenland, the world's largest island. The Danes sent scientists on an expedition to map the Arctic sea floor near Greenland to claim their rights to drill for Arctic oil and gas. Canada announced plans to build a naval base above the Arctic Circle to keep an eye on the part of the Arctic that they claim. The U.S. Coast Guard sent a ship to cruise waters north of Alaska, too. But what really grabbed the world's attention was the expedition of two Russian mini-submarines. They planted a Russian flag on the sea floor at the North Pole, more than two miles (3.2 km) below the North Pole.

"I don't know why some people got nervous about (us) placing the flag there," Anatoli Sagalevich, one of the Russian commanders, told TIME. "The Americans placed their flag on the moon, and it doesn't mean the moon became theirs."

MELTING ARCTIC ICE

In many ways, the new race is like the old one. Arctic explorers still seek an easy shipping shortcut through polar waters, and nations still seek riches. Only now, instead of whales and fur, countries are after gold, diamonds, uranium and, most importantly, oil and natural gas.

What has changed recently is the climate. Global warming is making the Arctic easier to explore. Burning fossil fuels, such as oil, natural gas and coal, releases carbon dioxide into the atmosphere. That creates a heat-trapping blanket around the Earth, which melts ice.

Recent satellite images show that summer sea ice in the Arctic has shrunk to a record low. That is bad news for polar bears, which may disappear entirely from some areas within a few decades. The complex food chain that links fish, seals and polar bears is being disrupted. And that, in turn, disrupts the lives of native people.

Melting ice may make the dream of a northern sea route come true. If enough of the polar ice cap melts, a shipping lane may be practical, though only in summer.

The race for Arctic riches will go on for many years. It will be dangerous and expensive. Many people worry that this unspoiled wilderness could be harmed. "The Arctic is already under stress," climate scientist James Wang of the conservation group Environmental Defense told TFK. "Rather than having powerful nations rush to grab resources, there should be careful planning and international cooperation."

—By David Bjerklie

A nuclear-powered Soviet ice-breaker near the North Pole

HABITATS AND WILDLIFE

The land masses on earth consist of six different kinds of large regions called *biomes*. The environment of each biome reflects the climate, temperature and geographical features that exist there. Within a biome are many smaller areas called *habitats*. Wildlife thrive in their own habitats. For example, thick-furred animals live in the Arctic circle and color-changing chameleons thrive in lush forests filled with colorful plants. The relationship among various species of plants, animals and other creatures within their habitat is called an *ecosystem*.

BIOME	CLIMATE AND GEOGRAPHICAL FEATURES	EXAMPLES OF WILDLIFE
Tropical rainforest	Hot, humid, rainy; lush, dense trees and thick undergrowth	Monkeys, jaguars, anteaters, toucans, snakes, frogs, **parrots**
Temperate forest	Four seasons, moderate amount of rain; evergreen and deciduous trees, mushrooms	Deer, foxes, squirrels, frogs, rabbits, eagles, sparrows, black bears
Desert	Can be hot (Sahara, Africa) or cold (Antarctica), very little rain; sandy dunes and **cacti** or pure ice	Snakes, scorpions, camels, penguins
Grassland	Savannah: rainy and dry seasons; dusty soil, some trees. Prairie: hot summers, cold winters; rich soil, wildflowers, no trees. Steppe: cool winters, hot summers; dry soil	Zebras, elephants, lions, tigers, giraffes, **buffaloes,** cattle, sheep, horses, gophers, coyotes
Taiga	Occasional short periods of rain; snowy cold winters, cool wet summers; evergreens, rocky soil covered with twigs and evergreen needles, fungus	Elks, **grizzly bears,** moose, caribou, wolverines
Tundra	Very cold year-round, windy winters, very short summers, hardly any precipitation; treeless plain, moss, lichen, grasses, low shrubs, permafrost layer (soil that never gets soft enough to cultivate)	Small rodents, **polar bears,** wolves, owls, foxes, seals

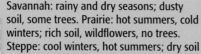

The Earth's Last Wildernesses

Cities and towns now stand where there used to be uninhabited ecosystems. Today, it's rare to find a truly wild part of the world. Conservation International compiled a list of 37 of the earth's last wild places. Here are a few:

THE AMAZON RAINFOREST, found in parts of Bolivia, Brazil, Colombia, Ecuador, French Guiana, Guyana, Peru, Suriname and Venezuela

THE SERENGETI, located in Kenya and Tanzania; famous for its national parks, game reserves and wildlife

THE MOJAVE DESERT, the dry, arid region of the southwestern United States

KIMBERLEY, a remote region in the northwest of Australia

THE SUNDARBANS, a mangrove forest and group of islands in Bangladesh and India; home to more than 250 species of birds and many endangered species, such as the Bengal tiger, estuarine crocodile and India python

THE NAMIB DESERT in Angola and Namibia; home to the highest sand dunes in the world

PATAGONIA, the southernmost region of South America

SOURCES OF ENERGY

The entire world relies on creating and using energy to heat homes, manufacture goods, grow and harvest food, transport products and complete many other processes. There are two kinds of energy sources—renewable and nonrenewable. **Renewable energy sources** are created repeatedly by nature and can be used repeatedly by people. **Nonrenewable sources**, also called **fossil fuels**, are in limited supply and will eventually be used up entirely.

Renewable Sources

BIOMASS is an energy source found in plants and animals. It includes such natural products as wood, corn, sugar cane, manure and plant and animal fats, and can also be found in organic trash. Biomass energy can be used in three ways:

- When burned, it creates steam that can be converted into electricity or captured to heat homes.
- Sources such as manure and organic trash give off a gas called **methane**, which can be used as fuel.
- Plant crops and plant and animal fats can be made into **ethanol** and **biodiesel**, two fuels used in transportation vehicles.

SUNLIGHT can be converted into heat and electricity.

- Solar cells absorb the heat from the sun and convert it to energy. **Solar cells** are used in calculators, watches and some highway signs.
- Solar power plants collect the sun's heat onto huge **solar panels**, which then heat water to produce steam. This steam moves an electrical generator. A similar system is used on a smaller scale in solar-powered homes.

WIND has been used as an energy source for centuries. For example, windmills were used to help grind grain. Today, wind towers much taller than those early windmills—usually about 20 stories high—are used to capture the power of wind. The wind turns giant blades connected to a long shaft that moves up and down to power an electrical generator.

WATER can produce energy called **hydropower**. Water pressure can turn the shafts of powerful electrical generators, making electricity. Waterfalls and fast-running rivers are major sources of hydropower because their natural flow creates pressure. Another way to harness hydropower is the "storage" method, in which dams are used to trap water in large reservoirs. When power is needed, the dams are opened and the water flows out. The water pressure created is then converted into energy.

GEOTHERMAL ENERGY uses the heat that rises from the earth's core, which is located about 4,000 miles (6,400 km) under the planet's surface. The most common way of harnessing geothermal energy involves capturing steam that comes from deep in the earth and emerges in volcanoes, fumaroles, hot springs and geysers (fountain-like bursts of shooting water). The steam, heat or hot water can be trapped in pipes that lead directly to electrical power plants and even to homes.

HYDROGEN is the most common element in the universe. It is everywhere, but it doesn't exist on its own. Instead, hydrogen atoms bind with the atoms of other elements to form such compounds as water (hydrogen + oxygen), methane (hydrogen + carbon) and ammonia (hydrogen + nitrogen). Up-to-date technology is being used to separate hydrogen molecules and turn the hydrogen gas into a liquid that can be used in fuel cells. These fuel cells can power vehicles and electrical generators.

Nonrenewable Sources

COAL is a hard rock made of carbon. It started out as decaying plant matter that was covered with many layers of earth. Over the course of millions of years, the pressure of all this dirt, as well as the earth's heat, transformed the matter into coal. Because coal takes so long to form, it cannot be manufactured for human use. Coal is the largest source of fossil fuel in the United States.

PETROLEUM is found deep within the earth and has to be drilled and piped up to the surface. It is made of decaying plant and animal remains that were trapped or covered with mud. Like coal, it was formed from pressure and heat over millions of years. In its "crude" state, before it is refined, it is known as petroleum. Petroleum can be refined into oil, gasoline or diesel fuel, which are used to power engines in vehicles, machines in factories and furnaces in homes.

NATURAL GAS was formed in the same way and over the same amount of time as coal and oil, except that it is the odorless byproduct of the decaying matter. The bubbles of gas are trapped underground and can be piped to the surface. Natural gas is used as a source of home heating as well as for grilling and cooking.

NUCLEAR ENERGY was developed in the 20th century. It relies on the heat given off when an atom is split (nuclear fission). In nuclear fission, the atoms of an element, Uranium-235, are hit with atomic particles called neutrons. The uranium atoms are split and give off lots of heat, which is used to boil water. The steam from this water powers electrical generators.

POLLUTION'S DEADLY EFFECTS

The Earth is constantly changing. Earthquakes, volcanoes, floods and other natural forces can alter the planet. Humans also leave their mark on the Earth through industrial development, over-farming and overpopulation. Sadly, many scientists are warning that humans are producing so much pollution that the planet may not be able to recover.

GLOBAL WARMING

Global warming is the most serious and immediate threat to our planet today.

Air pollution

The Sun's rays enter the Earth's atmosphere and energy from the Sun is absorbed into the plants, animals and land. The heat is then radiated back into the atmosphere. While some of the heat goes back into space, some is trapped (like air in a greenhouse) by gases such as carbon dioxide (CO_2). This trapped heat keeps the planet warm enough for humans, plants and animals.

Carbon dioxide is produced in many ways, including when fossil fuels are burned to produce energy. Humans are currently producing far more CO_2 and other "greenhouse" gases than the atmosphere needs. As a result, the planet is getting warmer—about 1°F (.6°C) over the past century. Even a small temperature increase can have disastrous effects on Earth.

- The patterns of the earth's winds are shifting, causing climate changes around the world. Some areas are experiencing longer droughts, while others are getting too much rain and flooding. This results in a loss of crops and wildlife.
- The surface waters of the earth's oceans are getting warmer. Since hurricanes feed on warm water, they are getting stronger and more numerous.
- The earth's glaciers are melting, and this is causing a rise in sea levels.
- Tropical diseases are spreading into temperate regions that are becoming warmer.

SMOG

The word "smog" is a combination of the words "smoke" and "fog." Car and truck exhaust, the burning of wood, factory emissions and certain chemical processes release particles into the air. These particles contain pollutants, which can get trapped in the air close to the ground. This smog can be especially harmful to the elderly and people with asthma or other breathing problems.

ACID RAIN

Today, the earth's air contains many pollutants. Sulfur dioxide (SO_2) and nitrogen dioxide (NO_2) are two of the most common. These gases are released when fossil fuels such as coal and petroleum are burned by factories, vehicles and power plants. Acid rain is formed when water vapor in the air combines with SO_2 and NO_2 to form sulfuric and nitric acids. Acid rain falls to the ground and causes many problems, including:

- Breathing difficulties in people with respiratory illnesses.
- Killing trees and plants and poisoning streams, rivers and lakes. This, in turn, harms fish and other water-dwellers. The effects of this poisoning travel up the food chain to other water creatures and animals who eat fish, including humans.
- Eating away at stone and slowly destroying old buildings and monuments.

Melting glacier

GUESS WHAT? Based on the current rate of global warming, scientists say that within the next century the earth's average temperature will rise another 2°F to 6°F (1.2°C to 3.6°C).

OZONE DEPLETION

Somewhere between 9 and 31 miles (14 and 50 km) above the earth is the ozone layer. Made up of ozone gas, this layer protects the earth from the sun's ultraviolet (UV) radiation. If it weren't for that layer, everything on earth would die. In the past century, a hole slowly began developing in this layer due to the use of chemicals such as chlorofluorocarbons (CFCs). The thinner the ozone layer gets, the more harmful ultraviolet (UV) rays can reach the earth.

CFCs were found in aerosol cans and appliances like refrigerators.

CHEMICAL CONTAMINATION

Chemical contamination of the earth comes in different forms, the most common being pesticides (used to kill insects), herbicides (which kill weeds) and fertilizers (used to enrich the soil), as well as the chemical waste products of factories, especially those that work with metals and plastics. In large amounts, these contaminants can hurt people and wildlife.

OIL SPILLS

Oil spills are particularly devastating to the ocean environment because of their widespread effects on marine life. The oil poisons, blinds, suffocates and kills sea creatures. It also harms the birds and land animals that come into contact with polluted water or food sources.

A rescue worker finds an otter killed by an oil spill.

Toxins from landfills seep into soil.

TRASH

In 2006, more than 251 million tons of garbage was produced in the United States. That comes to about 4.6 pounds (2.07 kg) of waste per person each day.

The greatest danger to wildlife is caused by non-organic trash, such as plastics, metal, Styrofoam and glass. These items don't decompose quickly but may take months, years or even centuries to break down. Some of these items are particularly harmful, such as clear plastic bags, which can be mistaken for food by animals or can trap marine life inside them. Plastic rings from six-pack beverage containers can strangle seabirds and small marine animals who don't see them floating in the water.

Record Breaker

How far back do trash heaps go? The oldest known dumps, found in South Africa, contain such things as 140,000-year-old shells, as well as bones, human and animal waste, charcoal and pieces of pottery. By sifting through such ancient "landfills," called middens, archaeologists learn a great deal about the diet and lifestyle of the people throughout history.

The Three Rs

One way to control the amount of trash that finds it way to landfills is to remember the three Rs: REDUCE, REUSE and RECYCLE. Today, the United States recycles nearly 35% of all waste. That's about twice as much as was recycled in 1993 and 3½ times as much as was recycled in 1980.

What Happens at a Recycling Plant?

GLASS Glass bottles and scraps are separated by color: clear, green or brown. The glass is broken into small pieces called **cullet.** The cullet is then moved along a track where screens, magnets and suction hoses remove any paper labels and plastic caps from the batch. Soda ash, silica and limestone are added to the cullet. The mixture is heated until it melts and poured into molds in the shape of bottles. Finally, air is blown into the neck of each mold to create hollow bottles.

PAPER Paper is separated according to type: white paper, newspaper and cardboard. Each type is shredded and mixed with water and chemicals to remove ink and glue. The mixture, called **pulp,** is washed, bleached and poured onto screens, where it drains. The remaining water is pressed out of the pulp, which is then dried between heated rollers. The resulting new rolls of paper, newsprint or cardboard can be cut into different sizes and reused.

This pulp will be made into fencing and other materials.

PLASTIC Plastic bottles and containers are washed and separated according to the kinds of chemicals that are in the plastic. The objects are ground into small particles or flakes and melted into long strings, which are finally cut into **pellets.** The pellets are sent to factories to make new bottles, containers and other items.

METAL Recycled metal cans are usually aluminum or tin-coated steel. The aluminum and steel cans are separated using magnets. The tin coating is removed from the steel cans using chemicals and an electrical current. The tin is sent to other factories to be processed into new coatings. The process for the steel and aluminum cans is basically the same. The cans' lids are removed and the cans are flattened. The metal is shredded into small pieces and melted. The molten metal is poured into blocks called **ingots,** which are then sent to factories to be melted again, this time into sheets. The sheets can be cut and assembled into new cans, aluminum foil or steel for vehicles and airplanes.

Cardboard packaged and ready to be recycled

WHAT CAN YOU DO TO HELP PROTECT THE EARTH?

Recycle glass, paper and metal objects.

Don't litter. Always clean up your picnic area or campsite.

Entertain yourself in ways that don't use electricity: read a book, play a board game, make a craft, ride your bike or play a sport.

Instead of opening new bottles of water all the time, rinse each bottle, refill it with tap water and reuse it several times.

Turn off the water while you brush your teeth.

Learn how to make compost from yard waste and cooking scraps.

Use cloth towels and napkins instead of paper ones.

Never throw out something in good condition that someone else might use, such as outgrown clothes, an old bike or used eyeglasses. Look for places that recycle these items.

Turn off any lights, computers and other electrical devices you're not using.

Organize a group of friends and their parents to host a bake sale or talent show to raise money to for an environmental group.

Plant a tree.

Take cloth bags (instead of asking for paper or plastic ones) when you go grocery shopping—and remind your parents to keep extra cloth bags in the car.

Use rechargeable batteries in electronic toys and gadgets.

Visit state or national parks and learn about efforts to protect natural habitats and the wildlife they support.

GUESS WHAT?

Recycling is on the rise! Today, 52% of all paper, 31% of all plastic soft drink bottles, 45% of all aluminum cans, 63% of all steel packaging and 67% of all major appliances are recycled.

TFK TOP 5 Paper-Recycling Countries

The U.S. recycles about 320 pounds (145 kg) of paper for each of its citizens every year. These countries recycle the most paper per 1,000 of their citizens each year. The United States is seventh.

1. Sweden: 186 tons
2. Austria: 182 tons
3. Switzerland: 179 tons
4. Germany: 176 tons
5. Netherlands: 162 tons

Source: Food and Agricultural Organization of the United Nations

Water Pollution

The trash left by beach-goers and garbage purposefully tossed overboard by people on ships can be extremely harmful to the wildlife in and around our oceans. Objects that are thrown onto streets and highways also end up in sewers and are carried by streams and rivers into our lakes, seas and oceans. Here are some of the items found during the Ocean Conservancy's International Coastal Cleanup effort from 2000–2007.

Item	Count
Fishing line and fishing nets	649,745
Balloons	421,610
Six-pack holders	252,309
Crab/lobster traps	79,820
Syringes	53,011

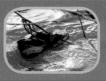

Source: Ocean Conservancy

THE FOOD PYRAMID

Since 2-year-olds and 80-year-olds don't have the same dietary requirements, the Department of Agriculture has introduced 12 different versions of the food pyramid. Depending on your age, gender, height, weight and how often you exercise, your dietary needs will be different.

| GRAINS | VEGETABLES | FRUITS | MILK | MEAT & BEANS |

OILS Oils are not a food group, but you need some for good health. Get your oils from fish, nuts and liquid oils such as corn oil, soybean oil and canola oil.

Based on the new food pyramid, here are the recommended food amounts for a 9-year-old girl and an 11-year-old boy of average height and weight, who both exercise 30 to 60 minutes per day.

	9-YEAR-OLD GIRL	11-YEAR-OLD BOY
GRAINS	5 ounces	6 ounces
VEGETABLES	2 cups	2½ cups
FRUITS	1½ cups	2 cups
MILK	3 cups	3 cups
MEAT AND BEANS	5 ounces	5½ ounces

Easy Meal Tips:

• To add more whole grains to your diet, eat whole-wheat bread instead of white bread and brown rice instead of white rice.

• Keep frozen vegetables in the freezer. That way, if you don't have any fresh veggies on hand, you can just pop them in the microwave for a quick and easy addition to any meal.

• There are countless cool ways to add more fruit to your diet. Top cereal with bananas or strawberries, or toss some blueberries into pancake or waffle batter. Try meat dishes that incorporate fruit, such as pork chops with applesauce, or add pineapples or peaches to kabobs on the grill.

• When cooking meat, fish or poultry, try to broil, grill, roast or poach it rather than frying it.

NUTRITIONAL BODY BUILDERS

PROTEIN This nutrient helps your body maintain and repair its cells and grow new ones. Proteins are found in meat, milk, eggs and other animal products. They're also found in legumes and grains.

CARBOHYDRATES are converted into sugars in your body. These sugars travel in the bloodstream and into your cells to give them energy. Simple carbohydrates are found in sweets such as fruit, candy, soda, molasses and table sugar; complex carbohydrates are more nutritious. They are found in multi-grain bread, brown rice, pasta and in vegetables such as potatoes.

FATS These substances are important in the production of hormones, as well as in developing and maintaining the brain and protecting the nervous system. Fats are also important in helping your body use some vitamins. Unsaturated fats are found in fish and some plants, such as olives, avocados, corn and soybeans. Saturated fats come from animal products, such as butter, cheese and non-skim milk. Trans fats are found in many processed foods.

FIBER This is an important substance in all healthy bodies. Fiber, also known as roughage, is what helps your body move food easily through the digestive system. Fiber is found in the shells of whole grains (rice, oats, wheat, barley) as well as the skins of fruits and vegetables.

VITAMINS Found in all kinds of food, vitamins play many roles in maintaining good health. Here are some of the most common vitamins and some foods in which each vitamin can be found.

VITAMIN A	carrots, pumpkins, sweet potatoes, eggs, milk
B VITAMINS	SEE TYPES BELOW
B1 (also known as thiamin)	beans, pork, whole-grain cereals, sunflower seeds peanuts, tomato juice
B2 (also known as riboflavin)	spinach, peas, mushrooms, oysters
B3 (also known as niacin)	fish, meat, potatoes, peanuts, eggs
B5	whole-grain cereals, meat, fish
B6	nuts, brown rice, fish, chicken, soybeans, watermelon, bananas
B9 (also known as folic acid)	broccoli, asparagus, beans, fortified breakfast cereals, liver, orange juice
B12	meat, milk, eggs, poultry
VITAMIN C	citrus fruits, strawberries, melons, spinach, broccoli
VITAMIN D	milk, eggs, liver, salmon, sardines
VITAMIN E	peanut butter, avocados, salad dressings made with vegetable oil, tofu, sunflower seeds
VITAMIN K	cheese, kale, parsley, broccoli, Brussels sprouts

MINERALS Like vitamins, these substances are found in many kinds of foods and help the body grow and stay healthy. Here are some of the most common minerals, one food in which each mineral is found and some parts of the body that mineral helps.

CALCIUM	yogurt	keeps bones and teeth healthy
IRON	eggs	good for red blood cells
POTASSIUM	bananas	good for muscles
SODIUM	salt	helps keep the body hydrated
ZINC	fish	good for a healthy immune system

CALORIES AND YOUR HEALTH

Calories measure the amount of energy your body can get from a certain quantity of food. Calories can be stored in your body as fat or used right away when your body changes carbohydrates into sugar.

HI-CAL OR LOW-CAL? IT'S UP TO YOU. You can make wise choices about what you eat throughout the day. Consider these meals and the calories in each serving.

Hi-Cal Breakfast
fried egg	92
2 strips bacon	75
toast with butter	163
small milkshake	300

Hi-Cal Lunch
4-oz. hamburger	445
French fries	230
small milkshake	300

Hi-Cal Dinner
4 oz. macaroni and cheese	245
slice apple pie	450
8 oz. soda	160

Hi-Cal Snacks
jelly doughnut	270
4 chocolate chip cookies	180
chocolate candy bar	140

Low-Cal Breakfast
hard-boiled egg	75
2 soy sausages	75
1 oz. bran cereal with 1% milk	100
8 oz. orange juice	105

Low-Cal Lunch
1 cup vegetable soup	145
½ turkey sandwich on whole wheat bread	260
8 oz. apple juice	110

Low-Cal Dinner
grilled skinless chicken breast	175
1 cup peas	125
1 cup carrots	55
8 oz. skim milk	85

Low-Cal Snacks
½ cup fat-free fruit yogurt	60
apple	50
banana	105

Childhood Obesity

Over the past 25 years, the number of kids and teens who are overweight has increased by more than 100%. In fact, today about one in six young people ages 6 to 19 is overweight. This is because kids are spending more time watching television, surfing the Internet and playing video games and less time exercising. Being overweight can be a serious problem at any age, but when it happens in the early years, it can lead to a disease called type 1 diabetes and to serious heart problems later on. Controlling your weight means increasing the amount of exercise you get and limiting the number of calories you take in each day. School-age children should eat somewhere between 1,600 and 2,500 calories per day.

What's Up with the Tomato?

Is it a fruit? Is it a vegetable? The difference between fruits and vegetables is that fruits contain seeds and vegetables don't. The tomato is actually a fruit, because it is the ovary of the tomato plant. The ovary of a plant is where the plant's seeds are found. People are often confused about this because tomatoes are usually used in cooking the way other vegetables are used.

TFK TOP 5 Garden Vegetables

Although the tomato is a fruit, the government still considers it a vegetable. Whatever you call it, the tomato is tops in U.S. gardens. Here are the veggies that people plant the most.

1. Tomatoes
2. Beans
3. Cucumbers
4. Peppers
5. Leafy Greens

Source: U.S. Department of Agriculture

MONKEY BRAINS AND OTHER FUNKY FOODS FROM AROUND THE WORLD

In the Amazon rainforest of Ecuador, people eat LEMON ANTS. The insects got their name because of their tangy, lemony taste.

NUTRIA are rodents that look like beavers but have tails like rats. They have been hunted for years for their fur, but because they have overpopulated swamps in Louisiana, people have recently started to eat them.

In Hong Kong, some people actually eat MONKEY BRAINS right out of the monkey's skull.

In Indonesia, people eat MONKEY TOES deep-fried in oil.

MENUDO is a Mexican soup made from the stomach lining of a cow.

CASU MARZU, or "rotten cheese," made on the Italian island of Sardinia, has fly larvae, or maggots, crawling inside it. The cheese is good to eat if the maggots are moving. If they aren't, the cheese is toxic.

HEAD CHEESE isn't a cheese but a kind of Swedish lunchmeat. It is made by boiling the head of a pig or cow. The meat is then chopped up and put in a mold, along with its boiled liquid. After it is chilled, the jellied loaf is sliced and served.

HAGGIS, a traditional Scottish dish, is made by stuffing the stomach of a sheep with oatmeal, onions and chopped sheep organs. The haggis is then steamed and served.

In Thailand, GRASSHOPPERS are fried in oil and eaten.

In South Korea, people eat the larvae, or grubs, of SILK WORMS.

SANGUINACCIO is a pudding or sausage made from pig's blood. It has many variations throughout Italy.

STEAK AND KIDNEY PIE is a traditional English dish using the meat and kidneys of a cow.

Different native groups in the Arctic Circle eat raw or cooked BLUBBER, which is the fat of whales, seals and other sea mammals.

In Indonesia, some people eat FRUIT BATS. On the island of Sulawesi, they are cooked in coconut milk. In the country's capital, Jakarta, they are smoked.

In the Italian region of Tuscany, cooks use the crowns, or combs, of roosters to make a stew called CIBREO.

In Slovenia, DORMICE STEW is a popular dish prepared from mice that are specially fattened for this purpose.

In the Canadian province of Newfoundland, a pie is made from SEAL FLIPPERS. They are boiled with vegetables, covered with pastry dough and baked.

TFK GEOGRAPHY

A TIMELINE OF EXPLORERS

Leif Ericsson

Approximately 1000 A.D.	**Leif Ericsson** landed in a section of North America that he dubbed "Vinland." The exact location of Vinland is unknown, but many people think it was either Nova Scotia, Canada, or New England.
1271–95	**Marco Polo,** a Venetian merchant, traveled throughout Asia.
1405–1433	Under the command of Zheng He, fleets of Chinese ships sailed as far as southeast Africa.
1433	Portuguese explorer Gil Eannes sailed past Cape Bojador in western Africa, which was thought to be the end of the world at the time.
1488	Bartholomeu Dias from Portugal led the first European expedition to round the Cape of Good Hope at the southern tip of Africa.
1492	**Christopher Columbus** left Spain, hoping to sail to the West Indies. Instead, he and his crew landed in the Bahamas and visited Cuba, Hispaniola (which is now split into Haiti and the Dominican Republic) and other small islands.
1497–99	Vasco da Gama led the first European expedition to India by sea via the Cape of Good Hope.
1513	Vasco Núñez de Balboa from Spain sailed to the Pacific Ocean. **Juan Ponce de León** explored Florida and the Yucatan Peninsula in Mexico.
1519–21	While exploring Mexico, **Hernán Cortés** conquered the Aztec empire.

Marco Polo

Christopher Columbus

Juan Ponce de León

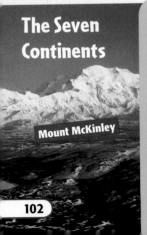

Hernán Cortés

The Seven Continents

Mount McKinley

ANTARCTICA
HOW BIG IS IT?
5,100,000 square miles
(13,209,000 sq km)
HIGHEST POINT?
Vinson Massif
16,066 feet (4,897 m)
LOWEST POINT?
Ice covering—8,327 feet
(2,538 m) below sea
level

NORTH AMERICA
(including Central America
and the Caribbean)
HOW BIG IS IT?
9,449,000 square miles
(24,474,000 sq km)
HIGHEST POINT?
Mount McKinley
20,320 feet (6,194 m)
LOWEST POINT?
Death Valley—282 feet
(86 m) below sea level

SOUTH AMERICA
HOW BIG IS IT?
6,879,000 square miles
(17,819,000 sq km)
HIGHEST POINT?
Mount Aconcagua
22,834 feet (6,960 m)
LOWEST POINT?
Valdes Peninsula
131 feet (40 m)
below sea level

Ferdinand
Magellan

1519–22 Ferdinand Magellan's **expedition circumnavigated, or sailed around, the globe.**

1524 Giovanni da Verrazano was the first European to reach New York harbor.

Jacques
Cartier

1532–33 Francisco Pizarro conquered the Inca Empire in South America.

1534 Jacques Cartier **of France explored Canada's St. Lawrence River.**

1541 Spaniard Hernando de Soto crossed the Mississippi River.

1577 Sir Francis Drake of England explored California's coastline.

Henry Hudson

1607–11 Henry Hudson **visited the Chesapeake, Delaware and New York Bays, and was the first European to sail up the Hudson River.**

1776 James Cook visited and named the Sandwich Islands (now Hawaii).

1804–06 Meriwether Lewis and William Clark explored the Louisiana Purchase lands, reaching the Pacific Ocean in November 1805.

1909 Robert Peary **is credited as the first to reach the North Pole, though new evidence suggests he might have actually been as much as 30 to 60 miles (48 to 97 km) away.**

Robert Peary

1911 Roald Amundsen, **the first man to travel the Northwest Passage, reached the South Pole.**

Roald Amundsen

1953 Edmund Hillary **and** Tenzing Norgay **climbed to the top of Mount Everest.**

Edmund Hillary and
Tenzing Norgay

AFRICA
HOW BIG IS IT?
11,608,000 square miles
(30,065,000 sq km)
HIGHEST POINT?
Mount Kilimanjaro
19,340 feet (5,895 m)
LOWEST POINT?
Lake Assal—512 feet
(156 m) below sea level

EUROPE
HOW BIG IS IT?
3,837,000 square miles
(9,938,000 sq km)
HIGHEST POINT?
Mount Elbrus
18,510 feet (5,642 m)
LOWEST POINT?
Caspian Sea—92 feet
(28 m) below sea level

ASIA
(including the Middle East)
HOW BIG IS IT?
17,212,000 square miles
(44,579,000 sq km)
HIGHEST POINT?
Mount Everest
29,035 feet (8,850 m)
LOWEST POINT?
Dead Sea—1,349 feet
(411 m) below sea level

AUSTRALIA
(including Oceania)
HOW BIG IS IT?
3,132,000 square miles
(8,112,000 sq km)
HIGHEST POINT?
Mount Kosciusko
7,316 feet (2,228 m)
LOWEST POINT?
Lake Eyre—52 feet
(16 m) below sea level

WHAT'S THAT?

ALTITUDE is the height of an object above sea level. It tells you how tall a mountain or other area is.

The **EQUATOR** is an imaginary line drawn all the way around the world. It is located halfway between the North and South poles. Above the equator, you will find the northern hemispheres and below, the southern hemispheres.

A group of scattered islands is called an **ARCHIPELAGO.** Many archipelagoes have formed in isolated parts of the ocean. Examples include Hawaii, the Philippines, Indonesia and Fiji.

An **ATOLL** is a coral island or group of coral islands often made up of a reef surrounding a lagoon.

ISTHMUS is an easy word to remember: It rhymes with Christmas! It's a narrow piece of land that connects two larger areas. The most famous example is Panama, which connects Central and South America.

Record Breaker
Greenland is the largest island in the world. It is almost entirely covered with ice.

An **OASIS** is a small green area in a desert region. Water is usually present at an oasis.

A **CANYON** is a deep, narrow valley with steep sides. The Grand Canyon in the United States and the Copper Canyon in Mexico are well-known examples.

The state of Florida is an example of a **PENINSULA,** which is a piece of land that is surrounded on three sides by water.

GUESS WHAT?
Many scientists believe that all of the land on Earth was once a single, enormous supercontinent called Pangaea. It broke apart to become the seven continents we have today.

A **PLATEAU** is a mountain with a wide, flat top. Plateaus are a common feature in the landscape of the Southwest.

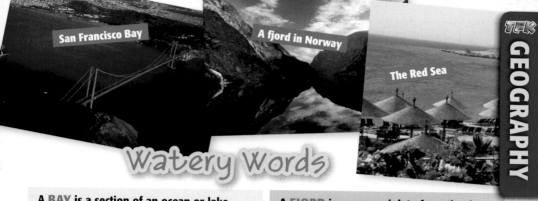

San Francisco Bay

A fjord in Norway

The Red Sea

Watery Words

A **BAY** is a section of an ocean or lake that fills an indentation in the coastline. Large bays are usually called **GULFS**. Examples include San Francisco Bay and the Gulf of Mexico.

A **CANAL** is a man-made waterway. The Suez and Panama Canals are two well-known examples built to provide shorter passageways for people and goods. Venice, Italy, is famous for its canals.

At the mouth of a river, water will often branch out into a triangle-shaped area called a **DELTA**. Known for their diverse wildlife, **ESTUARIES** form in deltas. They are partially separated bodies of water where the salt water from the ocean mixes with freshwater from the river. Rivers with deltas include the Nile and the Mississippi, while the Chesapeake Bay and Puget Sound are estuaries.

A **FJORD** is a narrow inlet of sea that is bordered by steep cliffs. There are many fjords along the coastline of Norway.

A **SEA** is an inland body of water. It is often filled with salt water and is sometimes connected to the ocean. Examples include the Red Sea and the Mediterranean Sea.

A **STRAIT**, sometimes called a **CHANNEL**, is a narrow strip of water connecting two larger bodies of water. The Bering Strait is between Alaska and Russia. The English Channel separates Great Britain and France.

Record Breaker
At 3,212 feet (979 m), Angel Falls in Venezuela is the tallest waterfall in the world.

GUESS WHAT?
The deepest point in the oceans is the Marianas Trench. Located in the Pacific Ocean, it is 35,827 ft (10,924 m) deep, which is more than six times as deep as the Grand Canyon!

A canal in Venice, Italy

A river delta in Quebec, Canada

Explore the Past

1325
IBN BATTUTA, of Morocco, sets out for the Middle East, China and Russia.

1499
AMERIGO VESPUCCI, of Italy, sets sail. He reaches a land later named for him.

1541
HERNANDO DE SOTO, of Spain, discovers the Mississippi River.

1604
SAMUEL DE CHAMPLAIN, of France, starts the first French colony in Canada.

<< **Read this timeline to learn more about other explorers. Then answer the questions.**

1. **When did Ibn Battuta begin his journeys?**
_____

2. **True or False: Samuel de Champlain started a French colony on the Mississippi River.**
_____

3. **Hernando de Soto set out how many years after Amerigo Vespucci?**
_____

ANSWERS ON PAGE 244

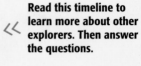

Mystery Person

CLUE 1: I am a Portuguese explorer. In 1519, I began the first journey to circumnavigate, or travel around, the world.

CLUE 2: My crew and I were the first Europeans to cross the Pacific Ocean. I died before the end of the voyage.

CLUE 3: A strait in South America bears my name.

WHO AM I? _____

ANSWERS ON PAGE 244

Record Breaker
Located in North Africa, the Sahara Desert is the largest desert in the world. Its rolling sands cover around 3.5 million square feet (325,160 sq m).

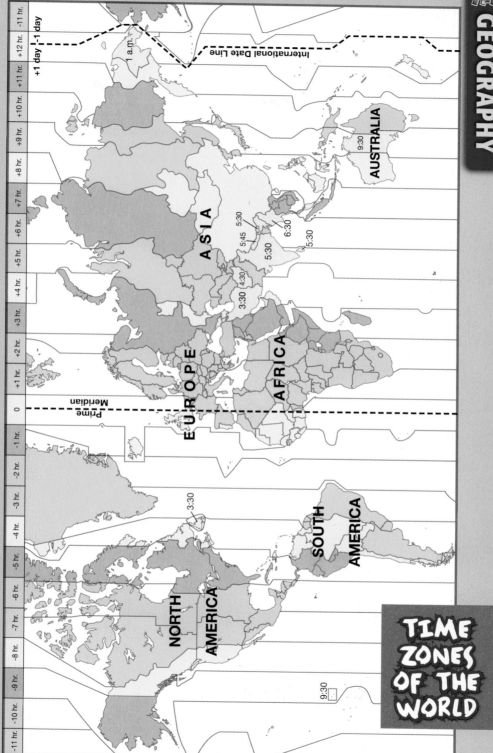

TIME ZONES OF THE WORLD

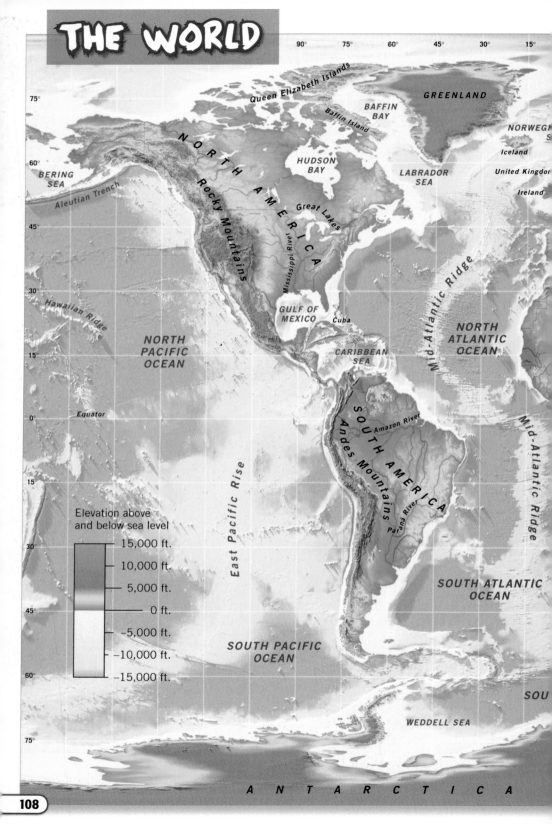

THE WORLD

ARCTIC OCEAN

15° 30° 45° 60° 75° 90° 105° 120° 135° 150° 165°

S i b e r i a

A S I A

Baltic
Sea

U R O P E

Ural Mts.

River

90

Lena River

Sea of
Okhotsk

Alps

Gobi

45°

Mt. Everest
World's
highest point
29,035 ft.

Black
Sea

Caspian
Sea

Aral
Sea

Huang River

Honshu

Kuril-Kamchatka
Trench

30°

Mediterranean Sea

Euphrates R.

Chang River

Japan Trench

NORTH
PACIFIC
OCEAN

Sahara

Persian
Gulf

Indus River

Himalayas

Ganges R.

South
China
Sea

15°

Nile River

Red Sea

ARABIAN
SEA

BAY OF
BENGAL

Mekong R.

Challenger Deep
World's greatest
ocean depth
-36,198 ft.

A F R I C A

Congo River

Borneo

Equator

0°

New Guinea

Central Indian Ridge

INDIAN
OCEAN

Sumatra

Ninety East Ridge

Java

Java Trench

Great Barrier Reef

15°

Kalahari
Desert

Madagascar

A U S T R A L I A

30°

Southwest Indian Ridge

North
Island

South
Island

45°

Maps always show a
distorted view of the
Earth because they
are not curved in
three dimensions.

60°

OCEAN

75°

109

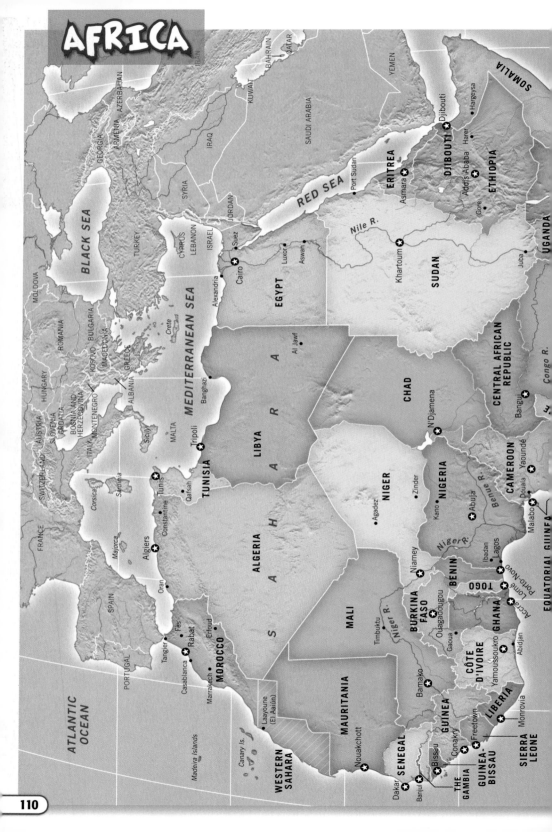

AFRICA

ATLANTIC OCEAN

BLACK SEA

MEDITERRANEAN SEA

RED SEA

MOLDOVA
ROMANIA
BULGARIA
KOSOVO
MACEDONIA
GREECE
ALBANIA
HUNGARY
CROATIA
SLOVENIA
BOSNIA AND HERZEGOVINA
MONTENEGRO
AUSTRIA
SWITZERLAND
ITALY
FRANCE
SPAIN
PORTUGAL
GEORGIA
ARMENIA
AZERBAIJAN
TURKEY
SYRIA
CYPRUS
LEBANON
ISRAEL
JORDAN
IRAQ
KUWAIT
BAHRAIN
QATAR
SAUDI ARABIA
YEMEN

Corsica
Sardinia
Crete
Sicily
MALTA
Majorca
Minorca
Canary Is.
Madeira Islands

SOMALIA
Djibouti
DJIBOUTI
Hargeysa
Harer
Addis Ababa
Asmara
ERITREA
ETHIOPIA
Gore
Port Sudan
UGANDA
Juba

Nile R.
Khartoum
SUDAN

Congo R.
CENTRAL AFRICAN REPUBLIC
Bangui

EGYPT
Alexandria
Cairo
Suez
Luxor
Aswan
Al Jawf

LIBYA
Tripoli
Banghazi

CHAD
N'Djamena

NIGER
Agadez
Zinder

CAMEROON
Yaoundé
Douala
Malabo
EQUATORIAL GUINEA

NIGERIA
Kano
Abuja
Ibadan
Lagos
Benue R.
Niger R.

TUNISIA
Tunis
Qafsah
Constantine

ALGERIA
Algiers
Oran

S A H A R A

MOROCCO
Tangier
Rabat
Casablanca
Marrakech
Fes
Erfoud

WESTERN SAHARA
Laayoune
(El Aaiún)

MAURITANIA
Nouakchott

MALI
Timbuktu
Bamako

BENIN
TOGO
Porto-Novo
Lomé
Accra
GHANA
CÔTE D'IVOIRE
Yamoussoukro
Abidjan

BURKINA FASO
Ouagadougou
Gaoua
Niamey
Niger R.

SENEGAL
Dakar
THE GAMBIA
Banjul
GUINEA-BISSAU
Bissau
GUINEA
Conakry
Freetown
SIERRA LEONE
Monrovia
LIBERIA

110

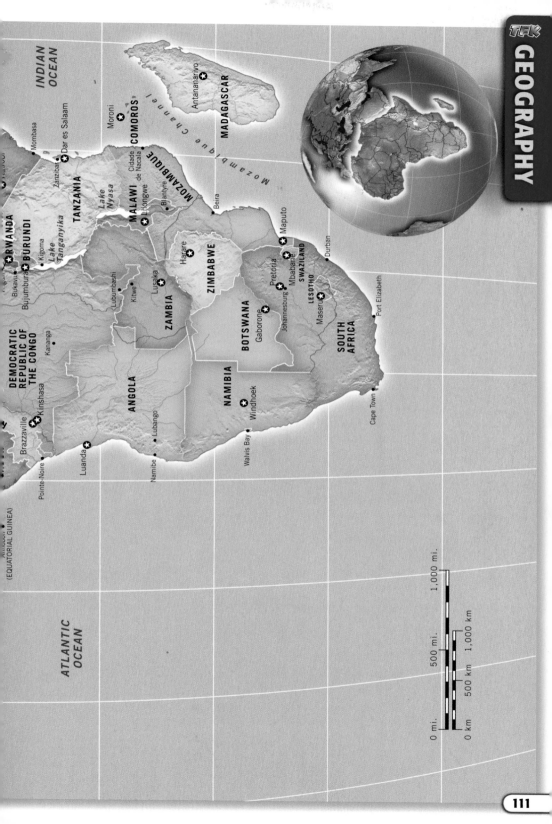

INDIAN OCEAN

MADAGASCAR

Antananarivo

Moroni

COMOROS

Mombasa

Dar es Salaam

Mozambique Channel

Zanzibar

TANZANIA

Cidade
de Nacala

Lake
Nyasa

MALAWI

MOZAMBIQUE

RWANDA

BURUNDI

Kigoma

Lilongwe

Blantyre

Beira

Bukavu

Bujumbura

Lake
Tanganyika

Lubumbashi

Kitwe

Lusaka

Harare

ZIMBABWE

Maputo

Pretoria

Mbabane

SWAZILAND

Durban

DEMOCRATIC
REPUBLIC OF
THE CONGO

Kananga

ZAMBIA

Johannesburg

LESOTHO

Maseru

Kinshasa

Brazzaville

ANGOLA

Lubango

BOTSWANA

Gaborone

SOUTH
AFRICA

Port Elizabeth

Pointe-Noire

Luanda

Namibe

NAMIBIA

Windhoek

Walvis Bay

Cape Town

ATLANTIC
OCEAN

(EQUATORIAL GUINEA)

1,000 mi.

500 mi.

1,000 km

0 mi.

500 km

0 km

1,000 km

ASIA AND THE MIDDLE EAST

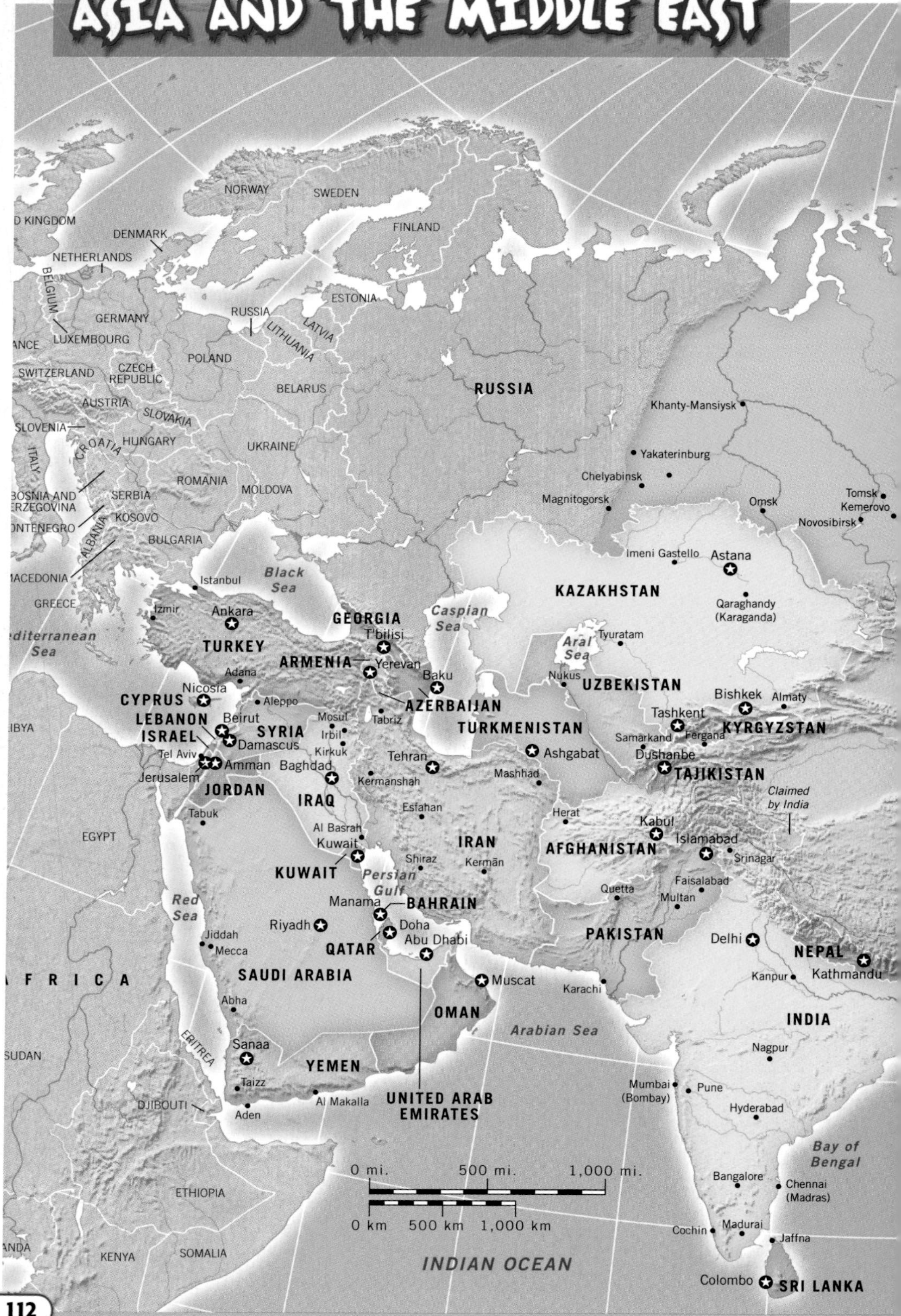

NORWAY
SWEDEN
FINLAND
D KINGDOM
DENMARK
NETHERLANDS
BELGIUM
GERMANY
RUSSIA
ESTONIA
ANCE
LUXEMBOURG
LITHUANIA
LATVIA
SWITZERLAND
CZECH
REPUBLIC
POLAND
BELARUS
Khanty-Mansiysk
AUSTRIA
SLOVAKIA
SLOVENIA
HUNGARY
UKRAINE
Yakaterinburg
ITALY
CROATIA
ROMANIA
MOLDOVA
RUSSIA
Chelyabinsk
BOSNIA AND
ERZEGOVINA
SERBIA
Magnitogorsk
Omsk
Tomsk
Kemerovo
ONTENEGRO
ALBANIA
KOSOVO
BULGARIA
Novosibirsk
MACEDONIA
Imeni Gastello
Astana
GREECE
Istanbul
Black
Sea
Caspian
Sea
KAZAKHSTAN
Qaraghandy
(Karaganda)
Izmir
Ankara
GEORGIA
T'bilisi
Aral
Sea
Tyuratam
diterranean
Sea
TURKEY
Adana
ARMENIA
Yerevan
Baku
Nukus
UZBEKISTAN
Bishkek
Almaty
Nicosia
Aleppo
AZERBAIJAN
Tashkent
CYPRUS
LEBANON
Beirut
SYRIA
Mosul
Tabriz
TURKMENISTAN
Samarkand
Fergana
KYRGYZSTAN
LIBYA
ISRAEL
Tel Aviv
Damascus
Irbil
Kirkuk
Tehran
Ashgabat
Dushanbe
TAJIKISTAN
Amman
Baghdad
Mashhad
Jerusalem
JORDAN
Kermanshah
Claimed
by India
IRAQ
Esfahan
Herat
Kabul
EGYPT
Tabuk
Al Basrah
Islamabad
Srinagar
Kuwait
IRAN
AFGHANISTAN
Shiraz
Kermān
KUWAIT
Persian
Gulf
Quetta
Faisalabad
Multan
Manama
BAHRAIN
Red
Sea
Jiddah
Riyadh
Doha
Abu Dhabi
PAKISTAN
Delhi
Mecca
QATAR
Karachi
NEPAL
Kanpur
Kathmandu
AFRICA
SAUDI ARABIA
Abha
Muscat
INDIA
OMAN
Arabian Sea
Nagpur
SUDAN
Sanaa
Mumbai
(Bombay)
Pune
Hyderabad
ERITREA
Taizz
YEMEN
DJIBOUTI
Al Makalla
UNITED ARAB
EMIRATES
Bay of
Bengal
Aden
Bangalore
Chennai
(Madras)
ETHIOPIA

0 mi.   500 mi.   1,000 mi.

0 km   500 km   1,000 km

Cochin
Madurai
Jaffna

KENYA
SOMALIA
INDIAN OCEAN
Colombo
SRI LANKA

ARCTIC OCEAN

Bering
Sea

Cherskiy

Tiksi

Verkhoyansk

RUSSIA

Magadan

Kamchatka
Peninsula

Yakutsk

Sea of
Okhotsk

Petropavlovsk-
Kamchatskiy

S I B E R I A

oyarsk

sk

Irkutsk

Khabarovsk

Sakhalin

Sapporo

Harbin

Ulaanbaatar

Changchun

Vladivostok

MONGOLIA

G o b i

Shenyang

JAPAN

Jinxi

N. KOREA

Hohhot

Beijing

P'yongyang

Nagoya

Tokyo

Tianjin

Seoul

Kyoto

Taiyuan

Jinan

Taegu

Kobe

Osaka

S. KOREA

Pusan

Lanzhou

Qingdao

Hiroshima

Fukuoka

Xi'an

Nagasaki

CHINA

Hefei

Shanghai

Chengdu

Wuhan

PACIFIC
OCEAN

Chongqing

Naha

TAN

Fuzhou

Taipei

Xiamen

GLADESH

Liuzhou

Guangzhou

TAIWAN

aka

Nanning

Macao

Kao-hsiung

Mandalay

ttagong

Hanoi

Hong Kong

NMAR
RMA)

LAOS

Luzon

Baguio

Chiang Mai

Vientiane

Quezon City

angoon

Da Nang

Manila

THAILAND

VIETNAM

PHILIPPINES

Bangkok

Cebu

CAMBODIA

Phnom
Penh

Ho Chi Minh City

Davao

Phuket

Songkhla

Borneo

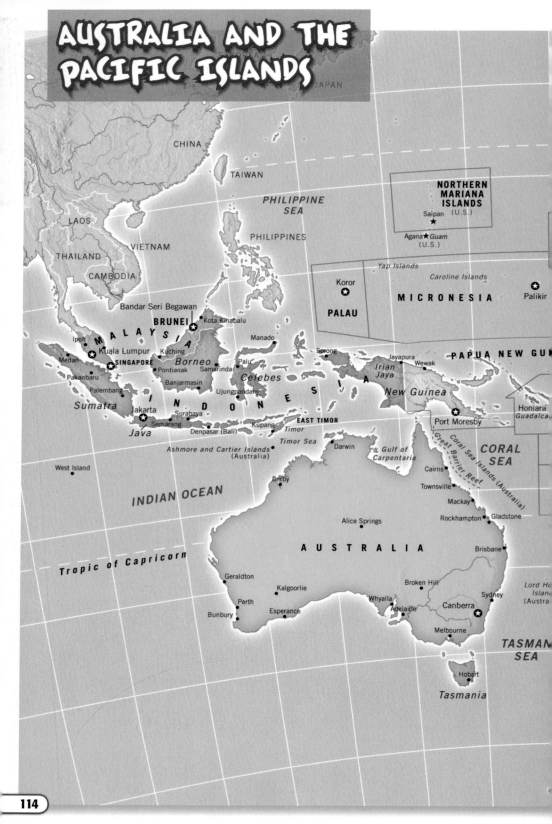

JAPAN

CHINA

TAIWAN

PHILIPPINE SEA

LAOS

VIETNAM

THAILAND

PHILIPPINES

CAMBODIA

NORTHERN MARIANA ISLANDS (U.S.)
Saipan ★

Agana ★ Guam (U.S.)

Yap Islands

Caroline Islands

Koror ◉

PALAU

M I C R O N E S I A

Palikir ◉

Bandar Seri Begawan

BRUNEI

Kota Kinabalu

M A L A Y S I A

Ipoh

Kuala Lumpur ✪ Kuching

Medan

SINGAPORE ✪ Pontianak

Borneo

Pakanbaru

Palembang

Banjarmasin

Samarinda

Manado

Celebes

Sorong

Jayapura

Wewak

Irian Jaya

P A P U A   N E W   G U I

Sumatra

Jakarta ✪

Surabaya

Semarang

Java

Denpasar (Bali)

EAST TIMOR

Ujungpandang

Kupang

Timor

New Guinea

Port Moresby ●

Honiara ●
Guadalca

I N D O N E S I A

Samarinda

Palu ●

Ashmore and Cartier Islands (Australia)

Timor Sea

Darwin ●

Gulf of Carpentaria

Great Barrier Reef

Coral Sea Islands (Australia)

CORAL SEA

West Island ●

INDIAN OCEAN

Derby ●

Cairns ●

Townsville ●

Mackay ●

Rockhampton ● Gladstone ●

Alice Springs ●

A U S T R A L I A

Brisbane ●

Tropic of Capricorn

Geraldton ●

Kalgoorlie ●

Broken Hill ●

Whyalla ●

Perth ●

Esperance ●

Bunbury ●

Adelaide ●

Lord He Island (Austra

Sydney ●

Canberra ✪

Melbourne ●

TASMAN SEA

Hobart ●

Tasmania

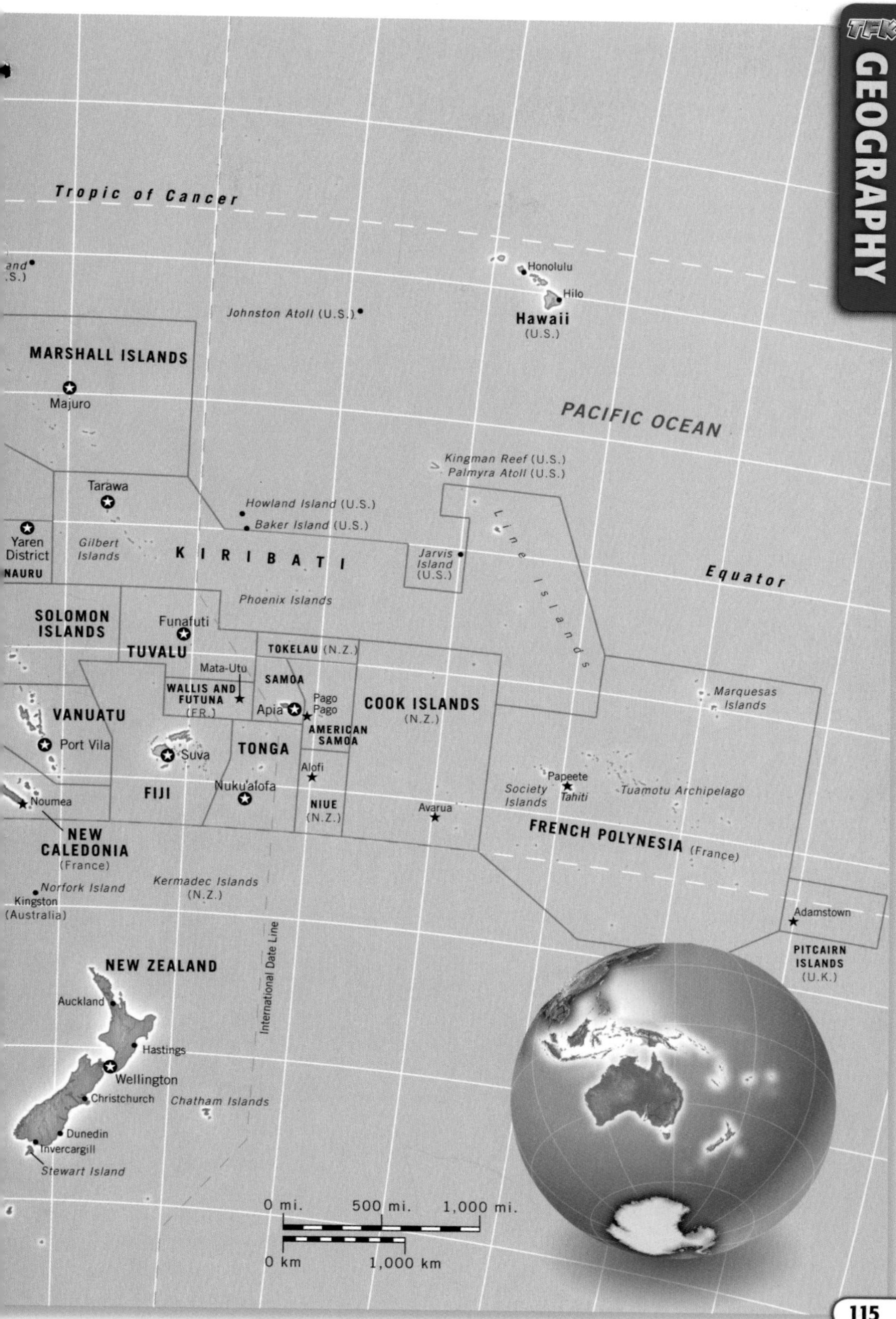

Tropic of Cancer

...and•
(U.S.)

Johnston Atoll (U.S.) •

Honolulu•
Hilo•

Hawaii
(U.S.)

MARSHALL ISLANDS

✪
Majuro

PACIFIC OCEAN

Kingman Reef (U.S.)
Palmyra Atoll (U.S.)

Tarawa
✪

Howland Island (U.S.)
• Baker Island (U.S.)

✪
Yaren
District

NAURU

Gilbert
Islands

K I R I B A T I

Jarvis
Island
(U.S.)

Line Islands

Equator

**SOLOMON
ISLANDS**

Phoenix Islands

Funafuti
✪

TUVALU

TOKELAU (N.Z.)

Mata-Utu

**WALLIS AND
FUTUNA**
(FR.)

SAMOA

Apia ✪ ★ Pago
Pago

COOK ISLANDS
(N.Z.)

Marquesas
Islands

VANUATU

✪ Port Vila

Suva
✪

TONGA

**AMERICAN
SAMOA**

Alofi
★

Papeete
★
Tahiti

Society
Islands

Tuamotu Archipelago

★ Noumea

FIJI

Nuku'alofa
✪

NIUE
(N.Z.)

Avarua
★

FRENCH POLYNESIA (France)

**NEW
CALEDONIA**
(France)

Kermadec Islands
(N.Z.)

Norfork Island
Kingston
(Australia)

Adamstown
★

**PITCAIRN
ISLANDS**
(U.K.)

International Date Line

NEW ZEALAND

Auckland

Hastings

✪ Wellington

Christchurch Chatham Islands

Dunedin
Invercargill

Stewart Island

0 mi.	500 mi.	1,000 mi.

0 km	1,000 km

EUROPE

ICELAND
Reykjavik ☆

Arctic Circle

FAROE ISLANDS
(Denmark)
Torshavn ·

SHETLAND ISLANDS

Trondheim ·

ORKNEY ISLANDS

NORWAY
Bergen ·
Oslo ☆
Gävle ·

Stavanger ·

HEBRIDES

SWEDEN
Göteborg ·

0 mi.   300 mi.   600 mi.

0 km   300 km   600 km

Aberdeen ·
Glasgow ·
Edinburgh ·
Belfast ·

DENMARK
Ålborg ·
Copenhagen ☆
Malmö ·

IRELAND ☆
Dublin ☆

UNITED KINGDOM
Liverpool · Leeds ·
Manchester ·
Sheffield ·

NORTH SEA

Birmingham ·

NETHERLANDS
Hamburg ·
Amsterdam ☆
Bremen ·
Berlin ☆
London ☆
The Hague ☆
Rotterdam ·

GUERNSEY (U.K.)
JERSEY (U.K.)
Calais ·
Antwerp ·
Essen ·
Poznan ·

Le Havre ·
Lille ·
Düsseldorf ·
Cologne ·
Bonn ·
GERMANY
Wroclaw ·

BELGIUM
LUXEMBOURG
Brussels ☆
Frankfurt ·

Paris ☆
Luxembourg ☆
Prague ☆
CZECH REPUBLIC
Brno ·

ATLANTIC OCEAN

Strasbourg ·
Stuttgart ·
Bratislava ☆

Nantes ·
Dijon ·
LIECHTENSTEIN
Munich ·
Vienna ☆

FRANCE
Zürich ·
Vaduz ☆
AUSTRIA

BAY OF BISCAY
Bern ☆
Geneva ·
SWITZERLAND
HUNGA

Bordeaux ·
Lyon ·
SLOVENIA
Ljubljana ☆
Trieste ·
Zagreb ☆

Porto ·
Bilbao ·
Turin ·
Milan ·
CROATIA

Toulouse ·
Genoa ·
SAN MARINO
BOSNIA AND HERZEGOVINA

Lisbon ☆
Madrid ☆
Andorra la Vella ☆
Marseille ·
MONACO ☆
Florence ·
☆ **SAN MARINO**
Sarajevo ·

PORTUGAL
SPAIN
Barcelona ·
ANDORRA
Bastia ·
ITALY
Rome ☆
MONTENE

Faro ·
Seville ·
Valencia ·
Majorca
Corsica
Vatican City ☆
ADRIATIC SEA

Málaga ·
Palma ·
Sardinia
Naples ·
Bari ·

Gibraltar ·

MEDITERRANEAN SEA
Cagliari ·
Kerki

Palermo ·
Messina ·

MOROCCO
ALGERIA
Sicily

A F R I C A
TUNISIA
Valletta ☆
MALTA

116

Murmansk

Pechora

ASIA

Arkhangel'sk

Oulu

FINLAND

R U S S I A

Tampere

rku Helsinki

Izhevsk

St. Petersburg

Tallinn

ESTONIA

Kazan

Nizhniy Novgorod

IC

Riga LATVIA

Moscow

THUANIA

Samara

Vilnius

Smolensk

A

Minsk

Saratov

Lipetsk

BELARUS

Homyel'

Voronezh

KAZAKHSTAN

ND

Brest

Kiev

Kharkiv

Volgograd

L'viv

Derazhnya

Voroshilovgrad

UKRAINE

Gorlovka

Makeyevka

Zhdanov

Rostov

Chisinau

Iasi

Odessa

Mykolavia

Groznyy

ROMANIA

Kerch'

MOLDOVA

Simferopol'

de

Bucharest

Sevastopol'

Craiova

Constanta

BLACK SEA

na

Sofia

Varna

BULGARIA

kopje

CEDONIA

Istanbul

essaloniki

T U R K E Y

Volos

EECE

Izmir

Athens

SYRIA

IRAN

Crete

CYPRUS

IRAQ

LEBANON

NORTH AMERICA AND CENTRAL AMERICA

ICELAND
Greenland Sea
Tasiilaq (Ammassalik)
Narsarsuaq
GREENLAND (Denmark)
Nuuk (Godthab)
Labrador Sea
St. John's
Island of Newfoundland
Happy Valley Goose Bay
Davis Strait
Iqaluit
CANADA
Qaanaaq (Thule)
Baffin Bay
Baffin Island
Chisasibi (Fort George)
Alert
HUDSON BAY
Moosonee
Queen Elizabeth Islands
Kaujuitoq (Resolute)
Churchill
Arctic Circle
Victoria Island
Banks Island
ARCTIC OCEAN
Winnipeg
Beaufort Sea
Echo Bay
Yellowknife
Regina
Saskatoon
Inuvik
Prudhoe Bay
Barrow
Edmonton
Calgary
Helena
Alaska (U.S.)
Whitehorse
Fairbanks
Juneau
Vancouver
Seattle
Boise
RUSSIA
Nome
Anchorage
Valdez
Victoria
Olympia
Portland
Salem
Bethel
Kodiak
Bering Sea
Aleutian Islands

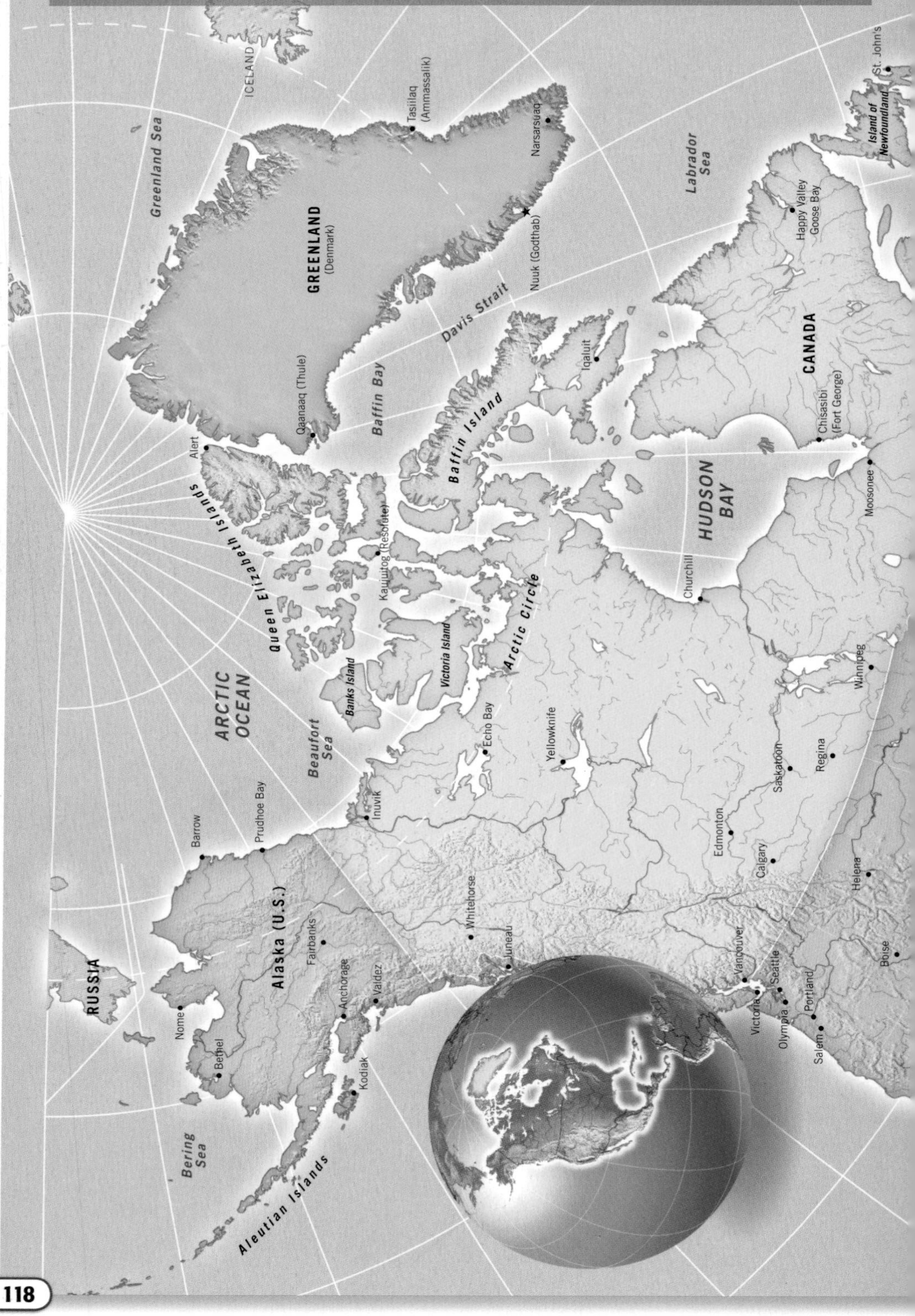

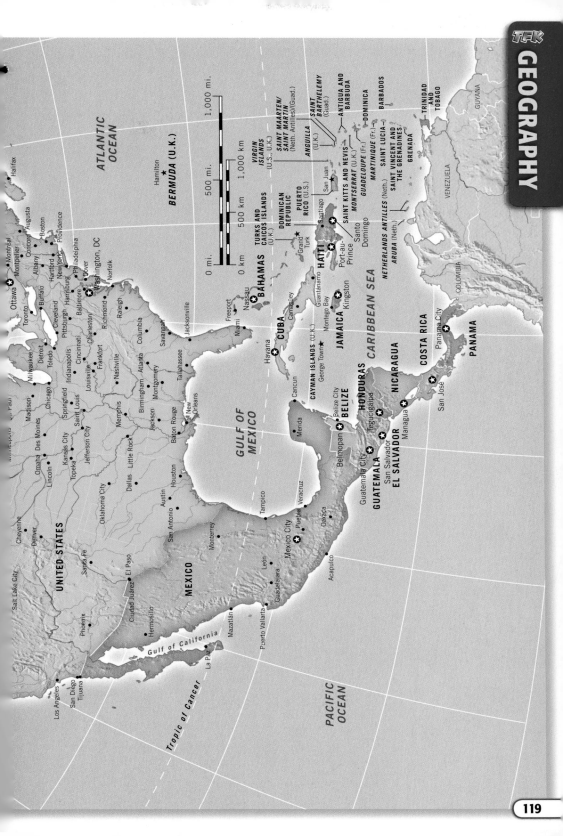

ATLANTIC OCEAN

Halifax

BERMUDA (U.K.)

Hamilton

1,000 mi.

500 mi.   1,000 km

0 mi.   500 km

Montréal
Ottawa
Montpelier
Concord Augusta
Albany Boston
Toronto Hartford Providence
Buffalo New York
Detroit Cleveland Philadelphia
Milwaukee Pittsburgh Harrisburg Dover
Chicago Toledo Baltimore Washington, DC
Cincinnati Norfolk
Madison Springfield Indianapolis Frankfort
Des Moines Saint Louis Louisville Richmond Raleigh
Omaha Kansas City Nashville Columbia
Lincoln Topeka Jefferson City Memphis Atlanta Columbia
Charleston
Savannah
Jacksonville

UNITED STATES

Cheyenne
Denver
Santa Fe
Oklahoma City
Dallas Little Rock
Austin Jackson Birmingham Montgomery
Baton Rouge Tallahassee
Phoenix San Antonio Houston New Orleans
El Paso

Salt Lake City

Los Angeles
San Diego
Tijuana

Ciudad Juárez
Hermosillo

MEXICO

Monterrey
Chihuahua
León Tampico
Guadalajara Mexico City
Puebla
Veracruz
Morelia Oaxaca
Puerto Vallarta
Mazatlán Acapulco

La Paz

Gulf of California

Tropic of Cancer

PACIFIC OCEAN

GULF OF MEXICO

Mérida
Cancún

Miami
Freeport
Nassau
BAHAMAS

TURKS AND CAICOS ISLANDS (U.K.)
Grand Turk

Havana
CUBA
Camagüey

Santiago

Guantánamo Bay
Montego Bay
Kingston
JAMAICA

CAYMAN ISLANDS (U.K.)★
George Town

HAITI
Port-au-Prince

DOMINICAN REPUBLIC
PUERTO RICO (U.S.)
San Juan
Santo Domingo

VIRGIN ISLANDS (U.S., U.K.)

ANGUILLA (U.K.)

SAINT MAARTEN/ SAINT MARTIN (Neth. Antilles)/(Guad.)

SAINT BARTHÉLEMY (Guad.)

ANTIGUA AND BARBUDA
SAINT KITTS AND NEVIS
MONTSERRAT (U.K.)
GUADELOUPE (Fr.)
DOMINICA
MARTINIQUE (Fr.)
SAINT LUCIA
BARBADOS
SAINT VINCENT AND THE GRENADINES
GRENADA

NETHERLANDS ANTILLES (Neth.)
ARUBA (Neth.)

CARIBBEAN SEA

TRINIDAD AND TOBAGO

VENEZUELA

GUYANA

COLOMBIA

BELIZE
Belmopan
Belize City

HONDURAS
Tegucigalpa

GUATEMALA
Guatemala City

EL SALVADOR
San Salvador

NICARAGUA
Managua

COSTA RICA
San José

PANAMA
Panama City

119

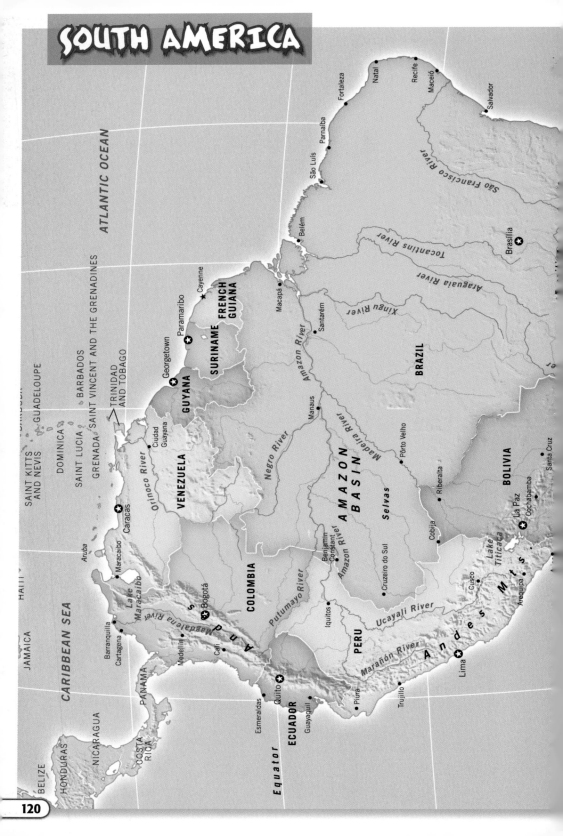

SOUTH AMERICA

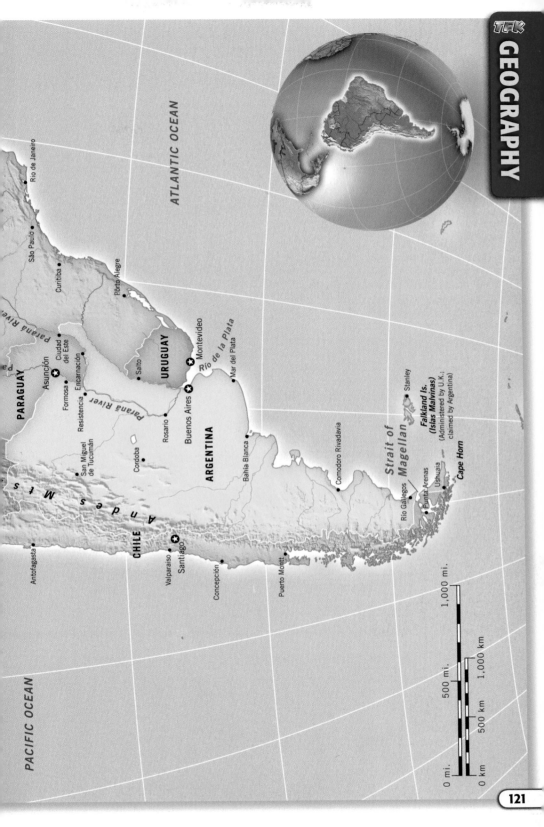

ATLANTIC OCEAN

Rio de Janeiro

São Paulo

Curitiba

Pôrto Alegre

Paraná River

Ciudad del Este

Asunción

PARAGUAY

Formosa

Encarnación

Resistencia

Salto

Montevideo

URUGUAY

Río de la Plata

Mar del Plata

San Miguel de Tucumán

Paraná River

Rosario

Buenos Aires

ARGENTINA

Córdoba

Bahía Blanca

Comodoro Rivadavia

Stanley

Falkland Is. (Islas Malvinas)
(Administered by U.K.; claimed by Argentina)

Strait of Magellan

Cape Horn

Río Gallegos

Punta Arenas

Ushuaia

Antofagasta

Andes Mts

Valparaíso

Santiago

CHILE

Concepción

Puerto Montt

PACIFIC OCEAN

0 mi.   500 mi.   1,000 mi.

0 km   500 km   1,000 km

121

THE CONSTITUTION OF THE UNITED STATES

In May 1787, a convention was held in Philadelphia to create a new set of rules by which this young nation would govern itself. George Washington was unanimously voted to preside over the gathering of 55 representatives of 12 states (Rhode Island refused to take part). James Madison of Virginia, who later became the fourth U.S. President, was chiefly responsible for the success of the convention.

Some leaders (Federalists) wanted to have a strong central government, while others (Anti-Federalists or Republicans) wanted the strongest powers to remain with the states. There were many heated debates, but on September 17, 1787, the Constitution of the United States was approved unanimously by the convention. By June 1788, it was ratified by ¾ of the states and, on March 4, 1789, it took its place as the supreme law of the land.

The Constitution begins with a passage called the preamble, which states the document's purpose:

GUESS WHAT?

The Constitution is housed at the National Archives Building in Washington, D.C. It is a four-page document, kept in a bullet-proof case that is sealed with helium and water vapor inside to preserve the document. Only the first and last pages are regularly on display, but on September 17 of each year, the anniversary of the day the Constitution was signed, all four pages are shown.

"We the people of the united States, in order to form a more perfect union, establish justice, insure domestic tranquility, provide for the common defense, promote the general welfare, and secure the blessings of liberty to ourselves and our posterity, do ordain and establish this Constitution for the united States of America."

James Madison is known as the "Father of the Constitution."

George Washington

The Bill of Rights

When the Congress-approved version of the Constitution was sent to the states for ratification, some state legislatures refused to approve it. Thanks to the efforts of James Madison and Thomas Jefferson, ten "amendments," known as the "Bill of Rights," were added to the Constitution. The Bill of Rights made it clear that individuals had certain personal freedoms that couldn't be taken away by the government. This document was ratified by ¾ of the states in 1791 and is considered a part of the Constitution.

Thomas Jefferson

AMENDMENT I declares the rights of freedom of religion, speech and the press. It also guarantees the right to assemble peacefully and to petition the government to hear and resolve any citizen's complaints or injustices.

AMENDMENT II guarantees citizens the right to own and use firearms to defend their country.

AMENDMENT III states that in peacetime a soldier cannot stay in a citizen's home without the owner's consent. In wartime, any such arrangement must be made according to the law.

AMENDMENT IV protects citizens, their belongings and their homes from being searched without a reasonable cause and prior legal consent.

AMENDMENT V says that no person can be tried for a non-military peacetime crime without having the crime first determined by a grand jury. It also states that a person cannot be tried twice for the same crime nor be forced to testify against himself or herself. Private property may not be taken by the government for public use without fair payment to the owner.

AMENDMENT VI guarantees citizens the right to a speedy public trial by jury. If accused, a person has the right to know what they are accused of, to be confronted by witnesses to the crime and to have an attorney and witnesses on behalf of their defense.

AMENDMENT VII states that the outcome of a trial can be determined by a jury and that any further appeal process must be done according to the law.

AMENDMENT VIII guarantees that reasonable amounts be set for fines and bail, which is a sum of money provided by a prisoner so that he or she may leave prison while awaiting trial. This amendment also prohibits cruel and unusual punishment for convicted criminals.

AMENDMENT IX declares that citizens have rights other than those stated in the Constitution.

AMENDMENT X guarantees that any powers not assigned to the federal government as provided in the Constitution belong to the states and the people.

Jury trial

Other Amendments

The framers of the Constitution always meant for the document to be a "work in progress," which would change and grow with the needs of a maturing nation. In the years since the Bill of Rights was ratified, 17 amendments have been added to the Constitution.

The 13th Amendment abolishing slavery was one of a trio of amendments passed after the Civil War.

After the passage of the 18th Amendment, prohibition agents destroyed alcohol all around the country.

AMENDMENT XI (1795) says that a state can't be sued by a citizen of another state or by a foreigner.

AMENDMENT XII (1804) further describes the way the President and Vice President are elected, namely by the electors of each state.

AMENDMENT XIII (1865) abolishes slavery or any kind of forced service.

AMENDMENT XIV (1868) defines a U.S. citizen as anyone born in the country or who comes to this country and is granted citizenship. U.S. citizenship can't be taken away from a citizen. The amendment also says that all citizens have equal protection under U.S. laws. No citizen who has been involved with any activity to overthrow the U.S. government or who has given aid to an enemy of the U.S. government can hold public office.

AMENDMENT XV (1870) gives the right to vote to all male citizens regardless of their "race, color, or previous condition of servitude."

AMENDMENT XVI (1913) gives Congress the right to collect income taxes from citizens.

AMENDMENT XVII (1913) allows for direct election of senators by the people of their states. In the case of death, disability or removal of a senator, the governor of that senator's state can appoint a temporary substitute until the people can hold another election.

AMENDMENT XVIII (1919) prohibits the making, selling and shipping of alcoholic beverages into and within the United States.

AMENDMENT XIX (1920) gives women the right to vote in all elections.

AMENDMENT XX (1933) describes the starting dates of the terms of President, Vice President and members of Congress. It also states that Congress must meet at least once a year and that if no presidential or vice presidential candidate receives a majority of electoral votes by the time their terms of office begin, the House of Representatives can choose the President and the Senate can choose the Vice President.

Franklin Roosevelt, seen here at his fourth inauguration, is the only President to have served for more than two terms.

AMENDMENT XXI (1933) repealed Amendment XVIII (Prohibition).

AMENDMENT XXII (1951) limits the length of the term of office of the presidency to two (four-year) terms.

AMENDMENT XXIII (1961) allows the District of Columbia to appoint electors to participate in the election of the President and Vice President.

Lyndon Johnson is sworn in after President Kennedy's assassination.

AMENDMENT XXIV (1964) eliminates the requirement of paying a poll tax in order to vote.

AMENDMENT XXV (1967) states that upon the death, removal or permanent disability of the President, the Vice President would become President. It also allows for a temporary succession if the President is unable to perform the duties of the office for a limited period of time. After such a period, the President can assume the office once again.

AMENDMENT XXVI (1971) extends the right to vote to U.S. citizens who have reached the age of 18.

An 18-year-old voter casts her ballot for the first time.

AMENDMENT XXVII (1992) states that a change in the salary of members of Congress can't be determined until those members have been elected.

GUESS WHAT?

Only five proposed amendments were passed by Congress, yet failed to be ratified by ¾ of the states:

1789: Anyone who accepts a title of nobility or office from a king or foreign power without Congress' permission gives up his U.S. citizenship.

1861: No constitutional amendment can be made that gives Congress the power to interfere with any state's laws regarding slavery.

1926: Congress has the power to "limit, regulate and prohibit the labor of persons under 18 years of age."

1972: Equality of rights under the law shall be given to women.

1978: The District of Columbia shall have the same rights of representation and election as all the other states (this would have repealed Amendment XXIII).

THE BRANCHES OF GOVERNMENT

The Constitution divides the basic structure of the U.S. government into three branches: the Legislative, Executive and Judicial branches. This provides a "separation of powers" among three equally important sectors—one that makes laws, another that carries out those laws and a third that determines whether those laws are constitutional. This system of "checks and balances" ensures that no single branch becomes too powerful.

THE LEGISLATIVE BRANCH

The Legislative branch was the first of the three branches of government to be created by the Constitution. The U.S. Legislature, known as Congress, is a "bicameral" structure, which means that it has two chambers: the House of Representatives and the Senate. The House of Representatives is based on state population, while the Senate gives every state equal representation. Both chambers hold hearings to gather information on bills being considered. Every bill must be approved by both chambers in order to become a law.

THE HOUSE OF REPRESENTATIVES includes 435 representatives chosen based on the population of each state, with a minimum of one representative for each state. The larger a state's population, the more representatives it has. For example, California has 53 representatives, while Montana has one. Representatives are elected to two-year terms every even-numbered year. The Speaker of the House presides over the sessions. The House of Representatives has the following special powers and responsibilities:

- creating bills that allow the government to collect taxes and spend money
- electing the President in the event that no candidate receives a majority of electoral votes
- voting to impeach the President, Vice President and other elected officials

The Senate questions Supreme Court nominee John Roberts.

THE SENATE
This chamber of Congress includes 100 senators, two for each state. Senators are elected to six-year terms, with $1/3$ of the Senate being elected every even-numbered year. The Vice President (or President Pro Tempore, in the Vice President's absence) presides over the sessions. The Senate has the following special powers and responsibilities:

- ratifying, or approving, treaties made by the President
- accepting or rejecting (by majority vote of all senators) the President's appointments of Supreme Court justices and federal judges, ambassadors, Cabinet secretaries and other high-level executive-branch officials
- holding trials of officials impeached by the House of Representatives and convicting or acquitting them

The House held impeachment hearings in 1998.

GUESS WHAT?

The political party with the most members in either chamber is called the "majority party." The other is called the "minority party." In each chamber, each party selects a leader, who coordinates party strategy and schedules when bills are introduced, and a whip, who tries to get party members to vote the same way for each bill considered.

THE EXECUTIVE BRANCH

When George Washington was inaugurated as President of the United States on April 30, 1789, it was the beginning of the Executive branch of the U.S. government. The President, Vice President and Cabinet make up this branch.

THE PRESIDENT

The President serves a term of four years, with a maximum of two terms. A President must be a native-born U.S. citizen, at least 35 years old and have lived in the United States for at least 14 years. The President has the following powers and responsibilities:

President Clinton signing a bill.

- carrying out the laws of the land
- appointing U.S. ambassadors, Supreme Court justices, federal judges and Cabinet secretaries (who then must be approved by the Senate)

The presidential seal

- giving the annual State of the Union address to Congress
- receiving foreign ambassadors
- proposing treaties with other nations
- serving as commander in chief of the armed forces, sending troops overseas (but needs Congressional approval to declare war)
- calling both houses of Congress to meet in a special session
- approving or vetoing bills passed by Congress
- granting pardons for federal crimes

This book had to go to the printer before the election results were in!

go To read about the 2008 election, go to www.timeforkids.

THE VICE PRESIDENT

Under Article I of the Constitution, the Vice President presides over the Senate and only votes to break a tie. Article XXV allows the Vice President to assume the office of President under certain conditions. The Vice President must meet the same age and residential qualifications as the President.

THE CABINET Since 1789, Presidents have designated certain responsibilities to members of their Cabinet, called secretaries, who oversee separate executive departments. The very first Cabinet consisted of four secretaries: State, Treasury, War and the Attorney General. Today the Presidential Cabinet consists of 15 secretaries.

DEPARTMENT	WEB ADDRESS
State	www.state.gov
Treasury	www.ustreas.gov
Interior	www.doi.gov
Agriculture	www.usda.gov
Justice (Attorney General)	www.usdoj.gov
Commerce	www.commerce.gov
Labor	www.dol.gov
Defense	www.defenselink.mil
Housing and Urban Development	www.hud.gov
Transportation	www.dot.gov
Energy	www.energy.gov
Education	www.ed.gov
Health and Human Services	www.dhhs.gov
Veterans Affairs	www.va.gov
Homeland Security	www.dhs.gov

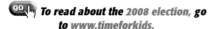

President and Commander in Chief Bush visited American troops in 2005.

GUESS WHAT? Madeleine Albright was the first woman Secretary of State of the United States.

THE JUDICIAL BRANCH

On February 2, 1790, the Supreme Court held its first session. The main task of the Judicial Branch, and of the Supreme Court in particular, is to see that the Constitution and the laws formed under its provisions are preserved and followed. The nine Supreme Court justices have the power to declare as unconstitutional any law or practice that doesn't comply with the laws of the land. The Courts also interpret the way an established law must be carried out.

Supreme Court justices and federal judges are appointed by the President and confirmed by the Senate. They serve for life or until they decide to resign or retire. The Supreme Court consists of eight associate justices and a chief justice. All decisions are made by a majority vote of the justices.

Supreme Court Justices (from left to right, first row): Anthony Kennedy, John Paul Stevens, Chief Justice John Roberts, Antonin Scalia, David Souter; (back row): Stephen Breyer, Clarence Thomas, Ruth Bader Ginsburg, Samuel Alito Jr.

Famous Supreme Court Cases

Marbury v. Madison (1803) Established the fact that the Constitution takes precedence over any other law, and that the Supreme Court has the power to decide what a law is.

Dred Scott v. Sandford (1856) Said that a slave was not a U.S. citizen. Established the fact that all residents (including slaveholders) in a U.S. territory must be treated equally and that Congress could not outlaw slavery in the U.S. territories.

Plessy v. Ferguson (1896) Upheld a Louisiana court decision that racial segregation was legal.

Brown v. Board of Education (1954) Declared that racial segregation in public schools was unconstitutional.

Miranda v. Arizona (1966) Determined that suspected criminals must be read their constitutional rights before being questioned by law enforcement officers.

Bush v. Gore (2000) Overturned a Florida Supreme Court decision to manually recount the state's votes in the presidential election, which originally gave a slight lead to George W. Bush over Al Gore. The decision was based on the fact that the process of counting votes varies from state to state and the Supreme Court didn't have jurisdiction in the way the process was regulated. As a result, George Bush won the election.

Kelo v. City of New London (2005) Said the government could take private land from owners without their consent to be used for private developments if the new developments are deemed to have a positive impact on the area. The owners must receive fair compensation for their land.

Massachusetts et al. v. Environmental Protection Agency et al. (2007) Declared that greenhouse gases are pollutants and that the EPA has the power to regulate them.

What Is a Filibuster?

Many colorful words and phrases describe U.S. political activities.

A **BULLY PULPIT** describes a special opportunity by office holders such as the President or members of Congress to hold people's attention and convince them of a certain idea or agenda. President Theodore Roosevelt used the word "bully" as a synonym for "terrific" and not "bossy." Today it might mean either one, depending on whether it is meant as criticism or praise.

GERRYMANDERING is the process of changing the boundaries of election districts to give one candidate or party a better chance of winning.

A political cartoon pokes fun at gerrymandering.

A **LAME DUCK** is a President or member of Congress who is serving his or her last term in office and not running for reelection. These leaders no longer have as much power or influence.

A **RIDER** is a proposal tacked on to another Senate bill, which may or may not have anything to do with the bill itself. If the bill passes, the rider automatically passes.

A **CHRISTMAS TREE BILL** contains lots of riders. Just like the different ornaments on a Christmas tree, the riders on the bill may be unrelated to one another, providing benefits to various kinds of groups.

A **POCKET VETO** is one strategy used by a President who doesn't want to approve a particular bill. The Constitution allows the President 10 days (not counting Sundays) to sign a bill that has already been passed by Congress. If the President doesn't act within that time, the bill automatically becomes a law. However, if Congress adjourns within that 10-day period and the President does not sign the bill, it's as if the President has put it in his or her "pocket."

A **FILIBUSTER** is a strategy used in the Senate to delay, change or defeat all or part of a bill. The goal of a filibuster is to stop a vote on the bill from taking place. Since a vote can only take place after debate ends, a filibuster extends the time in which the bill is debated in the hope that some senators might change their minds and vote a different way.

Beds are rolled into the Capitol so Senators can rest during a filibuster.

Mystery Person

TFK ?

CLUE 1: I was born in 1706, in Boston, Massachusetts.

CLUE 2: I was an inventor and a scientist. I flew a kite in a lightning storm to learn about electricity.

CLUE 3: I was a Founding Father of the United States. On September 17, 1787, I was one of 39 lawmakers to sign the U.S. Constitution.

WHO AM I? _____

ANSWERS ON PAGE 244

ANCIENT HISTORY

4000– 3500 B.C.	**Sumer, located in what is now Iraq, becomes the earliest known civilization. They develop a written alphabet.**
3500– 2600 B.C.	**People settle in the Indus River Valley in what is now India and Pakistan.**
2700 B.C.	**Minoan civilization begins on the island of Crete.**
approx. **2680** B.C.	**The Egyptian King, Khufu, finishes building the Great Pyramid at Giza. The Great Sphinx is completed soon after.**
2000 B.C.	**Babylonians develop a system of mathematics. The Kingdom of Kush in Africa becomes a major center of trade and learning.**
1792 B.C.	**Hammurabi becomes the ruler of Babylonia. He creates the first code of law, known as "Hammurabi's Code."**
1200 B.C.	**The Trojan War is fought between the Greeks and Trojans.**
approx. **1700– 1050** B.C.	**The Shang Dynasty is the first Chinese dynasty to leave written records.**
814 B.C.	**The city of Carthage, now located in Tunisia, is founded by the Phoenicians.**
753 B.C.	**According to the legend, Rome is founded by Romulus and Remus.**
563 B.C.	**Siddhartha Gautama, who becomes the Buddha, or "Enlightened One," is born. He will become the founder of the Buddhist religion.**
551 B.C.	**Chinese philosopher Confucius is born. His teachings on how people should treat one another are the foundations of Confucianism.**
508 B.C.	**Democracy is established in Athens, Greece.**
431 B.C.	**The Peloponnesian War breaks out between Sparta and Athens. In 404** B.C.**, Sparta finally wins the war and takes over Athens.**
334 B.C.	**Alexander the Great invades Persia. He eventually conquers lands from Greece to India, even crossing into North Africa.**
100 B.C.	**The great city of Teotihuacán is built in Mexico. Construction begins on the enormous Pyramid of the Sun.**
58 B.C.	**Julius Caesar leaves Rome for Gaul (France) and spends nine years conquering much of Central Europe. He is murdered in 44** B.C.
27 B.C.	**Octavian becomes the first Roman Emperor, ushering in a long period of peace. He is also known by the title Augustus.**

1200 B.C.

563 B.C.

334 B.C.

ca. 1 A.D.	**Jesus Christ is born. He is crucified by the Romans around 30** A.D.
66	**Jews rebel against Roman rule. The revolution is quashed by the Romans, who destroy Jerusalem in 70 and force many Jews into slavery.**
79	**Mount Vesuvius erupts, destroying the city of Pompeii.**
122	**Hadrian's Wall is built across northern Britain for protection from the "barbarian" tribes to the north.**
approx. 250	**The classic period of Mayan civilization begins and lasts until around 900. The Maya build impressive stone buildings and temples.**
330	**Constantine the Great chooses Byzantium as the capital of the Roman Empire and the city becomes known as Constantinople.**
476	**The Roman Empire collapses.**
622	**Muhammad, the founder of Islam, must flee from Mecca to Medina in what is called the Hegira. After his death in 632, Muslims conquer much of North Africa and the Middle East. In 711, they conquer Spain.**
800	**Charlemagne is crowned first Holy Roman Emperor by Pope Leo III.**
960	**The Song Dynasty begins in China. This dynasty is known for its advances in art, poetry and philosophy.**
ca. 1000– 1300	**During the classic period of Anasazi culture, Anasazi Indians in North America build their homes and meeting rooms into the sides of cliffs.**
1066	**At the Battles of Hastings, the Norman king, William the Conqueror, invades England and defeats English King Harold II.**
1095	**Pope Urban II delivers a speech urging Christians to capture the Holy Land from the Muslims. The fighting between 1096 and 1291 is known as the Crusades.**

approx. 1200	**The Inca Empire begins, eventually building elaborate stone structures in Cuzco and Machu Picchu, Peru. The Incas flourish until Spaniard Francisco Pizarro conquers them in 1533.**
1206	**A Mongolian warrior named Temujin is proclaimed Genghis Khan. He expands his empire hugely so that it covers most of Asia.**
1215	**A group of barons in England force King John to sign the Magna Carta, a document limiting the power of the King.**
1273	**The Hapsburg dynasty begins in Eastern Europe. It will remain a powerful force in the region until World War I.**
1325	**Aztecs begin building Tenochtitlán on the site of modern Mexico City.**
1337	**The Hundred Years' War breaks out between the English and the French. France finally wins in 1453.**
1347	**The Black Death, or bubonic plague, breaks out in Europe. It spreads quickly, killing more than one-third of Europe's population.**
1368	**The Ming Dynasty in China is founded by Buddhist monk Chu Yuan-Chang.**
1453	**Constantinople falls to the Ottoman Turks, ending the Byzantine Empire.**
1455	**Johannes Guttenberg invents the printing press. The Bible is the first book printed on the press. It becomes known as "the Guttenberg Bible."**

For information on historical exploration, see the Timeline of Explorers on page 102.

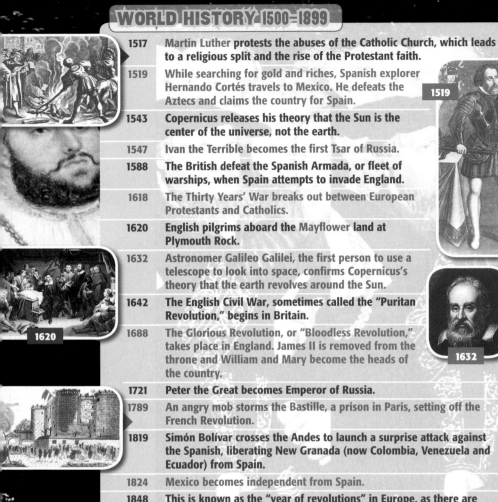

1517   **Martin Luther protests the abuses of the Catholic Church, which leads to a religious split and the rise of the Protestant faith.**

1519   **While searching for gold and riches, Spanish explorer Hernando Cortés travels to Mexico. He defeats the Aztecs and claims the country for Spain.**

1519

1543   **Copernicus releases his theory that the Sun is the center of the universe, not the earth.**

1547   **Ivan the Terrible becomes the first Tsar of Russia.**

1588   **The British defeat the Spanish Armada, or fleet of warships, when Spain attempts to invade England.**

1618   **The Thirty Years' War breaks out between European Protestants and Catholics.**

1620   **English pilgrims aboard the Mayflower land at Plymouth Rock.**

1632   **Astronomer Galileo Galilei, the first person to use a telescope to look into space, confirms Copernicus's theory that the earth revolves around the Sun.**

1642   **The English Civil War, sometimes called the "Puritan Revolution," begins in Britain.**

1620

1688   **The Glorious Revolution, or "Bloodless Revolution," takes place in England. James II is removed from the throne and William and Mary become the heads of the country.**

1632

1721   **Peter the Great becomes Emperor of Russia.**

1789   **An angry mob storms the Bastille, a prison in Paris, setting off the French Revolution.**

1819   **Simón Bolívar crosses the Andes to launch a surprise attack against the Spanish, liberating New Granada (now Colombia, Venezuela and Ecuador) from Spain.**

1824   **Mexico becomes independent from Spain.**

1848   **This is known as the "year of revolutions" in Europe, as there are upheavals in France, Italy, Germany, Hungary and other areas.**

1845   **A blight ruins the potato crop in Ireland. More than 1 million Irish starve to death, and another million leave for America to escape the famine.**

1859   **Charles Darwin writes The Origin of Species.**

1871   **A group of independent states unify, creating the German Empire.**

1884   **Representatives of 14 European countries meet at the Berlin West Africa Conference and divide Africa into areas of control.**

1893   **New Zealand becomes the first country to extend to women the right to vote. The Columbian Exposition (or Chicago World's Fair) is held.**

1894   **The Sino-Japanese War breaks out between China and Japan, who are vying for control of Korea. An 1895 treaty declares Korea independent.**

1898   **The Spanish-American War breaks out.**

1845

1899   **During the Boxer Rebellion, Chinese fight against Christian and foreign influences in their country. American, Japanese and European forces help to stop the fighting by 1901.**

1899

1904   **Japan declares war on Russia, beginning the Russo-Japanese War.** The countries clash over influence in Manchuria and Korea. Japan wins the conflict and becomes a world power.

1914   Austro-Hungarian Archduke Franz Ferdinand is assassinated, setting off a chain of events that begins World War I.

1917   **The United States enters World War I.** The Russian Revolution begins. The tsarist government is overthrown and, in 1922, the Soviet Union is formed.

1918   A devastating flu epidemic spreads quickly around the world, killing more than 20 million people.

1919   The Treaty of Versailles ends World War I.

1929   The U.S. stock market collapses, beginning the Great Depression.

1933   **Adolf Hitler** becomes Chancellor of Germany.

1936   The Spanish Civil War breaks out.

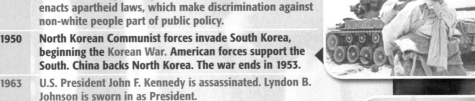

1933

1939   **World War II begins when Germany invades Poland.** France and Britain respond by declaring war on Germany. The United States declares neutrality.

1941   The Japanese launch a surprise attack on the United States, bombing U.S. ships at Hawaii's Pearl Harbor. In response, the U.S. declares war on Japan and both Germany and Italy declare war on the U.S.

1945   **Germany surrenders on May 7, ending the war in Europe.** In August, the United States drops two atomic bombs in Japan, on the cities of Hiroshima and Nagasaki. Japan surrenders, ending World War II.

1947   India and Pakistan become free of British colonial rule.

1948   Israel becomes a nation.

1949   Following China's Civil War, Mao Zedong sets up the Communist People's Republic of China. South Africa enacts apartheid laws, which make discrimination against non-white people part of public policy.

1950   **North Korean Communist forces invade South Korea, beginning the Korean War.** American forces support the South. China backs North Korea. The war ends in 1953.

1963   U.S. President John F. Kennedy is assassinated. Lyndon B. Johnson is sworn in as President.

1964   **The United States begins sending troops to Vietnam to aid South Vietnam in its civil war with North Vietnam.**

1967   The Six-Day War breaks out between Israel and neighboring Arab nations Egypt, Syria and Jordan. Israel seizes the Golan Heights, Gaza Strip, Sinai Peninsula and part of the West Bank of the Jordan River.

1973   **The Paris Peace Accords end the Vietnam War.** North Vietnam later violates the terms of the treaty and, in 1975, takes control of Saigon, the capital of South Vietnam. Egypt and Syria conduct a surprise attack on Israel, beginning the Yom Kippur War.

1978   U.S. President Jimmy Carter, Israeli President Menachem Begin and Egyptian President Anwar Sadat sign the Camp David Accords in an attempt to achieve peace in the Middle East.

1979	Religious leader Ayatollah Khomeini returns to Iran from exile and declares it an Islamic Republic.
1989	The Chinese army crushes a demonstration in Tiananmen Square, China, killing hundreds or thousands of students and protestors. The Berlin Wall is torn down and the city of Berlin, Germany, is reunified.
1990	Apartheid ends in South Africa. Nelson Mandela will be elected President four years later in the country's first free, multiracial elections. The Persian Gulf War begins when Iraq invades Kuwait.
1991	The Soviet Union dissolves. Croatia, Slovenia and Macedonia declare independence from Yugoslavia. The next year, Bosnia and Herzegovina declares independence, but war breaks out and does not end until 1995.
1994	Conflict between the Hutu majority and the Tutsi minority in Rwanda leads to a bloody civil war and genocide, which refers to the systematic killing of a racial or ethnic group.
2001	After the September 11th terrorist attacks in New York City and Washington, D.C., the United States declares an international war on terror, attacking the Taliban government in Afghanistan and searching for Osama Bin Laden and al Qaeda.
2003	With the aid of Britain and other allies, the United States invades Iraq. Though the government falls quickly, resistance and fighting continue. Dictator Saddam Hussein is captured and, in 2006, is executed for crimes against humanity. War in the Darfur region of Sudan begins, leading to a humanitarian crisis.
2004	An interim government is inaugurated in Iraq. Hamid Karzai becomes Afghanistan's president. A powerful tsunami kills nearly 300,000 people in Indonesia, Sri Lanka, India, Thailand and other Asian countries.
2006	Montenegro becomes independent from Serbia.
2007	Former Pakistani Prime Minister Benazir Bhutto is assassinated. The government of Myanmar (formerly known as Burma) violently cracks down on protestors, including Buddhist monks. A United Nations committee releases its report confirming the dangers of climate change.
2008	Kosovo declares its independence from Serbia.

2003

U.S. HISTORY

1607	English settlers found Jamestown in Virginia. The colony's leader, John Smith, is captured by Indians. According to legend, he is saved by Pocahontas.
1620	Pilgrims land at Plymouth, Massachusetts.
1626	Dutchman Peter Minuit buys the island of Manhattan from the Canarsie Indians.
1692	Accusations of witchcraft lead to the Salem Witch Trials and executions of 19 people.
1770	Tensions between British soldiers and colonists erupt in the Boston Massacre when British troops kill five men.
1773	Colonists protest a tax on tea by dressing up as Indians and dumping tea into Boston Harbor. Known as the Boston Tea Party, the protest angers the British, who pass other harsh laws.

1775	Paul Revere warns the colonists that the British are coming. The Battle of Lexington and Concord is the first fight of the American Revolution. The British surrender at Yorktown, Virginia, in 1781.
1776	Drafted by Thomas Jefferson, the Declaration of Independence is signed and the American colonies declare independence.
1787	The U.S. Constitution is written and submitted to the states for ratification. By the end of the year, Delaware, Pennsylvania and New Jersey have accepted it.
1789	George Washington becomes the first President of the United States.
1791	The Bill of Rights, written mostly by James Madison, becomes part of the Constitution.
1803	Thomas Jefferson buys the Louisiana Territory from France.
1812	The War of 1812 breaks out between the United States and Britain because of trade and border disputes, as well as disagreements about the freedom of the seas. In 1814, the Treaty of Ghent ends the war.
1823	President James Monroe issues the Monroe Doctrine, warning that the Americas are not open for colonization.
1836	Texas declares independence from Mexico. In response, the Mexican Army attacks and kills the 187 Texans defending the Alamo.
1838	In what is known as the "Trail of Tears," 16,000 Cherokee Indians are forced to leave their land in Georgia and relocate to a reservation in Oklahoma. Roughly a quarter of them die.
1846	The Mexican-American War begins. At the end of the fighting in 1848, Mexico cedes California and New Mexico (which also includes present-day Arizona, Utah and Nevada) to the United States. In return, the U.S. agrees to pay Mexico $15 million.
1848	John Sutter strikes gold in California, kicking off the California gold rush.
1860	Tensions between the North and the South over slavery, taxes and representation reach their boiling point, and South Carolina secedes from the United States.
1861	Mississippi, Florida, Alabama, Georgia, Louisiana and Texas secede from the Union, and the Confederate government is formed. The first shots of the American Civil War are fired at Fort Sumter in Charleston Harbor in South Carolina. Virginia, Arkansas, Tennessee and North Carolina also secede from the Union.
1862	The Homestead Act promises 160 acres of land to anyone who remains on the land for five years. This law encourages settlers to move west.
1863	President Abraham Lincoln issues the Emancipation Proclamation, which frees all slaves in the Confederate states. The Battle of Gettysburg is the bloodiest battle of the Civil War.

1776

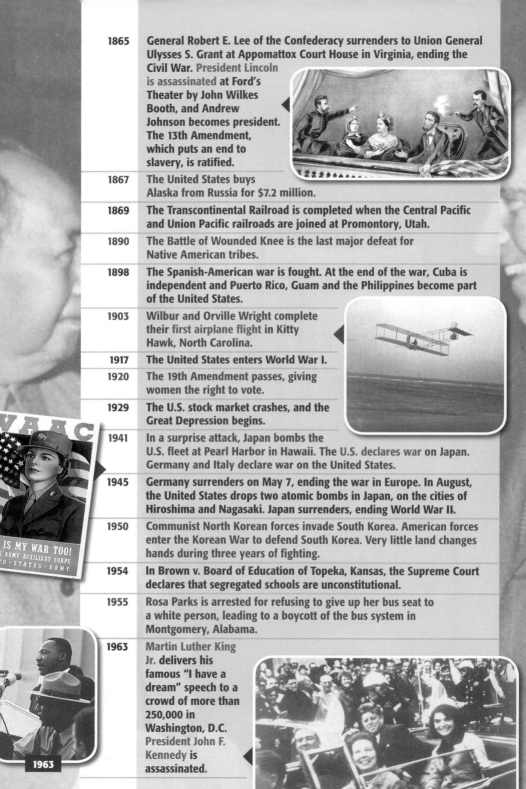

1865	**General Robert E. Lee of the Confederacy surrenders to Union General Ulysses S. Grant at Appomattox Court House in Virginia, ending the Civil War.** President Lincoln is assassinated at Ford's Theater by John Wilkes Booth, and Andrew Johnson becomes president. The 13th Amendment, which puts an end to slavery, is ratified.
1867	The United States buys Alaska from Russia for $7.2 million.
1869	The Transcontinental Railroad is completed when the Central Pacific and Union Pacific railroads are joined at Promontory, Utah.
1890	The Battle of Wounded Knee is the last major defeat for Native American tribes.
1898	The Spanish-American war is fought. At the end of the war, Cuba is independent and Puerto Rico, Guam and the Philippines become part of the United States.
1903	Wilbur and Orville Wright complete their first airplane flight in Kitty Hawk, North Carolina.
1917	The United States enters World War I.
1920	The 19th Amendment passes, giving women the right to vote.
1929	The U.S. stock market crashes, and the Great Depression begins.
1941	In a surprise attack, Japan bombs the U.S. fleet at Pearl Harbor in Hawaii. The U.S. declares war on Japan. Germany and Italy declare war on the United States.
1945	Germany surrenders on May 7, ending the war in Europe. In August, the United States drops two atomic bombs in Japan, on the cities of Hiroshima and Nagasaki. Japan surrenders, ending World War II.
1950	Communist North Korean forces invade South Korea. American forces enter the Korean War to defend South Korea. Very little land changes hands during three years of fighting.
1954	In Brown v. Board of Education of Topeka, Kansas, the Supreme Court declares that segregated schools are unconstitutional.
1955	Rosa Parks is arrested for refusing to give up her bus seat to a white person, leading to a boycott of the bus system in Montgomery, Alabama.
1963	Martin Luther King Jr. delivers his famous "I have a dream" speech to a crowd of more than 250,000 in Washington, D.C. President John F. Kennedy is assassinated.

WAAC

THIS IS MY WAR TOO!
WOMEN'S ARMY AUXILIARY CORPS
UNITED · STATES · ARMY

1963

1965	Malcolm X is killed. Race riots in the Watts section of Los Angeles are among the worst in U.S. history. President Lyndon Johnson authorizes air raids over North Vietnam.
1968	James Earl Ray shoots and kills Martin Luther King Jr. in Memphis, Tennessee. Riots break out across the country.
1973	The Vietnam War ends when peace accords are signed. Two years later, North Vietnam takes over Saigon, the capital of South Vietnam.
1974	Due to his involvement in the Watergate scandal, President Richard Nixon steps down as President. Gerald Ford becomes President.
1979	Islamic militants storm the U.S. embassy in Tehran, Iran. More than 60 Americans are held hostage for 444 days.
1986	The Challenger space shuttle explodes, killing seven crewmembers, including teacher Christa McAuliffe.
1991	After Iraq invades Kuwait, the United States begins bombing raids. The first Persian Gulf War ends quickly as Iraqi forces are driven from Kuwait.
1999	President Bill Clinton is acquitted of impeachment charges.
2000	In an extremely close election between Democrat Al Gore and Republican George W. Bush, the U.S. Supreme Court determines the outcome. Bush is declared the winner.
2001	On September 11, four passenger planes are hijacked. Two are flown into the World Trade Center in New York City, causing the two towers to collapse. Another is flown into the Pentagon near Washington, D.C. The fourth crashes into a field in Pennsylvania after passengers overpower the hijackers. The United States and Britain respond by attacking the Taliban government in Afghanistan, where terrorist Osama bin Laden is thought to be hiding. The U.S. government declares the "War on Terror."
2003	The space shuttle Columbia breaks apart during re-entry into Earth's atmosphere. Along with its allies from Britain and other countries, the United States invades Iraq. Saddam Hussein's government falls quickly, but resistance and fighting continue.
2005	Hurricane Katrina hits the Gulf Coast, destroying areas in Mississippi and Louisiana and along the southeast U.S. The levee system in New Orleans, Louisiana, cannot withstand the hurricane, and 80% of the city floods.
2007	The deadliest school shooting in U.S. history occurs when Seung-Hui Cho opens fire at Virginia Tech. Thirty-two students are killed and many others are wounded in the rampage. The minimum hourly wage is increased for the first time in 10 years—from $5.15 to $5.85—as part of a plan to get it to $7.25 by 2009.

2001

TNT Post

COOLEST INVENTIONS OF 2007

FROM TFK MAGAZINE

A dress that senses your mood and lets everyone know whether you are happy or sad. A machine that could help save your life. These are just a few of the recent gadgets, gizmos and bright ideas developed by inventors. Here are some of 2007's smartest notions and most interesting new products. Which is your favorite?

EXPRESS YOURSELF

If you're happy and you know it and you really want to show it, put on a Philips SKIN Probes outfit. The Bubelle dress uses sensors to pick up on your feelings. Lights in the dress change colors to match your mood.

MAIL AND GROW

How do you make your garden grow? Just peel off the plastic film on these stamps and plant them in dirt! Issued by a Dutch company, TNT Post, the stamps contain real flower seeds.

CITY WHEELS

Zoom, zoom, zoom. The City Car aims to change the way people travel in cities. Desiged by a team of researchers at the Massachusetts Institute of Technology, the electric cars stack together like shopping carts. The system could save energy. Passengers pick up and return the cars at stations. The cars should be running in 2011.

HEAD IN THE GAME

Relax, Mom! The HITS helmet records the location and force of impacts to a football player's head. The high-tech helmet sends data to a computer. A Web analysis helps parents and coaches see if a doctor is needed.

A FLYING ROBOT

Birds do it. Bees do it. And now a toy does it, too. FlyTech Dragonfly is the first remote-controlled toy to fly by flapping its wings instead of using a propeller. The dragonfly is sturdy yet ultralight, weighing just one ounce. It sells for $49.99.

Senz umbrella

SKINTIGHT SPACE SUIT

Astronauts will soon be able to shed some pounds—of heavy gear, that is. The Bio-Suit is formfitting spacewear developed by MIT professor Dava Newman. It is lighter than today's bulky suits and made of elastic materials that improve mobility.

THIS ROBOT CAN SEE YOU

What sets Domo apart from run-of-the-mill robots? This machine has the ability to recognize people and react to its surroundings. Created by two scientists at MIT, Domo can hold objects, place a cup on a counter and grasp your hands when you touch its spring-loaded ones. Its human-like eyes can even see who's watching.

TRANSFORMERS

High heels are not built for comfort. Now, in just three quick steps, towering high heels become comfy flats. Camileon Heels transform with just a tug, a click and a tuck. The unique design prevents the heel from collapsing or coming loose.

GOOD BLOOD

Scientists have developed a new machine that can convert anyone's blood to type O-negative. Only 7% of people have type O-negative blood. Those people are called "universal donors" because their blood can be given to help people of any blood type. The blood converter is now being tested on humans.

LET IT RAIN

Even Mary Poppins would want to trade in her old parasol for this sleek new model. Shaped like a bat wing, the stylish Senz umbrella can withstand winds up to 70 miles per hour without flipping inside out! For $55, the Senz will have you singing in the rain.

HEALING HAND

Even trained professionals find it hard to get CPR chest compressions right. Enter the CPR Glove, which was invented by three Canadian college students. The glove is embedded with sensors and chips that talk you through the proper CPR technique. The sensors measure the amount and frequency of pressure that is applied to the chest.

Early Inventions and Developments

2,600,000 B.C.	stone tools
1,420,000 B.C.	fire as a tool
38,000–10,000 B.C.	fishing, spear, bow and arrow, counting, drum, domestication of the dog, boat
7000–4000 B.C.	domestication of cattle and chickens, weaving, concrete, musical instruments (bone pipe and stringed harp), arithmetic
3500–2000 B.C.	wheel, writing, sundial, glass, candle, bronze, soap, papyrus, ink, library, school, irrigation, map, paved roads
1700–700 B.C.	alphabet, rubber, chocolate, shoe, steel, star navigation, dictionary, kite, false teeth, musical notation
650–30 B.C.	windmill, lighthouse, democracy, mirror, ice cream, steam power, book, calendar, insecticide, thumbprint to show identity
10–600 A.D.	detergent, paper, abacus, zoo, algebra, tea, toilet paper, matches, postal service
620–1000	chess, mail delivered by pigeons, comb, gunpowder, fork, golf, hospital, toothpaste, pizza, horse-drawn ambulance
1250–1699	eyeglasses, weighing scales, printing press, parachute, human-powered submarine, barometer, gun
1700–99	piano, steam engine, fire extinguisher, mercury thermometer, lightning rod, English-language dictionary, steam engine, steamboat, guillotine, bicycle, cotton gin

Timeline of
LIFE-CHANGING INVENTIONS

1830	sewing machine
1837	telegraph
1839	rubber
1850	refrigerator
1858	rotary washing machine
1862	plastic
1866	dynamite
1868	typewriter
1869	vacuum cleaner
1873	barbed wire
1876	microphone, telephone
1877	phonograph (record player)
1892	Diesel engine, escalator
1893	motion picture

Vulcanized rubber is a material that is strong but flexible and can withstand both hot and cold temperatures. Rubber wasn't always in this form. Originally, it was found oozing from trees. But in 1839, Charles Goodyear, spent long hours trying to create a practical form of rubber. He accidentally dropped a rubber-sulfur mixture onto a hot stove and was surprised to see that, in mere seconds, the rubber became solid and bendable. Today, the material is used in many objects, most notably in tires and shoes.

Dynamite was invented by Alfred Nobel. After his younger brother and four other people were killed in a factory explosion, Nobel wanted to find a safer way to handle explosives. When he died, the inventor left behind a fortune to provide yearly prizes for work in physics, chemistry, medicine and physiology, literature and world peace.

Rayon was the first man-made fiber ever developed. Made from wood or cotton pulp, it was originally known as "artificial silk." The name "rayon" was introduced in 1924.

Safety glass was accidentally invented by French scientist Edouard Benedictus in 1903. One day, as he was working in his lab, he accidentally knocked over a glass flask, which hit the floor but didn't shatter. In fact, the broken pieces mysteriously hung together. When Benedictus took a closer look, he realized that the flask held some liquid plastic that had evaporated into a thin solid coating. It was the plastic coating that held the broken pieces together. Benedictus started coating glass with this plastic and allowing it dry. This was the first safety glass!

1894	rayon fabric
1895	X-ray photography
1901	safety razor
1903	airplane, safety glass
1906	lightbulbs
1908	Ford Model T car, cellophane
1910	neon lamp
1911	air conditioning
1913	stainless steel
1914	gas mask
1921	lie detector
1922	insulin
1923	modern traffic light
1924	frozen food
1927	television
1928	penicillin
1931	electron microscope
1933	FM radio
1938	photocopier, Teflon, helicopter
1945	microwave, atomic bomb

Harry Brearley invented **stainless steel** while looking for a way to improve the quality of gun barrels.

Insulin, discovered by Canadian scientists in 1922, is a hormone created in the pancreas. It offers life-saving treatment for people who suffer from diabetes.

GUESS WHAT?
Microwave technology was born in 1946 when scientist Percy LeBaron Spencer was experimenting with radar waves. At one point, the waves melted a candy bar that was in his pocket but didn't burn a hole in his pants. Spencer knew he was on to something. Today, the microwave allows people to cook all kinds of things very quickly and safely.

GUESS WHAT?
The Popsicle was invented in 1905 when 11-year-old Frank Epperson, sitting on his back porch, mixed a popular drink of soda powder and water for himself. He somehow forgot about the mixture and left it overnight with the stirring stick still in the container. The cold overnight temperature froze the mixture and, the following morning, Epperson found a new frozen treat. About 3 million of the icy treats are now sold each year.

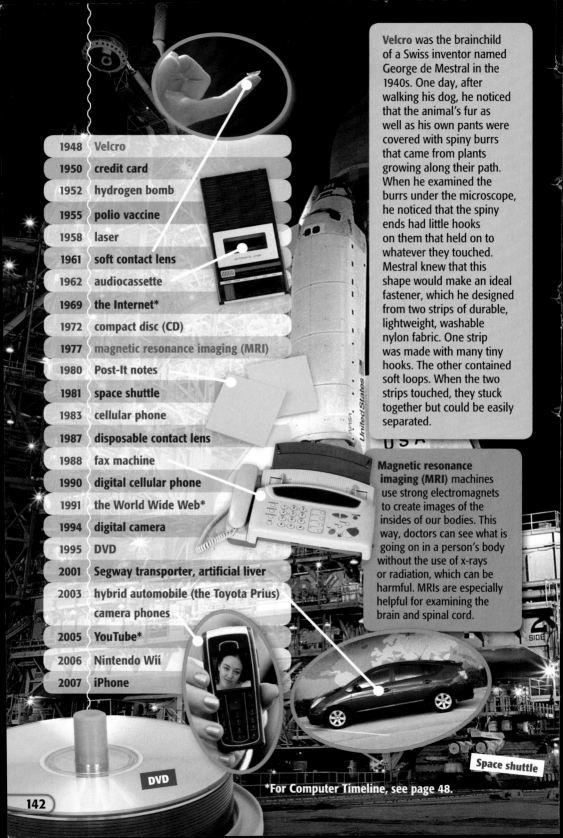

1948	Velcro
1950	credit card
1952	hydrogen bomb
1955	polio vaccine
1958	laser
1961	soft contact lens
1962	audiocassette
1969	the Internet*
1972	compact disc (CD)
1977	magnetic resonance imaging (MRI)
1980	Post-It notes
1981	space shuttle
1983	cellular phone
1987	disposable contact lens
1988	fax machine
1990	digital cellular phone
1991	the World Wide Web*
1994	digital camera
1995	DVD
2001	Segway transporter, artificial liver
2003	hybrid automobile (the Toyota Prius)
	camera phones
2005	YouTube*
2006	Nintendo Wii
2007	iPhone

Velcro was the brainchild of a Swiss inventor named George de Mestral in the 1940s. One day, after walking his dog, he noticed that the animal's fur as well as his own pants were covered with spiny burrs that came from plants growing along their path. When he examined the burrs under the microscope, he noticed that the spiny ends had little hooks on them that held on to whatever they touched. Mestral knew that this shape would make an ideal fastener, which he designed from two strips of durable, lightweight, washable nylon fabric. One strip was made with many tiny hooks. The other contained soft loops. When the two strips touched, they stuck together but could be easily separated.

Magnetic resonance imaging (MRI) machines use strong electromagnets to create images of the insides of our bodies. This way, doctors can see what is going on in a person's body without the use of x-rays or radiation, which can be harmful. MRIs are especially helpful for examining the brain and spinal cord.

Space shuttle

DVD

*For Computer Timeline, see page 48.

INVENTIONS AND TECHNOLOGY

Bright Ideas

Can you imagine the world without chocolate chip cookies or jeans? Thanks to these people, you don't have to. Match the inventor to his or her great invention.

ANSWERS ON PAGE 244

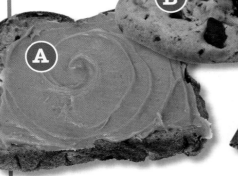

1. Levi Strauss went to California during the gold rush. Miners buttoned up his 1873 invention.

2. After his wife cut herself, Earle Dickson got to work. He found a solution that stuck.

3. Around 1830, Ruth Wakefield cooked up a delicious idea. She went on to write cookbooks.

4. Scientist George Washington Carver knew a lot about a little seed. He found 325 uses for it.

Mystery Person

CLUE 1: I was an American inventor born in Ohio in 1847.

CLUE 2: I invented the electric lightbulb. Before my invention, people and businesses used candles and gaslight.

CLUE 3: I held 1,093 patents for inventions. My work sparked great progress in the fields of electricity and communication.

WHO AM I? _____

ANSWERS ON PAGE 244

KEEPING LANGUAGES ALIVE

When any of the elderly members of the Yuchi (*yoo*-chee) tribe of Oklahoma tells a joke in his native language, chances are that only four other people will get it. That's right: Only five people in the world speak this American Indian tongue.

Experts say that every two weeks, a language disappears. At this rate, nearly half of the planet's 7,000 languages will be gone in 100 years. To draw attention to at-risk languages, the Living Tongues Institute for Endangered Languages and the National Geographic Society have joined forces on a project called Enduring Voices. In September 2007, the team announced the areas with the greatest number of endangered languages. The five hot spots are northern Australia, central South America, eastern Siberia, the southwestern United States and North America's upper Pacific coastal zone.

"North America is in dire straits," Greg Anderson, director of Living Tongues, told TFK. He says 54 native languages in Washington, Oregon and British Columbia, Canada, are in the most serious danger. Siletz Dee-Ni (sih-*lets dee*-nee), a language spoken on the Siletz reservation in Oregon, is believed to have just one fluent speaker.

One of the biggest threats to these languages is that they are being replaced by dominant languages like English. But when an ancient, native language is lost, some of the speakers' history is lost too.

Researchers hope to document and revitalize these languages. "We are eager to fire up a new generation of people to get involved," says Anderson. "But there are simply not enough trained people to do the work that is necessary."

—*By Claudia Atticot*

Illarion Ramos Condori, a speaker of Kallawaya, an endangered language of Bolivia

TFK TOP 5 Languages Spoken in the U.S.

1. **English (only)** 215,423,557 people
2. **Spanish** 28,101,052 people
3. **Chinese** 2,022,143 people
4. **French** 1,643,838 people
5. **German** 1,382,613 people

Source: U.S. Census Bureau

World's Most-Spoken Languages

RANK	LANGUAGE	NUMBER OF NATIVE SPEAKERS
1.	Chinese*	937,132,000
2.	Spanish	332,000,000
3.	English	322,000,000
4.	Bengali	189,000,000
5.	Hindi/Urdu	182,000,000
6.	Arabic*	174,950,000
7.	Portuguese	170,000,000
8.	Russian	170,000,000
9.	Japanese	125,000,000
10.	German	98,000,000

*includes different dialects

Source: The Summer Institute of Linguistics (SIL) Ethnologue Survey

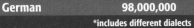

Serious Spelling

A record 286 kids participated in the 80th annual Scripps National Spelling Bee, held in Washington, D.C., on May 30–31, 2007. The winner, Evan O'Dorney from Danville, California, received a trophy and $35,000 in cash and scholarships. To win, he correctly spelled the words "schuhplattler," "Zoilus" and "papparadelle." His final word was "serrefine." Check out the other winning words below.

2007	serrefine
2006	ursprache
2005	appoggiatura
2004	autochthonous
2003	pococurante
2002	prospicience
2001	succedaneum
2000	démarche
1999	logorrhea
1998	chiaroscurist
1997	euonym
1996	vivisepulture
1995	xanthosis
1994	antediluvian
1993	kamikaze
1992	lyceum
1991	antipyretic
1990	fibranne

2007 winner Evan M. O'Dorney

THE NEWEST WORDS IN THE DICTIONARY

To keep its dictionary up-to-date, Merriam-Webster adds new words every year. Here is a sampling of the words added in 2007.

BOLLYWOOD (noun): the motion-picture industry in India

GINORMOUS (adjective): extremely large, humongous

SMACKDOWN (noun):
1. the act of knocking down or bringing down an opponent
2. a contest in entertainment wrestling
3. a decisive defeat
4. a confrontation between rivals or competitors

SNOWBOARDCROSS (noun): a snowboard race that includes jumps and turns

SUDOKU (noun): a puzzle in which numbers are to be filled in to a 9x9 grid of squares so that every row, every column and every 3x3 box contain the numbers 1 through 9

TELENOVELA (noun): a soap opera produced in and televised in or from many Latin-American countries

w00t!?!

Word of the year 2007

Merriam-Webster's Word of the Year is "w00t," a word first popularized on online gaming sites. It is not in the official dictionary yet, but could be included in the future. The 2004 word of the year, "blog," made the cut a year later. Check out the survey at www. m-w.com to help pick the next word of the year.

Commonly Misspelled Words

acceptable
a lot
argument
believe
broccoli
calendar
cemetery
changeable
collectible
definitely
embarrass
exercise
foreign
grateful
height
independent
judgment
ketchup
library
license
medieval
misspell
neighbor
occasionally
occurrence
pastime
receive
recommend
rhyme
rhythm
schedule
twelfth
until
vacuum
weather
weird

WORD WORDS

ANTONYM—a word that has the opposite meaning of another word
- hot and cold
- always and never

ALLITERATION—more than two words in a row that begin with the same consonant
- "The angry alligators ate a lot."
- "Careless cabbies cut corners and create chaos."

HOMOGRAPH—a word that is spelled the same as another word but has a different meaning
- "The girl with the bow in her hair took a bow after the performance."
- "I feel well enough today to help dig the well."

HOMOPHONE—a word that sounds the same as another but is spelled differently
- "I know the answer is no."
- "The two girls said they would like to go to the mall, too."

HYPERBOLE—an exaggeration
- "I have been waiting for an eternity."
- "I am so hungry I could eat a horse."

IDIOM—an informal phrase that cannot be understood just from the meanings of the words that make it up
- "She's the apple of my eye."
- "Oh my, it's raining cats and dogs out there!"

ONOMATOPOEIA—a word representing a sound
- "At the pet store, the cats meowed and the snakes hissed."
- "The cars vroomed past us."

METAPHOR—a figure of speech comparing two things without using the words "like" or "as"
- "Her answer was music to my ears."
- "He can eat anything—his belly is a bottomless pit."

SIMILE—a figure of speech comparing two things using the words "like" or "as"
- "Her smile shines like the sun."
- "Without his glasses, my dad is as blind as a bat."

SYNONYM—a word with the same or a similar meaning as another
- disgusting and gross
- purse and handbag
- chair and seat
- easy and simple

PALINDROME—a word or sentence that is the same when read forwards and backwards
Word examples: pop, eye, nun, deed, noon, kayak, Hannah, pullup, racecar
Sentence examples:
- Madam, I'm Adam.
- Was it a car or a cat I saw?

Where Words Come From

Saying that someone is "in the **limelight**" means that he or she is in the public eye or is the center of attention. Before the development of electric lights, theaters would burn lime to create the strong, bright lights needed for spotlights.

The **sandwich** was named after the Earl of Sandwich, who did not want to interrupt his card games to enjoy his meals. He asked his servants to bring him roast beef between two slices of bread. That way, he did not need utensils to eat and his fingers would not get greasy.

The word **sidekick** came from 19th-century pickpockets, who used slang to talk about their crimes. Pants were called "kicks" and the many pockets on a pair of trousers had different nicknames as well. "Side-kick" referred to the side pockets of trousers, which were the toughest to steal from. Eventually, the phrase began to refer to a friend, partner or person who was as close and trustworthy as the side-kick pocket.

The **teddy bear** was named for former president Theodore "Teddy" Roosevelt. According to the story, Roosevelt and his aides were hunting in 1902 but did not find any wildlife. So that he would not be disappointed, his hosts presented the president with a frightened bear cub. Teddy refused to shoot it, saying that it was "unsporting." Shortly afterward, a cartoon appeared in the *Washington Post*, poking fun at "Teddy's Bear." A shop owner in New York made a plush bear to put in the window by the cartoon, and it wasn't long before the name and the product began to catch on.

GUESS WHAT?
There are no English words that rhyme with orange, silver, purple or month.

TFK GAME Words in Spanish

Nearly 43 million Hispanic people live in the United States. Spanish is the second most widely spoken language in the country, after English.

Pretend that a friend has written you a letter in Spanish. Use the Word Bank to help you read the letter. Find each Spanish word in the bank. Then write its meaning on the line below.

WORD BANK

amiga = friend
en = in
gato = cat
hola = hello
México = Mexico
pájaro = bird
perro = dog
tengo = have
tu = your
un = a
vivo = live
y = and
yo = I

¡Hola!
_____
Yo vivo en México.
_____
Yo tengo un gato,
_____
un pájaro y un perro.
_____
Tu amiga,
_____
Pilar

ANSWERS ON PAGE 244

WHAT IS MATHEMATICS?

Mathematics is the study of figures and numbers. It deals with shapes, sizes, amounts and patterns. There are many branches of mathematics, such as arithmetic (addition, subtraction, multiplication and division), algebra, geometry, statistics and many more.

Common Formulas

To find the AREA of a TRIANGLE:
Multiply the base of the triangle by the height of the triangle. Divide by 2.

Area = ½ (base x height)

EXAMPLE:

Area = ½ (6 x 8) or Area = 24 square units

To find the AREA of a RECTANGLE:
Multiply the base of the rectangle by its height.

Area = base x height

EXAMPLE:

Area = 6 x 3 or Area = 18 square units

To find the AREA of a SQUARE:
Multiply the length of one side of the square by itself:

Area = side x side

EXAMPLE:

Area = 4 x 4 or Area = 16 square units

The **radius** of a circle is the length between the center of the circle and any point on the perimeter of the circle.

To find the AREA of a CIRCLE:
Multiply the radius by itself. Then multiply the product by 3.14 (which is also known as **pi** or **π**):

Area = radius x radius x 3.14 (or Area = πr^2)

EXAMPLE:

Area = 5 x 5 x 3.14 or Area = 78.5 square units

The **diameter** of a circle is the length of a straight line beginning on the perimeter of the circle, passing through the center and ending on the perimeter of the circle. The diameter is twice as long as the **radius**.

The **circumference** of a circle is the distance around the entire circle.
To find the CIRCUMFERENCE of a CIRCLE:
Multiply the diameter by 3.14.

Circumference = diameter x 3.14 or (Circumference = diameter x π)

EXAMPLE:

Circumference = 10 x 3.14 or Circumference = 31.4

Easy as Pi?

The number 3.14, used in some common mathematical formulas (above), is the shortened form of π, which is a Greek letter. It is pronounced "pi." The actual value of π continues for trillions of digits. Here are the first 50 digits after the decimal point:

3.14159265358979323846264338327950288419716939937510

Geometric Terms

An **angle** is formed every time two lines meet, or intersect.

A **right angle** is an angle that measures 90°.

An **acute angle** measures less than 90° and an **obtuse angle** measures more than 90°.

Parallel lines are straight lines that will never intersect.

Perpendicular lines form a right angle when they meet.

A **polygon** is a geometrical figure with three or more sides.

A **triangle** has three sides.

In an **equilateral triangle**, all sides are the same length.

An **isosceles triangle** has at least two sides of the same length.

In a **scalene triangle**, each side is a different length.

Scalene triangle

A **right triangle** is a triangle with a right angle. On a right triangle, the side opposite the right angle is called the **hypotenuse**.

A **quadrilateral** is a geometrical figure with four sides.

A **rectangle** is a quadrilateral with four right angles. A **square** is a rectangle with four equal sides.

A **trapezoid** is a quadrilateral with one set of parallel sides.

Trapezoid

A **parallelogram** is a quadrilateral with two pairs of parallel sides.

Parallelogram

A **rhombus** is a parallelogram with sides of equal length.

How to Round Numbers

A number can be rounded to any place value. Here's how to round a number to the nearest ten:

If a number ends with a 1, 2, 3 or 4, round it down to the nearest number that ends in 0. EXAMPLES:

22 should be rounded down to 20.
54 should be rounded down to 50.
631 should be rounded down to 630.

If a number ends with a 5, 6, 7, 8 or 9, round it up to the nearest number that ends in 0. EXAMPLES:

9 should be rounded up to 10.
87 should be rounded up to 90.
516 should be rounded up to 520.

Here's how to round a number to the nearest hundred:

If the last two digits of a number are 00 through 49, round it down to the nearest number that ends in 00. EXAMPLES:

122 should be rounded down to 100.
746 should be rounded down to 700.
1,314 should be rounded down to 1,300.

If the last two digits in a number end in 50 through 99, round it up to the nearest number that ends in 00. EXAMPLES:

189 should be rounded up to 200.
656 should be rounded up to 700.
3,791 should be rounded up to 3,800.

How to Average Numbers

Averages are used to get a sense of a group of numbers. You find the average by adding up the numbers in a group, then dividing the sum by the amount of numbers in the group.

For example, if you have three numbers, add them up and divide the sum by 3:

10+11+12=33 and 33÷3=11
The average of 10, 11 and 12 is 11.

If you have five numbers, add them up and divide the sum by 5:

31+34+29+30+21=145 and 145÷5=29.
The average of 31, 34, 29, 30 and 21 is 29.

Fractions

Fractions are used to express portions of a whole.

In a fraction, the number below the bar is called the denominator. The denominator is the total number of parts that a whole has been divided into.

The number above the bar is called the numerator. The numerator shows how many of these parts are in the fraction.

EXAMPLE: This circle has been divided into six equal parts. One of these parts is orange. The other five are hot pink. This can be expressed in fractions:
$\frac{1}{6}$ of the circle is orange
$\frac{5}{6}$ of the circle is hot pink

When the numerator is smaller than the denominator, it's a proper fraction. If the numerator is larger than the denominator, it is an improper fraction. This means the value of the fraction is greater than 1. For example, if 7 parts of the circle are blue, it could be expressed as $\frac{7}{6}$ or as $1\frac{1}{6}$.

Unless both the numerator and the denominator are the same, dividing the numerator by the denominator will turn a fraction into a decimal.

Decimals

Using decimals is a way to be more specific about numbers. They enable us to identify the numbers between two consecutive numbers, such as between 1 and 2 or between 54 and 55. The system of decimals is based on powers of ten. The placement of each digit to the right of the decimal point is important. The number in the first spot to the right of the decimal point is in the tenths place; the next number is in the hundredths. After that, there is the thousandths place, the ten thousandths place and so on. The further the number is from the decimal point, the smaller the amount.

EXAMPLE: 1.259872

tenths   thousandths   hundred thousandths
    hundredths   ten thousandths   millionths

Percents

Percents are similar to decimals in that they represent parts of a whole. Here are some common amounts expressed in fractions, decimals and percents:

FRACTION	DECIMAL	PERCENT
$\frac{1}{10}$	.1	10%
$\frac{1}{5}$	.2	20%
$\frac{1}{4}$	.25	25%
$\frac{1}{3}$	.33333	33%
$\frac{2}{5}$	.4	40%
$\frac{1}{2}$	.5	50%
$\frac{2}{3}$	.66667	66%
$\frac{3}{4}$	.75	75%
$\frac{4}{5}$	.8	80%
$\frac{9}{10}$	.9	90%
$\frac{4}{4}$	1	100%

Real Life Math

If you think math is just something you use in school, think again. You need math skills for lots of everyday tasks, such as:

- making a double batch of chocolate chip cookies or pancake batter
- giving the correct amount of change at the lunch counter
- keeping track of your sports team's scores and stats
- calculating the sale price of a toy you want to buy
- knowing how much money to leave as a tip after a restaurant dinner
- figuring out how long it will take to travel from one place to the next.

Abuzz About Numbers

Garden insects have crawled into three identical groups. Check out the bugs, then answer these questions.

1. Estimate the total number of bugs, without counting each bug. (Hint: There are 12 bugs in each magnifying glass.)

2. If each group has three ladybugs, how many ladybugs are there in all?

3. How many more caterpillars are there than bumblebees?

4. If each group has six ants and one bumblebee, what is the total number of ants and bumblebees?

5. Half of the bugs are ladybugs, caterpillars or bumblebees. How many is that?

ANSWERS ON PAGE 244

Incomes Around the World

The average annual income of residents of different countries varies greatly. The average annual income of a person in the United States is $43,800. How does that compare to other countries?

Afghanistan	$800
Albania	$5,700
Belize	$8,400
Chile	$12,600
China	$7,800
France	$31,200
Indonesia	$3,900
Iran	$8,700
Mexico	$10,700
Niger	$1,000
South Africa	$13,300
Sweden	$32,200
Turkey	$9,100
United Arab Emirates	$49,700
United Kingdom	$31,800
Vietnam	$3,100

How Much Is a Dollar Worth?

Look below to see how the value of the U.S. dollar has changed over time.

$1.00 from 1906 is worth $23.12 today.
$1.00 from 1956 is worth $7.42 today.
$1.00 from 1986 is worth $1.84 today.
$1.00 from 1996 is worth $1.28 today.

Source: www.measuringworth.com, 2006 estimates

Prices on the Rise

In May 2008, the cost of a stamp went up to $0.42. Look below to see how the cost of going to the movies or mailing a letter has changed in the last 50 years.

YEAR	COST OF MAILING A LETTER IN THE U.S.	AVERAGE U.S. MOVIE TICKET PRICE
2006	$0.39	$6.65
2002	.37	5.80
1995	.32	4.35
1988	.25	3.55
1981	.20	2.78
1978	.15	2.34
1974	.10	1.89
1971	.08	1.65

Sources: National Postal Museum and National Association of Theatre Owners

Top 10 Highest-Grossing U.S. Movies

1.	*Titanic* (1997)	$600,779,824
2.	*Star Wars* (1977)	$460,935,665
3.	*Shrek 2* (2004)	$436,471,036
4.	*E.T.: The Extra-Terrestrial* (1982)	$434,949,459
5.	*Star Wars: Episode I The Phantom Menace* (1999)	$431,065,444
6.	*Pirates of the Caribbean: Dead Man's Chest* (2006)	$423,032,628
7.	*Spider-Man* (2002)	$403,706,375
8.	*Star Wars: Episode III Revenge of the Sith* (2005)	$380,262,555
9.	*The Lord of the Rings: The Return of the King* (2003)	$377,019,252
10.	*Spider-Man 2* (2004)	$373,377,893

Source: www.IMDB.com, as of March 30, 2008

Top 10 Animated Flicks

	TITLE (YEAR)	MONEY MADE IN THE U.S. (GROSS)
1.	*Shrek 2* (2004)	$436,471,036
2.	*Finding Nemo* (2003)	$339,714,367
3.	*The Lion King* (1994)	$328,423,001
4.	*Shrek the Third* (2007)	$320,706,665
5.	*Shrek* (2001)	$267,652,016
6.	*The Incredibles* (2004)	$261,437,578
7.	*Monsters, Inc.* (2001)	$255,870,172
8.	*Toy Story 2* (1999)	$245,823,397
9.	*Cars* (2006)	$244,052,771
10.	*Aladdin* (1992)	$217,350,219

Source: www.IMDB.com, as of March 30, 2008

Top 10 TV Shows of 2007

	TV SHOW	PERCENTAGE OF HOMES WATCHING
1.	*American Idol*–Wednesday	17.3
2.	*American Idol*–Tuesday	16.8
3.	*Dancing with the Stars*–Monday	13.2
4.	*Dancing with the Stars*–Tuesday	12.2
5.	*NBC Sunday Night Football*	10.2
6.	*CSI*	10.1
7.	*Grey's Anatomy* (tie)	9.2
7.	*Samantha Who?* (tie)	9.2
9.	*House*	9.0
10.	*CSI: Miami*	8.9

Source: Nielsen Media Research
Note: Includes regularly-scheduled programs from
January 1–December 2, 2007

Top 10 Box Office Hits of 2007

RANK	FILM	MONEY MADE	OPENING DATE
1.	Spider-Man 3	$336,530,303	5/4/2007
2.	Shrek the Third	$321,012,359	5/18/2007
3.	Transformers	$319,071,806	7/3/2007
4.	Pirates of the Caribbean: At World's End	$309,420,425	5/25/2007
5.	Harry Potter and the Order of the Phoenix	$292,000,866	7/11/2007
6.	The Bourne Ultimatum	$227,471,070	8/3/2007
7.	300	$210,614,939	3/9/2007
8.	Ratatouille	$206,435,493	6/29/2007
9.	The Simpsons Movie	$183,106,242	7/27/2007
10.	Wild Hogs	$168,273,550	3/2/2007

Source: Nielsen EDI/The Hollywood Reporter
Note: Data from January 1–December 9, 2007 in the United States and Canada

Top 10 Movie Sequels of 2007

Many movie critics considered 2007 the "Year of the Sequels." Let's see how they did at the box office.

RANK	FILM	MONEY MADE	OPENING DATE
1.	Spider-Man 3	$336,530,303	5/4/2007
2.	Shrek the Third	$321,012,359	5/18/2007
3.	Pirates of the Caribbean: At World's End	$309,420,425	5/25/2007
4.	Harry Potter and the Order of the Phoenix	$292,000,866	7/11/2007
5.	The Bourne Ultimatum	$227,471,070	8/3/2007
6.	Rush Hour 3	$140,125,968	8/10/2007
7.	Live Free or Die Hard	$134,529,403	6/27/2007
8.	Fantastic Four: Rise of the Silver Surfer	$131,921,738	6/15/2007
9.	Ocean's Thirteen	$117,154,724	6/8/2007
10.	Evan Almighty	$100,462,298	6/22/2007

Source: Nielsen EDI/The Hollywood Reporter
Note: Data from January 1, 2007–December 9, 2007 in the United States and Canada.

Top 10 DVD Sales of 2007

TITLE	RELEASE DATE
1. Happy Feet	3/27/07
2. Transformers	10/16/07
3. 300	7/31/07
4. Night at the Museum	4/24/07
5. The Departed	2/13/07
6. Ratatouille	11/6/07
7. Casino Royale	3/13/07
8. Shrek the Third	11/13/07
9. Wild Hogs	8/14/07
10. The Pursuit of Happyness	3/27/07

Source: Nielsen VideoScan
Note: Data from January 1–November 18, 2007

2008 NICKELODEON KIDS' CHOICE AWARDS

MOVIES
FAVORITE MOVIE: Alvin and the Chipmunks
FAVORITE FEMALE MOVIE STAR: Jessica Alba
FAVORITE MALE MOVIE STAR: Johnny Depp
FAVORITE ANIMATED MOVIE: Ratatouille

TELEVISION
FAVORITE TV SHOW: Drake & Josh
FAVORITE TELEVISION ACTRESS: Miley Cyrus, Hannah Montana
FAVORITE TELEVISION ACTOR: Drake Bell, Drake & Josh

Josh Peck and Drake Bell

153

Daniel Day-Lewis, Tilda Swinton, Marion Cotillard, Javier Bardem

AND THE OSCAR GOES TO...

On February 24, 2008, the top names in Hollywood gathered at the Shrine Auditorium in Los Angeles for the Academy Awards.

BEST PICTURE: *No Country for Old Men*

BEST ANIMATED PICTURE: *Ratatouille*

BEST FEATURE DOCUMENTARY: *Taxi to the Dark Side*

BEST ACTOR: Daniel Day-Lewis, *There Will Be Blood*

BEST ACTRESS: Marion Cotillard, *La Vie en Rose*

BEST SUPPORTING ACTRESS: Tilda Swinton, *Michael Clayton*

BEST SUPPORTING ACTOR: Javier Bardem, *No Country for Old Men*

BEST DIRECTOR: Joel Coen and Ethan Coen, *No Country for Old Men*

BEST SONG: "Falling Slowly" from *Once*

BEST SCORE: *Atonement*, Dario Marianelli

BEST ORIGINAL SCREENPLAY: *Juno*, Diablo Cody

BEST VISUAL EFFECTS: *The Golden Compass*

The Golden Compass

2007 GOLDEN GLOBE–WINNING MOVIES

BEST MOTION PICTURE–DRAMA: **Atonement**

BEST MOTION PICTURE–MUSICAL OR COMEDY: **Sweeney Todd: The Demon Barber of Fleet Street**

BEST ACTOR–DRAMA: **Daniel Day-Lewis, There Will Be Blood**

BEST ACTOR–MUSICAL OR COMEDY: **Johnny Depp, Sweeney Todd: The Demon Barber of Fleet Street**

BEST ACTRESS–DRAMA: **Julie Christie, Away from Her**

BEST ACTRESS–MUSICAL OR COMEDY: **Marion Cotillard, La Vie en Rose**

BEST SUPPORTING ACTOR: **Javier Bardem, No Country for Old Men**

BEST SUPPORTING ACTRESS: **Cate Blanchett, I'm Not There**

BEST DIRECTOR: **Julian Schnabel, The Diving Bell and the Butterfly**

BEST SCREENPLAY: **Joel Coen and Ethan Coen, No Country for Old Men**

BEST FOREIGN LANGUAGE FILM: **The Diving Bell and the Butterfly**

BEST ANIMATED FILM: **Ratatouille**

Johnny Depp in *Sweeney Todd*

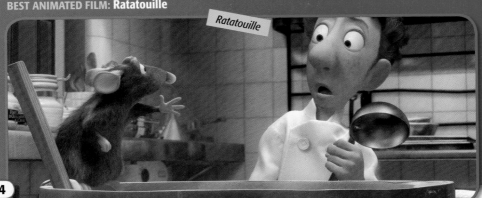

Ratatouille

2007 TEEN CHOICE AWARDS

MOVIES

CHOICE MOVIE, ACTION: *Pirates of the Caribbean: At World's End*
CHOICE MOVIE, DRAMA: *The Pursuit of Happyness*
CHOICE MOVIE, CHICK FLICK: *The Holiday*
CHOICE MOVIE, COMEDY: *Knocked Up*
CHOICE MOVIE, HORROR/THRILLER: *Disturbia*
CHOICE MOVIE ACTOR, DRAMA: Will Smith, *The Pursuit of Happyness*
CHOICE MOVIE ACTRESS, DRAMA: Jennifer Hudson, *Dreamgirls*
CHOICE MOVIE ACTOR, ACTION/ADVENTURE: Johnny Depp,
  Pirates of the Caribbean: At World's End
CHOICE MOVIE ACTRESS, ACTION/ADVENTURE: Keira Knightley,
  Pirates of the Caribbean: At World's End
CHOICE MOVIE ACTOR, COMEDY: Will Ferrell, *Talladega Nights:*
  The Ballad of Ricky Bobby, Blades of Glory
CHOICE MOVIE ACTRESS, COMEDY: Sophia Bush, *John Tucker Must Die*
CHOICE MOVIE VILLAIN: Bill Nighy, *Pirates of the Caribbean: At World's End*
CHOICE MOVIE BREAKOUT, MALE: Shia LaBeouf
CHOICE MOVIE BREAKOUT, FEMALE: Sophia Bush
CHOICE MOVIE DANCE: Channing Tatum and Jenna Dewan, *Step Up*
CHOICE MOVIE SCREAM: Steve Carell, *Evan Almighty*

Sanjaya

TELEVISION

CHOICE TV MOVIE: *High School Musical 2*
CHOICE TV SHOW, COMEDY: *Hannah Montana*
CHOICE TV SHOW, DRAMA: *Grey's Anatomy*
CHOICE TV SHOW, ANIMATED: *The Simpsons*
CHOICE TV SHOW, REALITY/VARIETY: *American Idol*
CHOICE TV ACTOR, COMEDY: *Steve Carell, The Office*
CHOICE TV ACTOR, DRAMA: *Hugh Laurie, House*
CHOICE TV ACTRESS, COMEDY: *Miley Cyrus, Hannah Montana*
CHOICE TV ACTRESS, DRAMA: *Hayden Panettiere, Heroes*
CHOICE TV BREAKOUT: *America Ferrera, Ugly Betty*
CHOICE TV SIDEKICK: *Allison Mack, Smallville*
CHOICE TV MALE REALITY/VARIETY STAR: *Sanjaya, American Idol*
CHOICE TV FEMALE REALITY/VARIETY STAR: *Lauren Conrad, The Hills*
CHOICE TV VILLAIN: *Vanessa Williams, Ugly Betty*

America Ferrera,
Ugly Betty

2007 MAJOR EMMY AWARDS

BEST DRAMA SERIES: *The Sopranos*
BEST ACTOR IN A DRAMA: James Spader,
  Boston Legal
BEST ACTRESS IN A DRAMA: Sally Field,
  Brothers & Sisters
BEST COMEDY SERIES: *30 Rock*
BEST ACTOR IN A COMEDY: Ricky Gervais, *Extras*
BEST ACTRESS IN A COMEDY: America Ferrera,
  Ugly Betty
BEST REALITY/COMPETITION PROGRAM:
  The Amazing Race

BEST REALITY PROGRAM: Kathy Griffin,
  My Life on the D-List
BEST CHILDREN'S PROGRAM: *Nick News*
  with Linda Ellerbee
BEST ANIMATED PROGRAM (ONE HOUR OR MORE):
  Where's Lazlo?
BEST ANIMATED PROGRAM (ONE HOUR OR LESS):
  South Park

FROM TFK MAGAZINE

5 QUESTIONS FOR MILEY CYRUS

Miley Cyrus plays two roles in the Disney Channel show *Hannah Montana*. By day, she's eighth grader Miley Stewart. By night, she's rock star Hannah Montana. "She goes in disguise and puts on wigs and tons of makeup," Miley told TFK Kid Reporter Emily Doveala. Miley's real-life dad, singer Billy Ray Cyrus, plays her father.

The *Hannah Montana* star's sold-out concert tour hit the big screen as a movie on February 1, 2008.

TFK: Why was the tour made into a film?

MILEY: We didn't want people to see only what happens onstage. The film goes behind the scenes, so people see the hard work that goes into [doing a tour]. They get to see it in the making.

TFK: What was it like touring with the Jonas Brothers?

MILEY: It was cool! They would pump everyone up before I came out. We have a lot of the same fans, so it doubled the excitement.

TFK: Do you have any preshow rituals?

MILEY: We all gather around and squeeze each other's hands. I squeeze the people next to me, and they squeeze the people next to them. We go around in a big circle, passing the energy.

TFK: What are some must-have items in your dressing room?

MILEY: Vitamin Water and protein bars that will keep my energy up onstage. And ketchup! Everyone makes fun of me because I eat so much ketchup.

TFK: What do you put ketchup on?

MILEY: Everything! I put ketchup on pizza, in macaroni and on the most random things. And I can't just have a little bit. I have to have gobs of it!

Top 10 Best-Selling Albums of 2007

	ALBUM	ARTIST
1.	Soundtrack	High School Musical 2
2.	Daughtry	Daughtry
3.	Minutes to Midnight	Linkin Park
4.	Soundtrack	Hannah Montana 2: Meet Miley Cyrus
5.	Dutchess	Fergie
6.	Long Road Out Of Eden	Eagles
7.	Graduation	Kanye West
8.	All the Right Reasons	Nickelback
9.	Konvicted	Akon
10.	Noel	Josh Groban

Source: Billboard 200/Nielsen SoundScan
Note: Data from January 1–December 2, 2007

Top 10 Songs Most Played on the Radio in 2007

	SONG	ARTIST	TIMES ON RADIO
1.	Buy U A Drank (Shawty Snappin')	T-Pain featuring Yung Joc	365,000
2.	Say It Right	Nelly Furtado	364,000
3.	Irreplaceable/Irreemplazable	Beyonce	363,000
4.	Big Girls Don't Cry	Fergie	360,000
5.	The Sweet Escape	Gwen Stefani featuring Akon	355,000
6.	It's Not Over	Daughtry	338,000
7.	Before He Cheats	Carrie Underwood	334,000
8.	Umbrella	Rihanna featuring Jay-Z	328,000
9.	How To Save A Life	Fray	314,000
10.	Home	Daughtry	299,000

Source: Billboard Hot 100 Airplay/Nielsen BDS
Note: Data from January 1–December 2, 2007

Fergie

2007 Best-Selling Ringtones

	ARTIST	SONG	TOTAL SALES
1.	T-Pain (feat. Yung Joc)	"Buy U A Drank (Shawty Snappin')"	2,279,00
2.	Mims	"This is Why I'm Hot"	2,088,000
3.	Shop Boyz	"Party Like a Rockstar"	1,732,000
4.	Soulja Boy	"Crank That"	1,609,000
5.	Akon	"Don't Matter"	1,471,000
6.	Huey	"Pop, Lock & Drop It"	1,398,000
7.	Sean Kingston	"Beautiful Girls"	1,379,000
8.	Hurricane Chris	"A Bay Bay"	1,376,000
9.	R. Kelly featuring T-Pain & T.I.	"I'm a Flirt"	1,147,000
10.	Nickelback	"Rockstar"	1,126,000

T-Pain & T.I.

Source: Billboard.com

Soulja Boy

2007's Top 10 Most Digitally Downloaded Songs

	SONG	ARTIST
1.	"Crank That"	Soulja Boy
2.	"Big Girls Don't Cry"	Fergie
3.	"The Sweet Escape"	Gwen Stefani featuring Akon
4.	"Makes Me Wonder"	Maroon 5
5.	"Hey There Delilah"	Plain White T's
6.	"Way I Are"	Timbaland
7.	"Buy U A Drank (Shawty Snappin')"	T-Pain featuring Yung Joc
8.	"Stronger"	Kanye West
9.	"Cupid's Chokehold"	Gym Class Heroes featuring Patrick Stump
10.	"Apologize"	Timbaland featuring OneRepublic

Source: Billboard Hot Digital Songs/Nielsen SoundScan
Note: Data from January 1–December 2, 2007

Jordin Sparks

American Idol

Since it first aired in June 2002, *American Idol* has been a hit! Many millions of viewers tune in to every episode and more than 30 million people have watched the last several season finales. And the winners were:

SEASON 6	Winner: Jordin Sparks	Runner-up: Blake Lewis
SEASON 5	Winner: Taylor Hicks	Runner-up: Katharine McPhee
SEASON 4	Winner: Carrie Underwood	Runner-up: Bo Bice
SEASON 3	Winner: Fantasia Barrino	Runner-up: Diana DeGarmo
SEASON 2	Winner: Ruben Studdard	Runner-up: Clay Aiken
SEASON 1	Winner: Kelly Clarkson	Runner-up: Justin Guarini

2007 GRAMMY AWARDS

RECORD OF THE YEAR: "Rehab," Amy Winehouse

ALBUM OF THE YEAR: *River: The Joni Letters*, Herbie Hancock

SONG OF THE YEAR: "Rehab," Amy Winehouse

BEST NEW ARTIST: Amy Winehouse

BEST FEMALE POP VOCAL PERFORMANCE: "Rehab," Amy Winehouse

BEST MALE POP VOCAL PERFORMANCE: "What Goes Around...Comes Around," Justin Timberlake

BEST POP PERFORMANCE BY A DUO OR GROUP WITH VOCALS: "Makes Me Wonder," Maroon 5

BEST DANCE RECORDING: "LoveStoned/I Think She Knows," Justin Timberlake

BEST ELECTRONIC/DANCE ALBUM: *We Are The Night*, The Chemical Brothers

BEST ROCK SONG: "Radio Nowhere," Bruce Springsteen

BEST ROCK ALBUM: *Echoes, Silence, Patience & Grace,* Foo Fighters

BEST ALTERNATIVE MUSIC ALBUM: *Icky Thump*, The White Stripes

BEST R&B SONG: "No One," Dirty Harry, Kerry Brothers and Alicia Keys, songwriters (Alicia Keys)

BEST R&B ALBUM: *Funk This*, Chaka Khan

BEST CONTEMPORARY R&B ALBUM: *Because of You*, Ne-Yo

BEST RAP PERFORMANCE BY A DUO OR GROUP: "Southside," Common featuring Kanye West

BEST RAP/SUNG COLLABORATION: "Umbrella," Rihanna featuring Jay-Z

BEST RAP SONG: "Good Life," Aldrich Davis, James Ingram, Quincy Jones, Faheem Rasheed Najm, Kanye West, songwriters (Kanye West featuring T-Pain)

BEST RAP ALBUM: *Graduation*, Kanye West

BEST COUNTRY SONG: "Before He Cheats," Josh Kear & Chris Tompkins, songwriters (Carrie Underwood)

BEST COUNTRY ALBUM: *These Days*, Vince Gill

BEST SCORE SOUNDTRACK ALBUM FOR MOTION PICTURE, TELEVISION OR OTHER VISUAL MEDIA: *Ratatouille*, Michael Giacchino (composer)

BEST SONG WRITTEN FOR MOTION PICTURE, TELEVISION OR OTHER VISUAL MEDIA: "Love You I Do" from *Dreamgirls*, Siedah Garrett & Henry Krieger, songwriters (Jennifer Hudson)

Amy Winehouse

Alicia Keys

Rihanna

Kanye West

2008 Nickelodeon Kids' Choice Awards

FAVORITE SONG: "Girlfriend," Avril Lavigne

FAVORITE MALE SINGER: Chris Brown

FAVORITE FEMALE SINGER: Miley Cyrus

FAVORITE MUSIC GROUP: The Jonas Brothers

MTV Music Video Awards

The MTV Music Video Awards took place on September 9, 2007, in Las Vegas. The Foo Fighters, Fall Out Boy, 50 Cent, Britney Spears, Kanye West and Timbaland were among the stars who took the stage to perform. Rihanna and Justin Timberlake were the evening's big winners.

BEST SINGLE: Rihanna featuring Jay-Z, "Umbrella"

QUADRUPLE THREAT: Justin Timberlake

BEST COLLABORATION: Beyoncé featuring Shakira, "Beautiful Liar"

MALE ARTIST OF THE YEAR: Justin Timberlake

FEMALE ARTIST OF THE YEAR: Fergie

BEST GROUP: Fall Out Boy

BEST NEW ARTIST: Gym Class Heroes

VIDEO OF THE YEAR: Rihanna featuring Jay-Z, "Umbrella"

BEST CHOREOGRAPHY: Justin Timberlake, "My Love"

BEST DIRECTION: Justin Timberlake, "What Goes Around...Comes Around"

BEST EDITING: Gnarls Barkley, "Smiley Faces"

Timberlake and Timbaland

Avril Lavigne

Teen Choice Awards

On August 26, 2007, Hilary Duff and Nick Cannon hosted the Teen Choice Awards at the Gibson Amphitheatre at Universal Studios in Hollywood. Kelly Clarkson, Avril Lavigne and Fergie performed for the crowd and surfboards were given to the winners, who were chosen by fans.

CHOICE MUSIC SINGLE: "Girlfriend," Avril Lavigne

CHOICE MUSIC MALE ARTIST: Justin Timberlake

CHOICE MUSIC FEMALE ARTIST: Fergie

CHOICE MUSIC RAP ARTIST: Timbaland

CHOICE MUSIC R&B ARTIST: Rihanna

CHOICE MUSIC ROCK GROUP: Fall Out Boy

CHOICE MUSIC BREAKOUT ARTIST, FEMALE: Vanessa Hudgens

CHOICE MUSIC BREAKOUT ARTIST, MALE: Akon

CHOICE MUSIC BREAKOUT GROUP: Gym Class Heroes

CHOICE MUSIC LOVE SONG: "With Love," Hilary Duff

CHOICE MUSIC R&B TRACK: "Beautiful Girls," Sean Kingston

CHOICE MUSIC RAP/HIP HOP TRACK: "The Way I Are," Timbaland (featuring Keri Hilson and D.O.E.)

CHOICE MUSIC ROCK TRACK: "Thnks Fr Th Mmrs," Fall Out Boy

CHOICE MUSIC PAYBACK TRACK: "What Goes Around...Comes Around," Justin Timberlake

CHOICE SUMMER ARTIST: Miley Cyrus

CHOICE SONG OF THE SUMMER: "Hey There Delilah," Plain White T's

Vanessa Hudgens

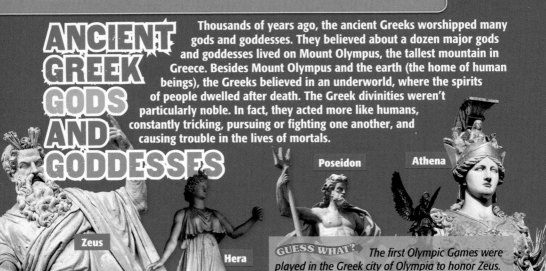

ANCIENT GREEK GODS AND GODDESSES

Thousands of years ago, the ancient Greeks worshipped many gods and goddesses. They believed about a dozen major gods and goddesses lived on Mount Olympus, the tallest mountain in Greece. Besides Mount Olympus and the earth (the home of human beings), the Greeks believed in an underworld, where the spirits of people dwelled after death. The Greek divinities weren't particularly noble. In fact, they acted more like humans, constantly tricking, pursuing or fighting one another, and causing trouble in the lives of mortals.

Poseidon

Athena

Zeus

Hera

GUESS WHAT? *The first Olympic Games were played in the Greek city of Olympia to honor Zeus.*

ZEUS, the ruler and most powerful of all the gods and goddesses, was known for his quick temper. He would hurl thunderbolts at anyone who angered him.

HERA, the sister and wife of Zeus, was the queen of the gods and goddesses. Always jealous of Zeus' many relationships, she caused trouble for the other women Zeus pursued. She was the protectress of married women and women in childbirth.

Zeus's brother, **POSEIDON,** ruled the oceans. The patron of sailors, he had the ability to create storms or calm the waters at will. The trident (a long-pronged fork) and the horse were his symbols.

Zeus's sister **DEMETER** was the goddess of the earth and the mother of Persephone. The ancient Greeks prayed to her for bountiful harvests.

Another of Zeus's sisters was **HESTIA,** the goddess of the hearth, or fireplace, of a home. In ancient Greek and Roman cities, the temples of Hestia contained a flame that was never allowed to burn out. People could always light their home fires using the flames from these temples.

The god of the underworld, **HADES,** was another brother of Zeus. He kidnapped and married Persephone, who ruled with Hades for six months of the year—during which time it would be autumn and winter on earth. Persephone returned to visit her mother in spring and summer.

Demeter

Persephone and Hades

HEPHAESTUS was the blacksmith of the gods and goddesses. He made their armor, helmets and shields, as well as metal cups, plates and other tools. A peace-loving son of Hera, Hephaestus lived in the depths of a volcano and walked with a limp.

ARES, the god of violence and war, was the son of Zeus and Hera. He was especially revered by the Romans and the Spartans (a Greek city of warriors), who would pray to him for victory before each battle.

APHRODITE, the goddess of love and beauty, was Hephaestus's wife but had relationships with Ares (a god), Adonis (a human) and many others. Her son **EROS** shot his arrows into the hearts of humans to make them fall in love. Some Greeks believed Aphrodite was the daughter of Zeus, but others believed she rose out of the sea.

The city of Athens, Greece, was named for **ATHENA,** the goddess of wisdom and crafts. According to the myth, Zeus suffered from a terrible headache and ordered Hephaestus to crack open his skull with an ax. Athena emerged, fully grown and dressed in armor.

APOLLO, a son of Zeus, was the god of light, medicine, music and the arts. Many Greeks believed that he drove the chariot of the sun across the sky each day. They also gathered at his temple in the city of Delphi to listen to a priestess, known as the Oracle, predict their future by communicating with Apollo.

ARTEMIS, the twin sister of Apollo, was a hunter, skilled with a bow and arrow. As her brother was linked with the Sun, she was linked with the moon. All wild animals were sacred to her, especially deer.

Artemis

HERMES was the son of Zeus and the messenger of the gods and goddesses. He wore a winged helmet and winged sandals. He was known for his swiftness and for his trickery. He also guided the souls of the dead into the underworld.

Apollo

Another son of Zeus, **DIONYSUS** was the god of wine, celebration and the theater. The Greeks believed he could also cause insanity in anyone he chose. During celebrations in his honor, plays would be performed. Among his symbols were the bull, snake and grapevine.

Greek Divinities, Roman Names

The ancient Romans conquered the Greeks. They adopted the Greek gods and goddesses but gave nearly all of them new names.

GREEK NAME	ROMAN NAME
Zeus	Jupiter
Hera	Juno
Poseidon	Neptune
Hades	Pluto
Demeter	Ceres
Hestia	Vesta
Hephaestus	Vulcan
Ares	Mars
Aphrodite	Venus
Eros	Cupid
Athena	Minerva
Artemis	Diana
Hermes	Mercury
Dionysus	Bacchus

ANCIENT HEROES

In stories, poems and songs, the Greeks and Romans celebrated heroes for their courage, strength and ability to overcome difficult obstacles.

HERACLES, the strongest human who ever lived, was quick-tempered and often got into trouble. For one of his misdeeds, he was ordered by the Oracle at Delphi to perform 12 great tasks, which included killing wild beasts and monsters.

ACHILLES was the most famous warrior of the Trojan War. Achilles' sea-nymph mother tried to make him immortal by dipping him in the Styx, the river of death. She held him by his heel, which was the only part of his body to remain mortal. When an arrow pierced that heel, he died. Even today, the term "Achilles' heel" refers to someone's weak spot.

ODYSSEUS, ruler of the kingdom of Ithaca, also fought in the Trojan War. He offended the god Apollo, who whipped up a storm that kept him from sailing home. Odysseus wandered the world for ten

Achilles

years, facing obstacles and challenges until, with Athena's help, he returned home. The book, *The Odyssey,* written by Homer, tells of this journey.

THESEUS is probably best-known for killing the half-man, half-beast known as the Minotaur. The Minotaur lived in the middle of a maze, or labyrinth. Theseus found his way in and out with the help of Ariadne, who gave him a silk thread to unravel going in and then rewind coming out.

161

PRESIDENTIAL ELECTIONS

Before the disputed election of 2000, many Americans forgot that our presidents are not chosen by majority vote. Instead, it is the electoral college that casts the final votes. Here's how the election process works in the United States.

1. Candidates announce that they are running for President.

In order to be eligible, a person must be a natural-born U.S. citizen at least 35 years of age. He or she must have been a U.S. resident for at least 14 years.

2. Let the campaigns begin!

The first part of the campaign is known as the nomination campaign, where several Democratic candidates and several Republican candidates compete against one another for votes within their party. Candidates crisscross the country giving speeches, raising money and trying to win the trust of the voters. They are also fighting for the support of the party delegates.

Hillary Clinton and Barack Obama debate.

3. Primary elections and caucuses take place.

To help decide which candidate from each party will win that party's nomination, states hold primary elections and caucuses to find out who the people support. Primaries are similar to the general election, although in many states people may only vote for candidates from their own political party. Some states hold what is called a caucus, where party leaders and citizens get together, discuss the issues, debate the candidates and then cast their votes. Caucus rules vary from state to state and are different for both political parties. At this stage, when a voter chooses a candidate, he or she is also choosing the delegates who will support that candidate at the national nominating convention.

4. Each party holds a national nominating convention.

In the summer before a presidential election, thousands of members from both parties gather together for a national convention. The delegates from each party cast their ballots for their chosen nominee. With rousing speeches, the nominee from each party is formally announced. Each nominee chooses a running mate, who will become Vice President if he or she is elected. These meetings also aim to whip up excitement for the upcoming election.

Gerald Ford wins his party's nomination in 1976.

5. The election campaign begins.

During this part of the process, the nominees from both major parties compete against one another for votes all around the country. Representatives from third parties (such as the Independent Party, the Green Party or the Libertarian Party) try to get voters to rally behind them as well.

President Carter campaigning

6. Citizens vote in the general election.
Every presidential election year, votes are cast on the Tuesday following the first Monday in November.

7. The Electoral College votes for President.
When the Constitution was being written in 1787, some of the founding fathers wanted Congress to be in charge of electing the President. Others felt that the citizens should be allowed to elect their leader by popular vote. So our early leaders put the electoral college in place as a compromise. With this system, a group of electors from each state actually chooses the President.

When voters cast their ballots on election day, it is as if they are voting for a group of electors rather than a particular candidate. Each state has a number of electors equal to the number of its Senators and Representatives. Washington, D.C., also has three electors. In most states, all of the electors must vote for the party that won the most votes in their state. Maine and Nebraska divide their electoral votes among the candidates. To win the presidency, a candidate must receive at least 270 out of the 538 possible electoral votes. If this majority is not reached, the House of Representatives chooses the President.

8. The new President is takes the oath of office.
On January 20, the country's new leader is inaugurated. He or she states the presidential oath, pledging to "preserve, protect and defend the Constitution of the United States."

The inauguration of George H.W. Bush in 1989

go 🔍 **To learn more about the 2008 election, go to** *www.timeforkids.com* **and search for** *"president"* **or** *"election."*

Presidential Succession

This list shows the order of people who would take over if a sitting President died, resigned or was removed from office.

1. **Vice President**
2. **Speaker of the House**
3. **President Pro Tempore of the Senate**
4. **Secretary of State**
5. **Secretary of the Treasury**
6. **Secretary of Defense**
7. **Attorney General**
8. **Secretary of the Interior**
9. **Secretary of Agriculture**
10. **Secretary of Commerce**
11. **Secretary of Labor**
12. **Secretary of Health and Human Services**
13. **Secretary of Housing and Urban Development**
14. **Secretary of Transportation**
15. **Secretary of Energy**
16. **Secretary of Education**
17. **Secretary of Veterans Affairs**
18. **Secretary of Homeland Security**

GEORGE WASHINGTON (SERVED 1789–1797)

BORN: Feb. 22, 1732, in Virginia; died: Dec. 14, 1799
POLITICAL PARTY: None (first term), Federalist
VICE PRESIDENT: John Adams
FIRST LADY: Martha Dandridge Custis

GUESS WHAT? When he was sworn in, Washington only had one tooth. He wore dentures!

JOHN ADAMS (SERVED 1797–1801)

BORN: Oct. 30, 1735, in Massachusetts; died: July 4, 1826
POLITICAL PARTY: Federalist
VICE PRESIDENT: Thomas Jefferson
FIRST LADY: Abigail Smith

GUESS WHAT? John Adams held the first fireworks display at the White House.

THOMAS JEFFERSON (SERVED 1801–1809)

BORN: April 13, 1743, in Virginia; died: July 4, 1826
POLITICAL PARTY: Democratic-Republican
VICE PRESIDENTS: Aaron Burr, George Clinton
FIRST LADY: Martha Wayles Skelton

GUESS WHAT? Jefferson had a pet mockingbird that he allowed to fly around the White House.

JAMES MADISON (SERVED 1809–1817)

BORN: March 16, 1751, in Virginia; died: June 28, 1836
POLITICAL PARTY: Democratic-Republican
VICE PRESIDENTS: George Clinton, Elbridge Gerry
FIRST LADY: Dorothy "Dolley" Payne Todd

GUESS WHAT? At 5 feet, 4 inches tall (162.5 cm), Madison was the shortest president.

JAMES MONROE (SERVED 1817–1825)

BORN: April 28, 1758, in Virginia; died: July 4, 1831
POLITICAL PARTY: Democratic-Republican
VICE PRESIDENT: Daniel D. Tompkins
FIRST LADY: Elizabeth "Eliza" Kortright

GUESS WHAT? Monroe was the third of five presidents to pass away on Independence Day. John Adams and Thomas Jefferson died on July 4th five years earlier.

JOHN QUINCY ADAMS (SERVED 1825–1829)

BORN: July 11, 1767, in Massachusetts; died: Feb. 23, 1848
POLITICAL PARTY: Democratic-Republican
VICE PRESIDENT: John C. Calhoun
FIRST LADY: Louisa Catherine Johnson

GUESS WHAT? At 14 years old, John Quincy Adams traveled to Russia, where he translated documents into French for the U.S. Minister to Russia.

ANDREW JACKSON (SERVED 1829–1837)

BORN: March 15, 1767, in South Carolina; died: June 8, 1845
POLITICAL PARTY: Democratic
VICE PRESIDENTS: John C. Calhoun, Martin Van Buren
FIRST LADY: Rachel Donelson Robards

GUESS WHAT? *Jackson fought in both the Revolutionary War and the War of 1812. He was the only president to do so.*

7

MARTIN VAN BUREN (SERVED 1837–1841)

BORN: Dec. 5, 1782, in New York; died: July 24, 1862
POLITICAL PARTY: Democratic
VICE PRESIDENT: Richard M. Johnson
FIRST LADY: Hannah Hoes

GUESS WHAT? *As Vice President, Martin Van Buren wore his pistols when he went to the Senate. At the time, the Senators often got into fights.*

8

WILLIAM HENRY HARRISON (SERVED 1841)

BORN: Feb. 9, 1773, in Virginia; died: April 4, 1841
POLITICAL PARTY: Whig
VICE PRESIDENT: John Tyler
FIRST LADY: Anna Tuthill Symmes

GUESS WHAT? *William Henry Harrison was in office for such a short time that his wife didn't even have time to move to Washington.*

9

JOHN TYLER (SERVED 1841–1845)

BORN: March 29, 1790, in Virginia; died: Jan. 18, 1862
POLITICAL PARTY: Whig
VICE PRESIDENT: None
FIRST LADIES: Letitia Christian (d. 1842); Julia Gardiner

GUESS WHAT? *Tyler was the first person to become president because someone else died in office. For this, he was called "His Accidency."*

10

JAMES K. POLK (SERVED 1845–1849)

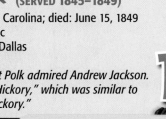

BORN: Nov. 2, 1795, in North Carolina; died: June 15, 1849
POLITICAL PARTY: Democratic
VICE PRESIDENT: George M. Dallas
FIRST LADY: Sarah Childress

GUESS WHAT? *President Polk admired Andrew Jackson. Polk was known as "Young Hickory," which was similar to Jackson's nickname, "Old Hickory."*

11

ZACHARY TAYLOR (SERVED 1849–1850)

BORN: Nov. 24, 1784, in Virginia; died: July 9, 1850
POLITICAL PARTY: Whig
VICE PRESIDENT: Millard Fillmore
FIRST LADY: Margaret Mackall Smith

GUESS WHAT? *Zachary Taylor was James Madison's second cousin.*

12

MILLARD FILLMORE (served 1850–1853)

BORN: Jan. 7, 1800, in New York; died: March 8, 1874
POLITICAL PARTY: Whig
VICE PRESIDENT: None
FIRST LADIES: Abigail Powers (d. 1853); Caroline Carmichael McIntosh

GUESS WHAT? *When Fillmore became president, 30 states made up the United States.*

13

FRANKLIN PIERCE (served 1853–1857)

BORN: Nov. 23, 1804, in New Hampshire; died: Oct. 8, 1869
POLITICAL PARTY: Democratic
VICE PRESIDENT: William R. King
FIRST LADY: Jane Means Appleton

GUESS WHAT? *Franklin Pierce recited his entire inaugural address from memory.*

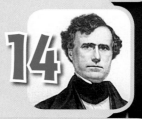

14

JAMES BUCHANAN (served 1857–1861)

BORN: April 23, 1791, in Pennsylvania; died: June 1, 1868
POLITICAL PARTY: Democratic
VICE PRESIDENT: John C. Breckinridge
FIRST LADY: None; his niece Harriet Lane acted as White House hostess

GUESS WHAT? *Southern states seceded from the Union during Buchanan's time as president. His Vice President, John C. Breckinridge, even fought for the Confederacy.*

15

ABRAHAM LINCOLN (served 1861–1865)

BORN: Feb. 12, 1809, in Kentucky; died: April 15, 1865
POLITICAL PARTY: Republican
VICE PRESIDENTS: Hannibal Hamlin, Andrew Johnson
FIRST LADY: Mary Todd

GUESS WHAT? *Lincoln was the first U.S. president to be assassinated.*

16

ANDREW JOHNSON (served 1865–1869)

BORN: Dec. 29, 1808, in North Carolina; died: July 31, 1875
POLITICAL PARTIES: Union, Democratic
VICE PRESIDENT: None
FIRST LADY: Eliza McCardle

GUESS WHAT? *Andrew Johnson held every elected political office at the local, state and national level. He was mayor, state representative, state senator, governor, congressman, senator, vice president and president.*

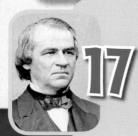

17

ULYSSES S. GRANT (served 1869–1877)

BORN: April 27, 1822, in Ohio; died: July 23, 1885
POLITICAL PARTY: Republican
VICE PRESIDENTS: Schuyler Colfax, Henry Wilson
FIRST LADY: Julia Boggs Dent

GUESS WHAT? *Grant was an accomplished horse rider and horse jumper. His high-jump record at West Point stood for more than 25 years.*

18

RUTHERFORD B. HAYES (served 1877–1881)

BORN: Oct. 4, 1822, in Ohio; died: Jan. 17, 1893
POLITICAL PARTY: Republican
VICE PRESIDENT: William A. Wheeler
FIRST LADY: Lucy Ware Webb
GUESS WHAT? *When he arrived in San Francisco in September 1880, Hayes became the first president to visit the West Coast.*

19

20

JAMES A. GARFIELD (served 1881)

BORN: Nov. 19, 1831, in Ohio; died: Sept. 19, 1881
POLITICAL PARTY: Republican
VICE PRESIDENT: Chester A. Arthur
FIRST LADY: Lucretia Rudolph
GUESS WHAT? *President Garfield had a dog named Veto.*

CHESTER A. ARTHUR (served 1881–1885)

BORN: Oct. 5, 1829, in Vermont; died: Nov. 18, 1886
POLITICAL PARTY: Republican
VICE PRESIDENT: None
FIRST LADY: Ellen Lewis Herndon
GUESS WHAT? *In one of his last official acts as president, Arthur dedicated the Washington Monument in February 1885.*

21

22

GROVER CLEVELAND (served 1885–1889)

BORN: March 18, 1837, in New Jersey; died: June 24, 1908
POLITICAL PARTY: Democratic
VICE PRESIDENT: Thomas A. Hendricks
FIRST LADY: Frances Folsom
GUESS WHAT? *Grover Cleveland and his young wife had a baby while he was in office. He was the first president to have a child born in the White House.*

BENJAMIN HARRISON (served 1889–1893)

BORN: Aug. 20, 1833, in Ohio; died: March 13, 1901
POLITICAL PARTY: Republican
VICE PRESIDENT: Levi P. Morton
FIRST LADIES: Caroline Lavina Scott (d. 1892); Mary Scott Lord Dimmick
GUESS WHAT? *Harrison lost the popular vote, but won more votes in the electoral college than his opponent, Grover Cleveland.*

23

24

GROVER CLEVELAND (served 1893–1897)

BORN: March 18, 1837, in New Jersey; died: June 24, 1908
POLITICAL PARTY: Democratic
VICE PRESIDENT: Adlai E. Stevenson
FIRST LADY: Frances Folsom
GUESS WHAT? *Cleveland was drafted to serve in the Civil War, but hired a substitute to fight for him. This was perfectly legal at the time.*

WILLIAM McKINLEY (served 1897–1901)

BORN: Jan. 29, 1843, in Ohio; died: Sept. 14, 1901
POLITICAL PARTY: Republican
VICE PRESIDENTS: Garret A. Hobart, Theodore Roosevelt
FIRST LADY: Ida Saxton
GUESS WHAT? *The $500 bill features a portrait of President McKinley. It was last printed in 1945.*

25

THEODORE ROOSEVELT (served 1901–1909)

BORN: Oct. 27, 1858, in New York; died: Jan. 6, 1919
POLITICAL PARTY: Republican
VICE PRESIDENT: Charles W. Fairbanks
FIRST LADY: Edith Kermit Carow
GUESS WHAT? *Theodore Roosevelt officially changed the name of the President's House, or Executive Mansion, to the "White House" in 1901.*

26

WILLIAM H. TAFT (served 1909–1913)

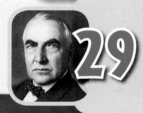

BORN: Sept. 15, 1857, in Ohio; died: March 8, 1930
POLITICAL PARTY: Republican
VICE PRESIDENT: James S. Sherman
FIRST LADY: Helen Herron
GUESS WHAT? *President Taft is one of two presidents buried in Arlington National Cemetery in northern Virginia. John F. Kennedy is the other.*

27

WOODROW WILSON (served 1913–1921)

BORN: Dec. 28, 1856, in Virginia; died: Feb. 3, 1924
POLITICAL PARTY: Democratic
VICE PRESIDENT: Thomas R. Marshall
FIRST LADIES: Ellen Louise Axson (d. 1914); Edith Bolling Galt
GUESS WHAT? *President Wilson was the first president to earn a doctorate, or Ph.D., which is the highest degree a university can grant a student.*

28

WARREN G. HARDING (served 1921–1923)

BORN: Nov. 2, 1865, in Ohio; died: Aug. 2, 1923
POLITICAL PARTY: Republican
VICE PRESIDENT: Calvin Coolidge
FIRST LADY: Florence King
GUESS WHAT? *Warren G. Harding was the first president to have his voice broadcast over the radio.*

29

CALVIN COOLIDGE (served 1923–1929)

BORN: July 4, 1872, in Vermont; died: Jan. 5, 1933
POLITICAL PARTY: Republican
VICE PRESIDENT: Charles G. Dawes
FIRST LADY: Grace Anna Goodhue
GUESS WHAT? *Calvin Coolidge found out at 2:30 a.m. that he was going to become president. President Harding had just died of a heart attack.*

30

HERBERT C. HOOVER (served 1929–1933)

31

BORN: Aug. 10, 1874, in Iowa; died: Oct. 20, 1964
POLITICAL PARTY: Republican
VICE PRESIDENT: Charles Curtis
FIRST LADY: Lou Henry

GUESS WHAT? *Herbert and his wife, Lou, spent time in China from 1899 to 1900. Back in the U.S., they would sometimes speak Chinese together so no one could understand them.*

FRANKLIN D. ROOSEVELT (served 1933–1945)

32

BORN: Jan. 30, 1882, in New York; died: April 12, 1945
POLITICAL PARTY: Democratic
VICE PRESIDENTS: John Garner, Henry Wallace, Harry S. Truman
FIRST LADY: Anna Eleanor Roosevelt

GUESS WHAT? *In 1921, at the age of 39, FDR contracted polio, or infantile paralysis, which left him with only partial use of his legs.*

HARRY S. TRUMAN (served 1945–1953)

33

BORN: May 8, 1884, in Missouri; died: Dec. 26, 1972
POLITICAL PARTY: Democratic
VICE PRESIDENT: Alben W. Barkley
FIRST LADY: Elizabeth "Bess" Virginia Wallace

GUESS WHAT? *After he retired, Truman referred to himself as "Mr. Citizen" rather than "Mr. President."*

DWIGHT D. EISENHOWER (served 1953–1961)

34

BORN: Oct. 14, 1890, in Texas; died: March 28, 1969
POLITICAL PARTY: Republican
VICE PRESIDENT: Richard M. Nixon
FIRST LADY: Marie "Mamie" Geneva Doud

GUESS WHAT? *Eisenhower was the first president licensed to fly an airplane.*

JOHN F. KENNEDY (served 1961–1963)

BORN: May 29, 1917, in Massachusetts; died: Nov. 22, 1963
POLITICAL PARTY: Democratic
VICE PRESIDENT: Lyndon B. Johnson
FIRST LADY: Jacqueline Lee Bouvier

35

GUESS WHAT? *Kennedy won the Pulitzer Prize for his book,* Profiles in Courage.

LYNDON B. JOHNSON (served 1963–1969)

36

BORN: Aug. 27, 1908, in Texas; died: Jan. 22, 1973
POLITICAL PARTY: Democratic
VICE PRESIDENT: Hubert H. Humphrey
FIRST LADY: Claudia Alta "Lady Bird" Taylor

GUESS WHAT? *Johnson left home at the age of 15, performing odd jobs for money. He briefly worked as an elevator operator and a grape picker.*

RICHARD M. NIXON (served 1969–1974)

BORN: Jan. 9, 1913, in California; died April 22, 1994
POLITICAL PARTY: Republican
VICE PRESIDENTS: Spiro T. Agnew, Gerald R. Ford
FIRST LADY: Thelma Catherine "Pat" Ryan
GUESS WHAT? *President Nixon was one of two presidents belonging to the Religious Society of Friends (or Quakers). Hoover was the other.*

37

GERALD R. FORD (served 1974–1977)

BORN: July 14, 1913, in Nebraska; died: Dec. 6, 2006
POLITICAL PARTY: Republican
VICE PRESIDENT: Nelson A. Rockefeller
FIRST LADY: Elizabeth "Betty" Anne Bloomer Warren
GUESS WHAT? *Ford held his daughter Susan's high school prom at the White House.*

38

JIMMY CARTER (served 1977–1981)

BORN: Oct. 1, 1924, in Georgia
POLITICAL PARTY: Democratic
VICE PRESIDENT: Walter F. Mondale
FIRST LADY: Rosalynn Smith
GUESS WHAT? *Born James Earl Carter, the 39th president, was the first sworn in using his nickname.*

39

RONALD REAGAN (served 1981–1989)

BORN: Feb. 6, 1911, in Illinois; died: June 5, 2004
POLITICAL PARTY: Republican
VICE PRESIDENT: George H.W. Bush
FIRST LADY: Nancy Davis
GUESS WHAT? *At 69 years old, Reagan was the oldest man elected to the presidency.*

40

GEORGE H.W. BUSH (served 1989–1993)

BORN: June 12, 1924, in Massachusetts
POLITICAL PARTY: Republican
VICE PRESIDENT: J. Danforth Quayle
FIRST LADY: Barbara Pierce
GUESS WHAT? *At Yale University, Bush was the captain of the baseball team.*

41

WILLIAM J. CLINTON (served 1993–2001)

BORN: Aug. 19, 1946, in Arkansas
POLITICAL PARTY: Democratic
VICE PRESIDENT: Albert Gore Jr.
FIRST LADY: Hillary Rodham
GUESS WHAT? *A talented saxophone player, Clinton once considered making a living as a musician.*

42

GEORGE W. BUSH (served 2001–2008)

43

BORN: July 6, 1946, in Connecticut
POLITICAL PARTY: Republican
VICE PRESIDENT: Richard B. Cheney
FIRST LADY: Laura Welch

GUESS WHAT? *George W. and his wife, Laura, have twin daughters. They are named Barbara and Jenna, after their grandmothers.*

?44

This book went to the printer before the 44th President of the United States was elected.

go! *To learn more about our new president, go to www.timeforkids.com.*

TFK GAME

Doodler in Chief

Being the President is a tough job. Doodling in meetings may help our leaders relax. Here are some drawings by U.S. Presidents. Match each President to his drawing.

ANSWERS ON PAGE 244

A

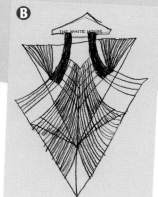
B

C

D

1. **When his mind drifted, John F. Kennedy may have been thinking, "From sea to shining sea."**

2. **Before he became President, former actor Ronald Reagan played a movie cowboy.**

3. **Lyndon B. Johnson and his staff were serious about keeping his scribbles, no matter how silly.**

4. **President Herbert Hoover never drew people. One of his doodle patterns was used on kids' clothing.**

TFK RELIGION

FIVE MAJOR FAITHS

There are about 20 major religions in the world, five of which have had the greatest influence on global culture: Judaism, Christianity, Islam, Hinduism and Buddhism.

Judaism

Jewish children light a Menorah.

Judaism began as a religion in the Middle East nearly 6,000 years ago with its founder, Abraham. Jews believe that there is one God and that God made a covenant, or agreement, with Abraham appointing him the leader of God's chosen people. The **Bible** (or Old Testament, as Christians refer to it) is the great book of Judaism, along with the **Talmud,** which includes many laws for daily living. Jewish worship includes readings from the **Torah** (the first five books of the Bible), written by God and given to Moses at Mount Sinai more than 3,000 years ago. The Torah begins with God's creation of the universe and includes the Ten Commandments. There are three basic practices in Judaism: Orthodox, Conservative and Reform. Orthodox Judaism is the most traditional, and Reform Judaism is the most modern. Judaism influenced the rise of Christianity and Islam, because all three religions claim Abraham as their ancestor.

The Torah

A stained glass window depicts Jesus Christ.

Christianity

Christianity is named after Jesus Christ, who is the founder and central figure of Christian worship. Christians believe that Jesus' mission as the son of God was to sacrifice his life in payment for the sins of humanity. Jesus, along with his 12 followers, called apostles, preached messages of love and compassion. Christians believe that Jesus and the apostles performed miracles, and these acts are recorded in the **New Testament** (an addition to the Jewish Bible). Christians believe that after Jesus' death by crucifixion (being nailed to a cross) in Jerusalem, he rose from the dead and went up to heaven. They also believe that he will return to earth on the Day of Judgment. There are many kinds of Christians, including Roman Catholics, Orthodox and Protestants (such as Episcopalians, Presbyterians, Baptists, Methodists, Lutherans and Evangelicals).

GUESS WHAT?

The ancient Egyptians believed that their ruler, known as the pharaoh, was a living god. When he died, his body was mummified (dried and wrapped in strips of cloth) so that he could live forever, ensuring that the people in his kingdom would continue to survive.

Christ was crucified around 30 A.D.

Islam

Islam is another major faith that traces its history back to Abraham. Muslims believe in the same god as Jews and Christians, whom they call Allah. Islam's founder and greatest prophet is Muhammad (570–632), and its great book is the **Qur'an.** Muslim devotion includes five practices, called the **Great Pillars:**

Muslims pray five times a day.

1. The statement of faith, which is "There is no God but Allah, and Muhammad is his prophet"
2. Praying five times a day
3. Giving to charity
4. Fasting from eating and drinking at certain times, including during the daylight hours of the month of Ramadan
5. Making a pilgrimage, or religious trip, to Mecca, Muhammad's birthplace, located in Saudi Arabia

Sunni and Shiite Muslims

The differences between Sunni and Shiite Muslims date back to the death of Muhammad in 632.

• Sunnis believed that Abu Bakr, a faithful follower of Muhammad, should be Muhammad's successor. Shiites disagreed, arguing that only someone with the same bloodline as Muhammad should lead the religion. Shiites backed Muhammad's cousin (and son-in-law), Ali ibn Abi Talib.

• The majority of Muslims are Sunnis, with only 10 to 15% following the Shiite branch of the religion. Sunnis are found throughout the Muslim world, with large populations in Indonesia, Pakistan, India, Bangladesh, Turkey, Iran and North Africa.

• Shiites are also found throughout the world, with large communities in Iraq, Iran, Yemen, Bahrain, Syria and Lebanon.

• Although both branches of the religion follow many of the same basic beliefs, adherents to the two branches follow different leaders and are often in conflict.

Many Muslim women wear head scarves.

Hinduism

The oldest of the five major faiths, Hinduism began more than 7,000 years ago in Asia. Hinduism as a religion appears in many forms. Some Hindus believe in only one God; others believe in many gods and goddesses. In general, Hindus believe that life is a journey of learning, and that how a person acts affects his or her destiny. They believe in reincarnation, in which a person's soul returns to earth in the form of another human being or other creature until that soul learns all its lessons and becomes perfect. Hinduism is the main religion in India and Nepal. Hindi sacred texts include the **Vedas** and **Upanishads.**

The Hindu god Krishna

Buddhism

Although many people think of Buddhism as a religion, it is more of a philosophy, or a way of life. That is because Buddhists don't believe in a specific god. Instead, they follow the teachings of their founder, Siddhartha Gautama (born in India about 563–483 B.C.) known as the Buddha. *Buddha* means "the Awakened One," and Buddhists believe that he "awoke" to the reality of what life is about, which he summed up in *"Four Noble Truths."*

A statue of Buddha

1. There is suffering in the world.
2. The cause of suffering is desire.
3. Suffering can be ended.
4. The way to end suffering is by following the "Noble Eightfold Path." This path involves correct ways to speak, act, work, improve oneself, be aware, concentrate, understand and think.

Like Hindus, many Buddhists believe in reincarnation. There are three main kinds of Buddhism (Theravada, Mahayana, Vajrayana), each following different beliefs, practices and rituals.

The Hindu god Shiva

DISCOVERIES FROM THE LAND DOWN UNDER

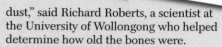

Marsupial lion skeleton

Australia's unique animals are among the most fascinating creatures on the planet. Roly-poly wallabies, duck-billed platypuses, cuddly koalas, flightless emus and prickly echidnas can be found only on that continent. But a recent fossil discovery reveals that Australia's ancient creatures were even more bizarre than their modern cousins.

About 500,000 years ago, kangaroos as tall as trucks, wombats weighing more than 400 pounds and fierce marsupial lions roamed the Land Down Under. Scientists call the animals "megamarsupials" for their giant size. A marsupial is a mammal whose infants develop in an external pouch.

Until a few years ago, scientists had assembled only bits and pieces of megamarsupial skeletons. In January 2007, Australian scientists announced that they had found a treasure trove of fossils, including the first-ever complete skeletons of marsupial lions.

LOCKED UP IN CAVES

In 2002, a team of cave explorers were soaking up the sights on the Nullarbor Plain in southern Australia. They came across several small openings in the ground that led to a series of extensive caves.

The explorers may have been the very first humans to set foot in the caves. They found "heaps of bones and complete skeletons of unusual animals that looked as fresh as if they had died yesterday," Gavin Prideaux told TFK. Prideaux, the lead scientist, examined the bones. He believes the animals accidentally fell through holes into the caves and died there.

In all, the scientists unearthed 69 well-preserved fossils of birds, mammals and reptiles. "Those animals had died a half-million years ago, but the caves had been locked up tight for so long that the fossils were barely covered in a layer of dust," said Richard Roberts, a scientist at the University of Wollongong who helped determine how old the bones were.

A giant wombat, two new species of parrots and eight new species of ancient kangaroos, including two tree-climbing varieties, were found. But scientists are most excited about finding complete skeletons of the marsupial lion, or *Thylacoleo carnifex* (*thy*-lack-oh-*lee*-oh *car*-nee-fex).

Eleven marsupial lion fossils were discovered. The lion was the largest carnivorous, or meat-eating, marsupial ever to roam Australia. The 220-pound prehistoric predator has fascinated scientists for more than a century. It had retractable thumb claws and a stronger jaw than any other animal its size.

WHY DID THEY GO EXTINCT?

Researchers had long believed that a drastic change in climate was responsible for the extinction of Australia's megamarsupials. But after studying the fossils found in Thylacoleo Cave, a team of scientists has developed a new theory. They believe that climate change alone cannot account for the animals' disappearance. "Current evidence tells us that the extinctions happened soon after people arrived, probably within a few thousand years. That points to humans as the cause," says Christopher Johnson, a scientist who consulted with the team.

For now, scientists are keeping the exact location of the caves a secret. They are eager to explore the area to find out more about what happened to Australia's megamarsupials and learn more about how they lived.

—By Claudia Atticot

TIMELINE OF THE EARTH

HADEAN ERA
4.5–3.8 billion years ago
Formation of solar system, Earth

ARCHAEAN ERA
3.8–2.5 billion years ago
Cooling of Earth's crust, formation of rocks and moving continental plates, life first appears in form of bacteria

PROTEROZOIC ERA
2.5 billion–543 million years ago Stable continents form, earliest forms of fungi and single-cell plants and animals

PALEOZOIC ERA
543–248 million years ago
Multi-cell plants, animals and fungi; later insects and marine animals

Trilobite

MESOZOIC ERA
248–65 million years ago Dinosaurs, birds, ferns

Dinosur fossil

CENOZOIC ERA
65 million years ago–present Amphibians, mammals, flowering plants, fish, humans

PALEOCENE EPOCH
65–54.8 million years ago
Platypuses, kangaroos

EOCENE EPOCH
54.8–33.7 million years ago
Rhinos, horses, zebras, deer, sheep, goats

OLIGOCENE EPOCH
33.7–23.8 million years ago
Cats, dogs

MIOCENE EPOCH
23.8–5.3 million years ago
Small birds, rodents

PLIOCENE EPOCH
5.3–1.8 million years ago
Giraffes, hippopotamuses, antelopes, gazelles

PLEISTOCENE EPOCH
1.8 million years ago–10,000 years ago Flowering plants, insects, primates, humans
400,000–200,000 years ago
Homo sapiens
200,000–30,000 years ago
Homo sapiens neandertalensis
130,000–present
Homo sapiens sapiens

A 15,000-year-old cave painting of a horse

5–4 million years ago
Australopithecus ramidus
4–2.7 million years ago
Australopithecus afarensis
3–2 million years ago
Australopithecus africanus

Artist's image of A. africanus

2.2–1.6 million years ago
Homo habilis
2.2–1 million years ago
Australopithecus robustus
2 million–400,000 years ago
Homo erectus

Human evolution

How Old Is Old?

SCIENTISTS USE DIFFERENT METHODS TO DETERMINE THE AGES OF VERY OLD OBJECTS OR LIVING THINGS.

DENDROCHRONOLOGY is the study of tree rings to determine a tree's age as well as the climate conditions it experienced. Tree rings can be observed by taking a cross-section of the tree's trunk. Each ring shows one year of the tree's life. Wide rings indicate mostly wet weather for that year; narrow rings indicate dry seasons.

CARBON-14 DATING is a scientific technique used to determine the age of cloth, plant fibers, wood and bones up to about 60,000 years old. Carbon 14 is a radioactive form of the element carbon that is absorbed by all living things, including humans. Every 5,700 years, the amount of Carbon 14 in anything is reduced by half. This is called the "half-life" of the atom. Using a special mathematical formula, scientists can figure out an object's age by determining how much Carbon 14 it still contains.

To determine the age of things that are billions of years old, scientists use similar techniques with other elements.

Record Breaker The oldest-determined piece of the earth, a zircon crystal, was found in Australia. It is between 4.3 and 4.4 billion years old.

BRANCHES OF SCIENCE

Astronomy

Geology

Science is the field of knowledge that systematically studies and organizes information and draws conclusions based on measurable results. Traditionally, scientists have classified their fields into three branches: physical sciences, Earth sciences and life sciences. Social sciences, technology and mathematics may also be included. Each branch has many fields of study; some are included here.

PHYSICAL SCIENCES These sciences study the properties of energy and matter, as well as their relationship to each other. **Physics** seeks to explain how the universe behaves through the workings of matter, energy and time. **Chemistry** is the study of chemical elements and how they interact on an atomic level. **Astronomy** is the study of space and its galaxies.

Chemistry

EARTH SCIENCES These sciences focus on the earth and study its composition and structure. **Geology** is the study of the earth's inner rock formations. **Geography** is concerned with the study and mapping of the earth's terrain. **Oceanography** focuses on Earth's oceans and their currents and habitats. **Meteorology** is the study of weather. **Paleontology** focuses on the remains of ancient plants and animals.

LIFE SCIENCES These sciences explore the nature of living things. **Biology** covers the study of how living things evolve, reproduce, thrive and relate to one another. **Botany** focuses on plants, **zoology** on animals and **microbiology** on microscopic organisms.

Paleontology

SOCIAL SCIENCES These sciences investigate how humans behave and live together. **Psychology** explores individual human behavior, while **sociology** analyzes human behavior in groups. **Anthropology** studies human physical traits as well as cultures and languages. **Economics** is the study of how money, goods and businesses affect society. **Law** focuses on the rules of society and **political science** studies governmental processes and institutions.

TECHNOLOGY This branch is concerned with the practical application of scientific knowledge. **Engineering** is concerned with the design and construction of objects, machines and systems. **Biotechnology** is the application of biological processes to create medicines and vaccines and to alter food and crops. **Computer science** focuses on meeting industrial needs by creating computers and new software.

MATHEMATICS This science differs from other branches because it deals with concepts rather than physical evidence. Its focus is on measuring numeric relationships, analyzing data and predicting outcomes. **Arithmetic** uses only numbers to solve problems, while **algebra** uses both numbers and unknown variables in the form of letters. **Geometry** is the study of two- and three-dimensional shapes. **Calculus** involves the computation of problems that contain constantly changing measurements. Nearly all sciences use mathematics in their research.

GUESS WHAT?
Exobiology is a very new life science. It focuses on the origins of life on Earth and around the universe and explores the possibility of life elsewhere in the universe.

Engineering

THE FIVE KINGDOMS

Every form of life belongs to one of five kingdoms.

MONERA

This kingdom consists of one-celled bacteria that don't have any nucleus. Some are able to move, while others can't. Some can make their own food to live on, while others need to feed on things outside themselves.

FUNGI

These creatures have more than one cell, and their cells have nuclei. Fungi generally can't move. They must rely on outside sources for their food. This kingdom includes molds, mushrooms and yeast.

PROTISTA

The one-celled creatures of this kingdom share the same characteristics as those in the monera kingdom except for the fact that they have a nucleus. Examples of protista are amoebas, paramecia and some one-celled algae.

PLANTS

The plant kingdom consists of multicellular organisms that have nuclei and remain in one place. In a process called photosynthesis, plants use sunlight and a chemical called chlorophyll to produce their own food. Some plants produce flowers and fruit; others don't. Examples of the plant kingdom are multicellular algae, ferns, mosses, trees, shrubs, wildflowers, fruits and vegetables.

ANIMALS

The animal kingdom consists of multicellular organisms that move and rely on outside sources for food. In general, they are the most complex creatures on Earth, with most having such abilities as communication and forming social groups. Examples of animals are sponges, jellyfish, insects, amphibians, fish and mammals, including humans.

Elements, Atoms, Molecules and Mixtures

ELEMENTS: Every substance in the world is made up of one or more elements. Elements are substances that can't be divided to form other substances. Some common elements are hydrogen, oxygen, nitrogen, carbon and sodium.

MOLECULES: These are formed when two or more atoms are joined in a chemical reaction. What results is a substance that has different chemical properties than the atoms that form it.

- Water is made up of molecules that contain two hydrogen atoms and one oxygen atom. Water is very different from either pure oxygen or pure hydrogen.
- Table salt is made up of molecules that contain one sodium atom and one chlorine atom.
- Carbon dioxide is made up of molecules that include one carbon atom and two oxygen atoms.

ATOMS: Every element contains atoms. An atom consists of two parts:

1. a **nucleus** that contains one or more **protons** and **neutrons**
2. one or more **electrons** that circle around the nucleus.

Protons are particles that have a positive electrical charge. Electrons are particles that have a negative electrical charge. Neutrons have no electrical charge. The opposite charges of protons and electrons cause an attraction between these particles. This attraction keeps the electrons spinning around the nucleus.

MIXTURES: Mixtures are combinations of molecules that are not chemically joined. The molecules can be separated out of the mixture at any time. Salt water is a mixture of the molecules of salt and water. The salt can be separated from the water if the water evaporates.

GUESS WHAT?

Diamonds and the graphite in pencils have something in common. They are both made of carbon. Their molecular structures are different, however, and that's what makes a diamond the hardest natural material on Earth and graphite one of the softest.

Pioneers in Science

ISAAC NEWTON
(1642–1727) A mathematician and physicist, Newton was the first to discover that white light is made up of light of different colors (known as the spectrum). He is best known for studies analyzing and predicting the motion and speed of objects in water, on the ground and in the air. His laws of gravitation and mechanics still greatly influence modern physicists and astronomers.

Newton

CHARLES DARWIN
(1809–82) Evolutionary biologist Charles Darwin caused a stir in 1859 with the publication of his book, *The Origin of Species.* His theory stated that certain mutations enable some species to better survive in their habitats. These mutations are then passed down to their offspring. As a result, species evolve, or develop new characteristics, over time.

Darwin

LOUIS PASTEUR
(1822–95) A chemist and biologist, Louis Pasteur was the first scientist to demonstrate that illnesses are caused by microscopic particles called "germs." He devoted his life to finding ways to kill bacteria and prevent disease in animals and people through vaccination. "Pasteurization" is the process used to rid milk of harmful bacteria.

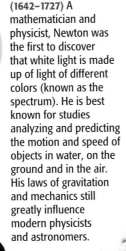

Pasteur

WANT TO BECOME A SCIENTIST?

Here are some different kinds of scientists, along with what they study.

ANTHROPOLOGIST	cultures, languages and the physical development of humans
ARCHAEOLOGIST	artifacts and ruins of past civilizations
ASTRONOMER	history, development and motion of things in the universe
BOTANIST	plants
CHEMIST	combinations and reactions of chemicals
COMPUTER SCIENTIST	computer design, creation of hardware and software programs
ECOLOGIST	structure and balance of environmental life systems
ENTOMOLOGIST	insects
EPIDEMIOLOGIST	causes, spread and control of diseases
ETHOLOGIST	animal behavior
GENETICIST	heredity and gene therapy
GEOLOGIST	Earth's structure; formation and composition of rocks, minerals and volcanoes
HERPETOLOGIST	reptiles and amphibians
ICHTHYOLOGIST	fish
METEOROLOGIST	climate, weather patterns and predictions
MICROBIOLOGIST	cellular life
OCEANOGRAPHER	ocean life and currents
ORNITHOLOGIST	birds
PHYSICIST	relationship between energy and matter
PHYSIOLOGIST	structures and functions within an organism
ZOOLOGIST	animals

Chemist

Botanist

Entomologist

Ornithologist

Ichthyologist

MARIE CURIE

(1867–1934) Working in Paris with her physicist husband, Pierre Curie, Marie Curie discovered the properties of two new chemical elements, radium and polonium. In 1903, they won the Nobel Prize in Physics. Eight years later, Marie Curie's work showing the practical uses of radioactivity earned her the Nobel Prize in Chemistry. Modern medical cancer treatments are based on her discoveries.

ALBERT EINSTEIN

(1879–1955) Albert Einstein changed the way scientists understand the concepts of time, gravity and planetary motion through his theories of relativity. He described how molecules move and proved that matter can be turned into energy and energy into matter.

JONAS SALK

(1914–95) In 1952, Salk created a vaccine against the polio virus, which causes paralysis. Salk's discovery saved the lives of hundreds of thousands of people and has prevented the disability of many more.

JANE GOODALL

(1934–) Ethologist and conservationist Jane Goodall spent decades working with African chimpanzees. She revealed the tool-making and communication skills of chimps and was the first to discover that chimpanzees eat meat as well as plants. Her work with chimps has also helped scientists understand more about what it means to be human. Today she continues to teach others about saving the environment, and chimpanzees in particular.

Einstein

Curie

Goodall

COOL SCIENCE FAQs

WHY DO CHILI PEPPERS BURN WHEN YOU EAT THEM?

Chili peppers contain a chemical substance called **capsaicin**. This substance produces a burning sensation. Scientists aren't sure why chili peppers have capsaicin in them, but some believe that this might be a natural defense mechanism to keep the peppers from being eaten by animals.

Capsaicin is an ingredient in pepper spray, a substance people use against attackers. Surprisingly, because capsaicin affects the nerves right underneath the skin, people who have chronic pain often apply creams that contain capsaicin to numb their skin and block their pain.

HOW LONG DOES IT TAKE FOR OBJECTS TO DECOMPOSE?

Objects decompose at different rates depending on how simple or complex their molecular structures are. For example, natural materials such as plants, animal waste, paper and eggshells can take several weeks to several months to completely decompose. But objects made of metal, plastic or petroleum products, such as Styrofoam cups, aluminum cans or plastic bottles, can take tens, hundreds or even thousands of years to decompose.

WHAT IS THE "GREENHOUSE EFFECT"?

The greenhouse effect is the process by which Earth's surface is warmed by gases trapped in the atmosphere, much like the air in a greenhouse is trapped and warms the plants growing inside. In itself, this effect is a good thing, because otherwise Earth's temperature would be colder by 60°F (15.5°C). The greenhouse effect relies on keeping Earth's temperature at certain levels, but it can become dangerous if global warming threatens to change the current balance and raise the atmospheric temperature. Even a rise in a few degrees can threaten life on Earth.

WHICH ELEMENTS MAKE UP THE HUMAN BODY?

About two-thirds of the human anatomy is made up of water, which means that oxygen and hydrogen are significant elements. Carbon is also very important in cell growth. Here's a breakdown of the most common elements found in the body:

Oxygen	65%
Carbon	18%
Hydrogen	10%
Nitrogen	3%
Calcium	1.5%
Phosphorus	1.0%
Potassium	0.35%
Sulfur	0.25%
Sodium	0.15%
Lithium, Strontium, Aluminum, Silicon, Lead, Vanadium, Arsenic, Bromine	trace amounts

WHY IS PLUTO NO LONGER CONSIDERED A PLANET?

Since its discovery in 1930, Pluto has always puzzled scientists. While it seemed to be a planet in shape, it seemed to be more like a comet in its small size. Also, its orbit around the Sun is out of line with the orbits of the other eight planets in the solar system. In addition, Pluto's only moon, Charon, is almost the same size as the planet itself—a trait that makes it different from all the other planets. In 2006, Pluto was declassified from a "true" planet to a "dwarf" planet by the International Astronomical Union, the organization that classifies and names all the bodies in space.

Pluto

REAL-LIFE CSI: Sleuthing with Science

SCIENCE

THE SCENE: A man lies dead face-up in a flower bed by the front door to a large mansion. When the CSI team arrives, they find that the man has been shot in the stomach. Muddy footprints head toward the empty garage, where tire marks lead down the driveway. The man has no identification on him, his clothes are torn and his hands are bloody, as if a struggle took place. What can the team do with these clues and others to solve the crime?

To Find Out About the Crime

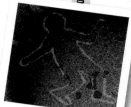

• A medical examiner can remove the bullet and send it to a ballistics lab, where it can be examined. Groove marks on the bullet will match the inside of the barrel of the gun that fired it.

• Casts and molds can be made of the footprints to determine the estimated heights and weights of possible suspects.

• The tire tracks can be compared with those made by a suspect's vehicle.

• The chemical composition of any unrecognizable material can be determined by various techniques, such as gas chromatography, mass spectrometry and laser ablation spectrometry. These processes burn a tiny part of the evidence, turning it into a gas, which is then analyzed for the elements it contains.

GUESS WHAT?

The markings in the iris, or colored part of the human eye, are different for every human being. Today there are machines that can scan these physical traits and record that data for future reference. Biometrics, the measurement of unique life characteristics, is becoming a special tool in the high-tech security field.

To Find Out About the Victim

• The medical examiner can do an autopsy on the body to determine the time of death. He or she would look for any substances in the stomach that might indicate food, drink or poison.

• The DNA of the victim's sweat, tears, saliva and blood can be analyzed to determine his identity. If the victim has been dead for a while, there may be flies or other insects on or in the body. A forensic entomologist (a scientist who specializes in insects) might be able to determine how long the body has been lying at the site.

• Information about the victim's teeth can be matched with local dental records to help in identification.

To Find Out About the Murderer

• If the medical examiner finds any foreign blood or hair at the scene, or skin under the victim's fingernails, the DNA of these samples can help to identify the person they came from.

• Investigators can dust objects that the murderer might have touched, such as the garage door handle, in order to find fingerprints.

• If a suspect is caught soon after the shooting, special tape can be touched to his or her fingers. When examined under an electron microscope, the tape will reveal whether any gunpowder is present.

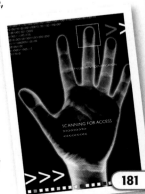

SCANNING FOR ACCESS

>>>

181

A GALACTIC GLOSSARY

The term **CELESTIAL BODY** refers to objects found in space, such as stars or planets.

Comet Hale-Bopp

Solar eclipse

Lunar eclipse

An **ECLIPSE** happens when one celestial body falls into the shadow of another. The most common types of eclipses are **solar** (when the Moon passes between Earth and the Sun) and **lunar** (when the full Moon passes through some portion of Earth's shadow). Sometimes stars eclipse one another, too. A lunar eclipse can be seen from the entire half of the earth facing it, while a solar eclipse can only be seen by people along a narrow path on the surface of Earth.

A **COMET** is made up mostly of dust and gases, and moves in an elliptical orbit around the Sun. An **elliptical orbit** is oval-shaped, rather than circular. Some comets may take less than 200 years to move around the Sun, others can take thousands of years. Because the paths of comets may take them deep into space before they come back toward the Sun, they are only seen for short periods of time. Halley's Comet, for example, is only seen on Earth every 76 years. Some scientists say that comets look like big, dirty snowballs.

GUESS WHAT?
The Moon's color depends on the amount of dust in the atmosphere.

A spiral galaxy

A **LIGHT YEAR** is the distance light travels in one year, about 6 million miles (9,656,000 km). Other than the Sun, the closest stars to Earth are Alpha and Proxima Centauri. They are 4.3 light years away.

A **GALAXY** is a large collection of stars, dust and gas held together by gravity. A typical galaxy consists of billions of stars. Everything we can see in the sky—the planets, the Sun, the stars—are all part of the **Milky Way** galaxy. It is estimated that there are 50 billion galaxies in the universe!

METEOROIDS are rocks found in space. They are usually fragments of comets or asteroids. When a meteoroid enters Earth's atmosphere, it usually burns up. If it does not, it is known as a **meteor** or a **falling star.** Meteors that hit the ground are called **meteorites.** The largest meteorite ever recorded fell in the Tunguska Basin in Siberia in 1908, destroying 770 square miles (2,000 sq km) of forest.

A crater left by a meteorite in Arizona

THE LIFE OF A STAR

BIRTH

Stars are formed when huge clouds of dust and gas collapse as they're pulled together by gravity. Young stars—really clusters of dust and gas—are called **protostars.** As protostars grow, they begin to generate heat. Once the heat and pressure build to a point where nuclear fusion can occur in a star's core, the star ignites and enters its "main sequence." Our Sun's main sequence will last for roughly 10 billion years.

GUESS WHAT? *Some stars never become hot enough to explode into a normal star. These are called* **brown dwarfs.**

Protostar

MIDLIFE

As stars get older, they expand, growing to many times their original size. During this growth spurt, they overtake and burn up the planets closest to them. Then their surface cools and begins to glow red. At this stage in their life cycle, they're called **red giants.** Eventually, over millions of years, the star will begin to collapse. The next stage depends on the mass of the star.

DEATH

A star the size of our Sun (and up to 1.5 times bigger) will collapse into a **white dwarf.** It will spend millions of years as a white dwarf, then it will cool off and end its life as a **black dwarf.**

A star that is much bigger than our Sun (1.5 to 3 times the size) will collapse much more quickly, exploding into a **supernova.** The core that remains after this explosion is extremely dense—so dense that the protons and electrons that make up the star are crushed together into neutrons. The resulting mass is called a **neutron star.**

When the biggest stars of all (those with more than 3 times the mass of our Sun) explode, the leftover core continues to collapse into itself. Scientists believe that all of this exploding and collapsing forms **black holes.** The gravity inside a black hole is so strong that nothing—not even light—can escape it.

GUESS WHAT? *A* **supergiant** *is a huge, bright star that has already completed its main sequence. The biggest star ever recorded is 10 million times as bright as the Sun.*

It's a Star! No, It's a Planet! No...

Stars and planets look almost exactly alike in the night sky, but there are a couple of ways to tell them apart. Because stars are so much farther away from us than planets, they twinkle. A planet's light remains steady.

White dwarfs

Supernova

NOAO

THE SOLAR SYSTEM

The Sun is at the center of our solar system. It consists mostly of ionized gas and supports life on Earth. Planets rotate around the Sun. Early astronomers were able to see the six closest planets to the Sun simply by looking up, but Uranus, Neptune and Pluto (which is now considered a dwarf planet) can only be seen by telescope. Mercury, Venus, Earth and Mars are called the terrestrial planets because they have solid, rocky bodies. The outer four planets do not have surfaces because they are made up of gases.

MERCURY

Because it's so close to the Sun, Mercury can only be seen within an hour or so of the rising or setting of the Sun.

HOW BIG IS IT? With a diameter of 3,032.4 miles (4,880 km), it is less than half the size of Earth.

WHERE IS IT? About 36 million miles (57.9 million km) from the Sun

HOW'S THE WEATHER? The average surface temperature is 332°F (167°C).

MOONS: 0 RINGS: 0

EARTH

About 70% of Earth is covered with water. Nearly all of Earth's water is found in the oceans, which are salty. Only 3% is drinkable freshwater.

HOW BIG IS IT? Earth has a diameter of 7,926.2 miles (12,756 km).

WHERE IS IT? About 92.9 million miles (149.6 million km) from the Sun

HOW'S THE WEATHER? The average surface temperature is 59°F (15°C).

MOONS: 1 RINGS: 0

VENUS

Venus is similar in size to Earth but has no oceans. It's covered by a layer of thick clouds, trapping heat in its atmosphere.

HOW BIG IS IT? With a diameter of 7,519 miles (12,100 km), it is a little smaller than Earth.

WHERE IS IT? About 67.24 million miles (108.2 million km) from the Sun

HOW'S THE WEATHER? The average surface temperature is 867°F (464°C).

MOONS: 0 RINGS: 0

MARS

Mars is prone to dust storms that engulf the entire planet. This makes for interesting geography, including giant sand dunes.

HOW BIG IS IT? With a diameter of 4,194 miles (6,794 km) it is roughly half as big as Earth.

WHERE IS IT? About 141.71 million miles (227.9 million km) from the Sun

HOW'S THE WEATHER? The average surface temperature is -82°F (-63°C).

MOONS: 2 RINGS: 0

GUESS WHAT? *A nice summer's day on Mars can get up to 80°F (26.7°C), but at night it can be as cold as -200°F (-128.9°C).*

The Sun

Mercury

Venus

Earth

Mars

JUPITER

Jupiter is the solar system's biggest planet. Four of its many moons are planet-size themselves.

HOW BIG IS IT? At 88,736 miles (142,800 km), its diameter is 11 times bigger than Earth's.

WHERE IS IT? About 483.9 million miles (778.3 million km) from the Sun

HOW'S THE WEATHER? The average surface temperature is -244°F (-153°C).

MOONS: 63 **RINGS:** 4

SATURN

Known as the "ringed planet," Saturn spins very quickly. It only takes 11 hours for the planet to rotate fully on its axis. Saturn's famous rings are made up of ice and rock.

HOW BIG IS IT? With a diameter of 74,900 miles (120,500 km), it is nine and half times the size of Earth.

WHERE IS IT? About 885.9 million miles (1.43 billion km) from the Sun

HOW'S THE WEATHER? The average surface temperature is -300°F (-184°C).

MOONS: 47 **RINGS:** About 1,000

URANUS

Uranus was discovered by William Herschel in 1781. The planet is surrounded by 11 narrow rings.

HOW BIG IS IT? With a diameter of 32,193 miles (51,810 km), it is about four times the size of Earth.

WHERE IS IT? About 1.78 billion miles (2.87 billion km) from the Sun

HOW'S THE WEATHER? The average surface temperature is -350°F (-210°C).

MOONS: 27 **RINGS:** 11

NEPTUNE

Neptune was the first planet located by mathematical predictions instead of observation.

HOW BIG IS IT? With a diameter of 30,775 miles (49,528 km), it is four times bigger than Earth.

WHERE IS IT? About 2.8 billion miles (4.5 billion km) from the Sun

HOW'S THE WEATHER? The average surface temperature is -370°F (-220°C).

MOONS: 13 **RINGS:** 7 rings made up of thousands of "ringlets"

GUESS WHAT?

Once every 248 years, Pluto moves inside the path of Neptune for about twenty years. The last time this happened was between January 23, 1979, and February 11, 1999.

Neptune

Uranus

Saturn

Jupiter

THE SPACE RACE

During the 1950s and 1960s, the United States and the Soviet Union competed to put the first person on the Moon.

1957 The Soviet Union launches *Sputnik 1*, the first artificial satellite, into Earth's orbit. *Sputnik 2* carries a dog, Laika, into space a month later.

1958 NASA begins operations.
The first American satellite, *Explorer 1*, goes into orbit.

1959 The Soviet *Luna 2* lands on the Moon, becoming the first human-made object to land on another celestial body.

1961 A chimpanzee named Ham survives the flight of the *Mercury 2*.
On April 12, Soviet cosmonaut Yuri Gagarin becomes the first human in space. Aboard the *Vostok 1*, he makes a single orbit of Earth.
On May 2, Alan Shepard becomes the first American in space.
In a speech before Congress, President Kennedy sets the goal of getting a man to the Moon by the end of the decade.

1963 Soviet Valentina Tereshkova becomes the first woman in space, orbiting Earth in *Vostok 6*.

1964 The Soviet *Voskhod 1* is the first mission to send multiple men into space.

1965 Soviet cosmonaut Alexei Leonov exits the *Voskhod 2* and goes on the first spacewalk.
Two months later, Edward White II, the pilot of *Gemini 4*, is the first American to go on a spacewalk.
In December, *Gemini 6* and *Gemini 7* fly within a few feet of each other, marking the first "space rendezvous."

1966 The unmanned Soviet probe *Luna 10* is the first object to orbit the Moon.
American *Surveyor 1*, also unmanned, lands on the Moon a month later and transmits photos and other information back to Earth.

1967 All three astronauts on the first *Apollo* mission die before takeoff when a fire breaks out in the cockpit. NASA makes numerous safety changes to their spacecraft.

1968 *Apollo 8* completes the first manned orbit of the Moon.
The first pictures of Earth are taken from space.

1969 Neil Armstrong and Buzz Aldrin of *Apollo 11* become the first men on the Moon.

1975 A U.S. *Apollo* spacecraft docks with a Soviet *Soyuz* spacecraft, becoming the first joint mission between the two countries.

Gemini 4

Gemini 6

GUESS WHAT?
Humans have brought 842 pounds of Moon rock and soil back to Earth.

The Huntsville Times
Man Enters Space
So Close, Yet So Far: Sighs Cape
U.S. Had Hoped For Own Launch
Soviet Officer Orbits Globe In 5-Ton Ship
Praise Is Heaped On Major Gagarin

Crew of *Apollo 11*

American Thomas P. Stafford and Russian Aleksey A. Leonov aboard the *Apollo Soyuz* Test Project

GUESS WHAT?
In 1983, Sally Ride became the first American woman in space. That same year, Guion S. Bluford became the first black American in space.

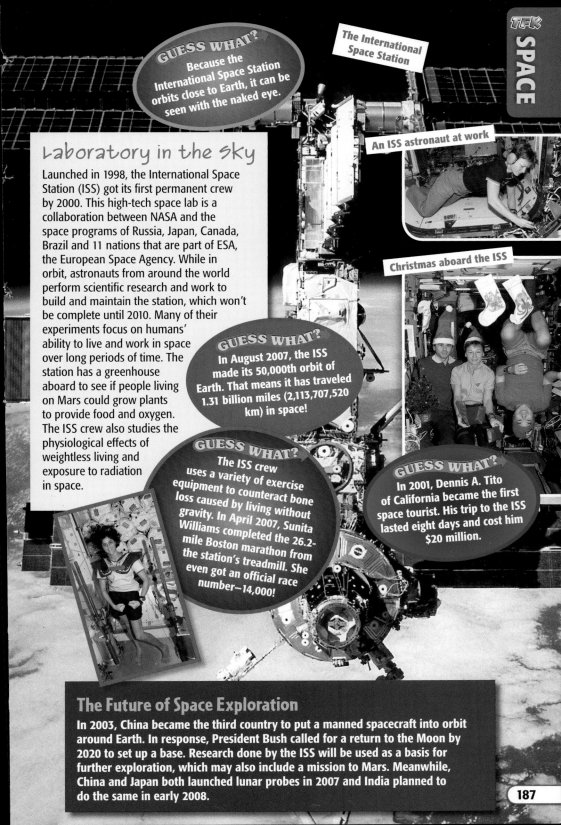

GUESS WHAT?
Because the International Space Station orbits close to Earth, it can be seen with the naked eye.

The International Space Station

An ISS astronaut at work

Christmas aboard the ISS

Laboratory in the Sky

Launched in 1998, the International Space Station (ISS) got its first permanent crew by 2000. This high-tech space lab is a collaboration between NASA and the space programs of Russia, Japan, Canada, Brazil and 11 nations that are part of ESA, the European Space Agency. While in orbit, astronauts from around the world perform scientific research and work to build and maintain the station, which won't be complete until 2010. Many of their experiments focus on humans' ability to live and work in space over long periods of time. The station has a greenhouse aboard to see if people living on Mars could grow plants to provide food and oxygen. The ISS crew also studies the physiological effects of weightless living and exposure to radiation in space.

GUESS WHAT?
In August 2007, the ISS made its 50,000th orbit of Earth. That means it has traveled 1.31 billion miles (2,113,707,520 km) in space!

GUESS WHAT?
The ISS crew uses a variety of exercise equipment to counteract bone loss caused by living without gravity. In April 2007, Sunita Williams completed the 26.2-mile Boston marathon from the station's treadmill. She even got an official race number—14,000!

GUESS WHAT?
In 2001, Dennis A. Tito of California became the first space tourist. His trip to the ISS lasted eight days and cost him $20 million.

The Future of Space Exploration

In 2003, China became the third country to put a manned spacecraft into orbit around Earth. In response, President Bush called for a return to the Moon by 2020 to set up a base. Research done by the ISS will be used as a basis for further exploration, which may also include a mission to Mars. Meanwhile, China and Japan both launched lunar probes in 2007 and India planned to do the same in early 2008.

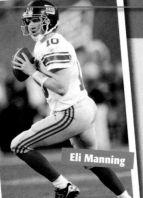
Eli Manning

Plaxico Burress

A SUPER STUNNER

Quarterback Eli Manning leads his team to a Giant win over the New England Patriots in Super Bowl XLII.

More than 70,000 football fans at the University of Phoenix Stadium in Glendale, Arizona, along with an estimated 97.5 million television viewers, witnessed one of the biggest upsets in football history on Sunday, February 3, 2008. The New York Giants came from behind to snatch a thrilling 17–14 victory over the New England Patriots in Super Bowl XLII. Coming into the big game, the undefeated Patriots seemed invincible.

THE UNDERDOGS WIN

The Giants scored the first three points of the game with a field goal, but then went scoreless until the fourth quarter. Still, their defensive line kept the game close. They fought aggressively, sacking Patriots' quarterback Tom Brady five times.

With 2:42 left in the game, Brady connected with Randy Moss, who scored a touchdown. The Patriots got the extra point and led by a score of 14–10. But the Giants did not give up. Wide receiver David Tyree used his head to score a stunning catch, which helped the Giants stay alive. With just 35 seconds remaining, the Giants brought the game home. Quarterback Eli Manning threw a 13-yard touchdown pass to wide receiver Plaxico Burress.

David Tyree's awesome catch

Lawrence Tynes's extra point was good and the Giants held a three-point lead.

The Pats tried to use the remaining seconds to score, but got nowhere. Victory belonged to the underdogs. "This is the greatest feeling in professional sports," said Burress, holding back tears. "For us to come out and win a world championship tonight—nobody gave us a shot."

This was the Giants' third Super Bowl win. The last time they won the game was in 1991. "It's the greatest victory in the history of this franchise, without question," said Giants' co-owner John Mara.

Manning was named the Most Valuable Player of the game. "It is an unbelievable game and an unbelievable feeling," he said.

ALMOST PERFECT

Brady had hoped to cap his team's undefeated season with a Super Bowl win. The team finished the season with a record 16 straight wins and no losses. Then they won two play-off games. Although the Giants brought the Patriots' dream of a perfect season to a screeching halt, the team remains proud of its winning ways. "Tonight doesn't take away from anything we have done over the course of the season," said Brady.

—By Claudia Atticot

GUESS WHAT?
Eli Manning was named the 2008 Super Bowl MVP. His older brother, Peyton, was 2007's Super Bowl MVP. This is the first time brothers have earned MVP titles in back-to-back Super Bowl games.

PRO FOOTBALL

Tom Brady

2007 Regular Season League Leaders

RANK	PLAYER	TEAMS	YARDS
PASSING YARDS			
1.	Tom Brady	New England Patriots	4,806
2.	Drew Brees	New Orleans Saints	4,423
3.	Tony Romo	Dallas Cowboys	4,211
RUSHING YARDS			
1.	LaDainian Tomlinson	San Diego Chargers	1,474
2.	Adrian Peterson	Minnesota Vikings	1,341
3.	Brian Westbrook	Philadelphia Eagles	1,333
RECEIVING YARDS			
1.	Reggie Wayne	Indianapolis Colts	1,510
2.	Randy Moss	New England Patriots	1,493
3.	Chad Johnson	Cincinnati Bengals	1,440

COLLEGE FOOTBALL

LSU team members celebrate.

HEISMAN TROPHY

Florida Gators quarterback Tim Tebow (15) won the 2007 Heisman Trophy. It was the first time in college football history that a sophomore won the distinguished prize. Tebow accomplished another first as well. He was the first Division I-A player to score at least 20 touchdowns running and 20 touchdowns passing. His regular season stats: 3,132 passing yards and 29 touchdowns; 838 running yards for 22 touchdowns. Tebow also got the most votes ever from the nationwide Heisman panel.

Record Breaker The 1972 Miami Dolphins is the only team to go undefeated from the start of the season through the Super Bowl.

BOWL CHAMPIONSHIP SERIES (BCS) NATIONAL CHAMPIONSHIP GAME (New Orleans, LA): Louisiana State 38, Ohio State 24

Other Bowl Games

CAPITAL ONE BOWL (Orlando, FL): Michigan 41, Florida 35
COTTON BOWL (Dallas, TX): Missouri 38, Arkansas 7
EMERALD BOWL (San Francisco, CA): Oregon State 21, Maryland 14
FIESTA BOWL (Glendale, AZ): West Virginia 48, Oklahoma 28
GATOR BOWL (Jacksonville, FL): Texas Tech 31, Virginia 28
LIBERTY BOWL (Memphis, TN): Mississippi State 10, Central Florida 3
ORANGE BOWL (Miami, FL): Kansas 24, Virginia Tech 21
ROSE BOWL (Pasadena, CA): Southern California 49, Illinois 17
SUGAR BOWL (New Orleans, LA): Georgia 41, Hawaii 10

SPORTS

TFK

189

BASEBALL

2007 Top Players

Record Breaker

On August 7, 2007, Barry Bonds of the San Francisco Giants hit his 756th home run, beating the previous record of 755 set by Hank Aaron in 1974. This achievement didn't come without controversy, as Bonds was linked to alleged use of "performance-enhancing drugs." By the end of the 2007 season, Bonds had hit a total of 762 home runs.

Jimmy Rollins

MOST VALUABLE PLAYER
American League: **Alex Rodriguez, third baseman, New York Yankees**
National League: Jimmy Rollins, **shortstop, Philadelphia Phillies**

CY YOUNG AWARD (BEST PITCHER)
American League: **C.C. Sabathia, Cleveland Indians**
National League: **Jake Peavy, San Diego Padres**

ROOKIE OF THE YEAR
American League: **Dustin Pedroia, Boston Red Sox**
National League: **Ryan Braun, Milwaukee Brewers**

HOME-RUN CHAMPIONS
American League: Alex Rodriguez, **New York Yankees, 54 home runs**
National League: **Prince Fielder, Milwaukee Brewers, 50 home runs**

BATTING CHAMPIONS
American League: **Magglio Ordonez, Detroit Tigers, .363 batting average**
National League: **Matt Holliday, Colorado Rockies, .340 batting average**

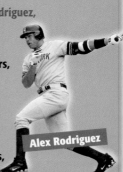

Alex Rodriguez

2007 WORLD SERIES: BOSTON RED SOX VS. COLORADO ROCKIES

In four straight games, the Boston Red Sox beat the Colorado Rockies 13–1, 2–1, 10–5 and 4–3. It was Boston's second World Series title in four years and its seventh World Series title in all. For a while it looked as if Boston wouldn't make it to the final Series. They trailed the Cleveland Indians three games to one in the American League Championship Series before coming back to win the league. They faced a tough opponent, as the Rockies swept all four games in the National League Championship Series against the Arizona Diamondbacks. Red Sox third-baseman Mike Lowell was named the Series' Most Valuable Player for his 7th-inning homer in the final game that won his team the championship.

Dalton Carriker

2007 LITTLE LEAGUE WORLD SERIES

Georgia's Warner Robins American Little League team beat the Tokyo Kitsuna Little League team from Tokyo, Japan, by a score of 3–2. They played before a crowd of 31,400 at Lamade Stadium in Williamsport, Pennsylvania. An eighth-inning home run hit by Dalton Carriker on a pitch by Japan's relief pitcher Junsho Kiuchi clinched the title for the United States—the third American win in a row (Columbus, Georgia, won in 2006 and Ewa Beach, Hawaii, won in 2005).

Record Breaker

Red Sox Manager Tony Francona is the first manager in Major League History to win his first eight World Series games.

BASKETBALL

NATIONAL BASKETBALL ASSOCIATION

TFK TOP 5 2006–07 NBA Scorers

NAME	TEAM	GAMES PLAYED	AVERAGE POINTS
1. Kobe Bryant	Los Angeles Lakers	77	31.6
2. Carmelo Anthony	Denver Nuggets	65	28.9
3. Gilbert Arenas	Washington Wizards	74	28.4
4. Dwyane Wade	Miami Heat	51	27.4
5. LeBron James	Cleveland Cavaliers	78	27.3

LeBron James

2007 NBA CHAMPIONSHIP
The San Antonio Spurs swept the Cleveland Cavaliers in four straight games.
GAME 1: Spurs 85, Cavaliers 76
GAME 2: Spurs 103, Cavaliers 92
GAME 3: Spurs 75, Cavaliers 72
GAME 4: Spurs 83, Cavaliers 82

WOMEN'S NATIONAL BASKETBALL ASSOCIATION

TFK TOP 5 2006–07 WNBA Scorers

NAME	TEAM	GAMES PLAYED	AVERAGE POINTS
1. Diana Taurasi	Phoenix Mercury	34	25.3
2. Seimone Augustus	Minnesota Lynx	34	21.9
3. Lisa Leslie	Los Angeles Sparks	34	20.0
4. Lauren Jackson*	Seattle Storm	30	19.5
5. Cappie Poindexter*	Pheonix Mercury	32	19.5

*Tied for most points on average

2007 WNBA CHAMPIONSHIP
The Phoenix Mercury beat the Detroit Shock three games to two.
GAME 1: Shock 108, Mercury 101
GAME 2: Mercury 98, Shock 70
GAME 3: Shock 88, Mercury 83
GAME 4: Mercury 77, Shock 76
GAME 5: Mercury 108, Shock 92

Seimone Augustus

COLLEGE BASKETBALL

2007 NCAA MEN'S DIVISION I CHAMPIONSHIP

TEAM	POINTS: 1ST HALF	POINTS: 2ND HALF	FINAL SCORE
Florida Gators	40	44	84
Ohio State Buckeyes	29	46	75

2007 NCAA WOMEN'S DIVISION I CHAMPIONSHIP

TEAM	POINTS: 1ST HALF	POINTS: 2ND HALF	FINAL SCORE
Tennessee Volunteers	29	30	59
Rutgers Scarlet Knights	18	28	46

TFK TOP 5 Team Sports for Kids

1. Basketball
2. Soccer
3. Baseball
4. Touch Football
5. Tackle Football

Source: The Sporting Goods Manufacturers Association

Florida vs. Ohio State

SOCCER

The men's and women's competitions for the top prize in soccer, the World Cup, take place every four years. The most recent men's game was in 2006, in which Italy beat France by a score of 5–3 in a penalty shoot-out. In 2007, it was the women's turn.

Brazil vs. Germany

2007 WOMEN'S WORLD CUP

The competition in Shanghai, China, pitted 16 nations against one another. In the finals, Germany shut out Brazil 2–0, making the Germans the first team in women's soccer history to keep their title from the previous World Cup. (In 2003, Germany beat Sweden 2–1 in extra time to take the Cup.) The Germany–Brazil match was the first Women's World Cup final between a European and a South American team. Germany also set another women's record by playing six matches without allowing the opposing team to score. Here are the final standings:

1ST PLACE: Germany   **2ND PLACE:** Brazil
3RD PLACE: United States   **4TH PLACE:** Norway

GUESS WHAT? *Germany's high scorer, Birgit Prinz, was the first woman to play in three separate World Cup tournaments (1995, 2003 and 2007).*

World Cup Winners

MEN
2006 ITALY
2002 BRAZIL
1998 FRANCE
1994 BRAZIL
1990 WEST GERMANY
1986 ARGENTINA
1982 ITALY
1978 ARGENTINA
1974 WEST GERMANY
1970 BRAZIL
1966 ENGLAND
1962 BRAZIL
1958 BRAZIL
1954 WEST GERMANY
1950 URUGUAY
(NO GAMES IN 1942 AND 1946)
1938 ITALY
1934 ITALY
1930 URUGUAY

WOMEN
2003 GERMANY
1999 UNITED STATES
1995 NORWAY
1991 UNITED STATES

HOCKEY

Teemu Selanne of the Mighty Ducks

THE 2007 STANLEY CUP

The Anaheim Ducks beat the Ottawa Senators 6–2 in the fifth game of the NHL championship to win the Stanley Cup. Going into the final game, the Ducks were ahead three games to one. The championship win was the Ducks' first since the team was formed in 1993.

Record Breaker
Patrick Roy holds the National Hockey League record as the goalie with the most winning games: 551.

Stanley Cup Champs

The Stanley Cup competition has been around since 1893. In 1926, it came under the administration of the National Hockey League. Here are winners from the past decade.

YEAR	WINNING TEAM
2007	ANAHEIM DUCKS
2006	CAROLINA HURRICANES
2004	TAMPA BAY LIGHTNING
2003	NEW JERSEY DEVILS
2002	DETROIT RED WINGS
2001	COLORADO AVALANCHE
2000	NEW JERSEY DEVILS
1999	DALLAS STARS
1998	DETROIT RED WINGS
1997	DETROIT RED WINGS

AUTO RACING

The National Association for Stock Car Auto Racing (NASCAR) oversees the biggest car racing series in the United States, The Nextel Cup. Drivers compete from February through November in 36 races, the last 10 of which are known as "The Chase." For every win in races 1 through 26, the driver gets 185 points. The 12 drivers who have accumulated the most points after Race 26 compete in The Chase.

Nextel Cup Series Champions, 1997–2007

YEAR	DRIVER	MAKE OF CAR
2007	Jimmie Johnson	Chevrolet
2006	Jimmie Johnson	Chevrolet
2005	Tony Stewart	Chevrolet
2004	Kurt Busch	Ford
2003	Matt Kenseth	Ford
2002	Tony Stewart	Pontiac
2001	Jeff Gordon	Chevrolet
2000	Bobby Labonte	Pontiac
1999	Dale Jarrett	Ford
1998	Jeff Gordon	Chevrolet
1997	Jeff Gordon	Chevrolet

2007 NEXTEL CUP TOP 3 POINTS WINNERS

	DRIVER	TOTAL POINTS
1.	Jimmie Johnson	6,723
2.	Jeff Gordon	6,646
3.	Clint Bowyer	6,377

Jimmie Johnson

THE INDIANAPOLIS 500

The Indy 500, as it is known, features Indy racing cars instead of stock cars.

The drivers complete 200 laps for a distance of 500 miles (804.7 km) in the oval Indianapolis Motor Speedway. The first race was held in 1911, and the sport has developed some quirky traditions. For example, the winner drinks milk as part of the Victory Lane celebration. In 2007, Dario Franchitti won the Indy 500.

CYCLING

2007 TOUR DE FRANCE

For 104 years, the Tour de France has tested cyclists' strength and endurance. The 2007 winner was 24-year-old Alberto Contador of Spain. He finished the grueling 2,142-mile (3,570-km) course through England, Belgium, Spain and France in 91 hours 26 seconds, beating the second-place rider, Australia's Cadel Evans, by 23 seconds.

Contador had a special reason to celebrate. In 2004, an artery in his brain burst as he was riding in a race in Spain. He collapsed and was rushed into surgery. During his recovery, he was inspired by the career of American cyclist Lance Armstrong, who survived cancer and won the Tour de France seven times. Three years after his illness, Contador won the yellow jersey (the Tour's champion symbol) as well as a white jersey, which is given to the best young rider.

Lance Armstrong

Recent Tour de France Winners

2007	Alberto Contador, Spain
2006	Oscar Pereiro, Spain*
2005	Lance Armstrong, USA
2004	Lance Armstrong, USA
2003	Lance Armstrong, USA
2002	Lance Armstrong, USA
2001	Lance Armstrong, USA
2000	Lance Armstrong, USA
1999	Lance Armstrong, USA
1998	Marco Pantani, Italy
1997	Jan Ullrich, Germany

*Awarded after Floyd Landis (USA) was stripped of his title because he was found guilty of using performance-enhancing drugs.

TENNIS

2007 Tennis Champs

Justine Henin

Australian Open (2007)
MEN'S SINGLES: **Roger Federer**
MEN'S DOUBLES: **Bob Bryan, Mike Bryan**
WOMEN'S SINGLES: **Serena Williams**
WOMEN'S DOUBLES: **Cara Black, Liezel Huber**

French Open (2007)
MEN'S SINGLES: **Rafael Nadal**
MEN'S DOUBLES: **Mark Knowles, Daniel Nestor**
WOMEN'S SINGLES: **Justine Henin**
WOMEN'S DOUBLES: **Alicia Molik, Mara Santangelo**

Wimbledon (2007)
MEN'S SINGLES: **Roger Federer**
MEN'S DOUBLES: **Arnaud Clément, Michaël Llodra**
WOMEN'S SINGLES: **Venus Williams**
WOMEN'S DOUBLES: **Cara Black, Liezel Huber**

U.S. Open (2007)
MEN'S SINGLES: **Roger Federer**
MEN'S DOUBLES: **Simon Aspelin, Julian Knowle**
WOMEN'S SINGLES: **Justine Henin**
WOMEN'S DOUBLES: **Nathalie Dechy, Dinara Safina**

Davis Cup (Men's International Team Tennis)
The United States team beat the Russian team by a score of four matches to one.

GOLF

2007 Major Event Winners

Men
MASTERS: **Zach Johnson**
BRITISH OPEN: **Padraig Harrington**
U.S. OPEN: **Angel Cabrera**
PGA CHAMPIONSHIP: **Tiger Woods**
U.S. AMATEUR CHAMPIONSHIP: **Colt Knost**

Women
LPGA CHAMPIONSHIP: **Suzann Pettersen**
U.S. WOMEN'S OPEN: **Cristie Kerr**
KRAFT NABISCO CHAMPIONSHIP: **Morgan Pressel**
WOMEN'S BRITISH OPEN: **Lorena Ochoa**
U.S. AMATEUR CHAMPIONSHIP: **María José Uribe**

GUESS WHAT?
The word *caddy* was first used by Mary, Queen of Scots, in 1552. It's short for *cadets*, which is what she called her assistants on the golf course. She is believed to be the first female golfer.

Zach Johnson

GYMNASTICS

Shawn Johnson

The 2007 World Gymnastics Championships were held in Stuttgart, Germany, in September. The women's teams competed in four events: the vault, uneven parallel bars, balance beam and floor exercise. The men's teams competed in six events: the rings, vault, parallel bars, high bar, pommel horse and floor exercise. The team from China won the men's all-around title, with the U.S. men's team coming in fourth place. But the U.S. women's team took the top all-around prize, as well as the all-around women's individual title, which went to Shawn Johnson.

WINTER SPORTS

Alpine Skiing

The *Fédération Internationale de Ski* (International Ski Federation or FIS) has organized international skiing competitions since 1924. The most recent Alpine World Ski Championship was held February 2–18, 2007 in Are, Sweden. The 2009 Championships are set to be held in Val d'Isère, France.

Anja Paerson

2007 Winners

SUPER GIANT SLALOM
MEN: **Patrick Staudacher (Italy)**
WOMEN: **Anja Paerson (Sweden)**

SUPER COMBINED
MEN: **Daniel Albrecht (Switzerland)**
WOMEN: **Anja Paerson (Sweden)**

DOWNHILL COMBINED
MEN: **Bode Miller (USA)**
WOMEN: **Anja Paerson (Sweden)**

DOWNHILL
MEN: **Askel Lund Svindal (Norway)**
WOMEN: **Anja Paerson (Sweden)**

GIANT SLALOM
MEN: **Askel Lund Svindal (Norway)**
WOMEN: **Nicole Hosp (Austria)**

SLALOM
MEN: **Mario Matt (Austria)**
WOMEN: **Sarka Zahrobska (Czech Republic)**

Cross-Country Skiing

Less steep than downhill skiing, cross-country skiing tests a racer's endurance over long distances, anywhere between 1 kilometer (0.6 mi) and 50 kilometers (30 mi). Andy Newell took top honors in the men's 2008 U.S. Cross Country Championships, while Kikkan Randall won for the women.

Snowboarding

The 2007 World Championship was held in Arosa, Switzerland, on January 14–20, 2007. Like alpine skiing, international snowboard events are governed by the FIS and championships are held every two years. The next championship will be held in the Gangwon Province of Korea in February 2009.

SNOWBOARDCROSS
MEN: **Xavier Delerue (France)**
WOMEN: **Lindsey Jacobellis (USA)**

PARALLEL GIANT SLALOM
MEN: **Rok Flander (Slovenia)**
WOMEN: **Ekaterina Tudigescheva (Russia)**

PARALLEL SLALOM
MEN: **Simon Schoch (Switzerland)**
WOMEN: **Heidi Neururer (Austria)**

BIG AIR
MEN: **Mathieu Crepel (France)**

HALFPIPE
MEN: **Mathieu Crepel (France)**
WOMEN: **Manuela Laura Pesko (Switzerland)**

Figure Skating

Figure skating is probably the most popular winter spectator sport. Here are some of the sport's most recent medalists.

The 2008 U.S. Figure Skating Championships
Saint Paul, Minnesota   January 20–27, 2008

WOMEN	MEN
1. Mirai Nagasu	1. Evan Lysacek
2. Rachael Flatt	2. Johnny Weir
3. Ashley Wagner	3. Stephen Carriere

2007 World Figure Skating Championships
Tokyo, Japan   March 19–25, 2007

PLACE	NAME	NATION
WOMEN		
1.	Miki Ando	Japan
2.	Mao Asada	Japan
3.	Yu-Na Kim	Korea
MEN		
1.	Brian Joubert	France
2.	Daisuke Takahashi	Japan
3.	Stephane Lambiel	Switzerland

SPORTS

TFK

BOBSLED, SKELETON AND LUGE

Bobsled, skeleton and luge test the speed and skill of athletes as individuals and teams speeding down long, deep, snow-packed ditches, packed with twists and turns. In the **bobsled,** the athletes are sitting. **Skeleton** is an individual sport, where athletes move head-first on a sled that can only be steered by shifting their body weight. In the **luge,** riders lie on their backs with their feet pointing in the direction of the run.

2007 Bobsled and Skeleton World Championship Winners

ALTENBERG, GERMANY
FEBRUARY 11–24, 2008

FOUR-MAN BOB: Andre Lange, Rene Hoppe, Kevin Kuske, Martin Putze (Germany)

BOB WOMEN: Sandra Kiriasis and Romy Logsch (Germany)

TEAM COMPETITION: Germany (Sebastian Haupt, Sandra Kiriasis, Berit Wiacker, Anja Huber, Matthias Hoepfner and Alex Mann)

SKELETON MEN Kristan Bromley (Great Britain)

SKELETON WOMEN: Anja Huber (Germany)

The 2008 Luge World Championship Winners

OBERHOF, GERMANY JANUARY 21–27, 2008

MEN: Felix Loch (Germany)

WOMEN: Tatjana Hüfner (Germany)

DOUBLES: André Florschütz and Torsten Wustlich (Germany)

Florschütz and Wustlich

ESPN'S X GAMES

Gretchen Bleiler

The **X Games,** created by the sports network ESPN in the mid-1990s, are yearly events for athletes who participate in some extreme sports.

2007 Summer X Games Winners

LOS ANGELES, CALIFORNIA • AUG. 2–5, 2007

SKATEBOARDING: Shaun White (men's vert), Chris Cole (men's street), Bob Burnquist (big air), Marisa Dal Santa (women's street), Lyn-Z Adams Hawkins (women's vert)

MOTO X: Ronnie Renner (step-up), Adam Jones (freestyle), Mark Burkhart (supermoto), Ricky Carmichael (racing)

BMX: Jamie Bestwick (vert), Daniel Dhers (freestyle park), Kevin Robinson (big air)

RALLY CAR RACING: Tanner Foust (driver), Chrissie Beavis (co-driver)

Shaun White

2008 Winter X Games Winners

ASPEN, COLORADO • JAN. 24–27, 2008

SNOWBOARDING: Gretchen Bleiler (women's superpipe), Lindsey Jacobellis (women's snowboarder X), Jamie Anderson (women's slopestyle), Shaun White (men's superpipe), Nate Holland (men's snowboarder X), Andreas Wiig (men's slopestyle), Torstein Horgmo (men's big air)

SKIING: Tanner Hall (men's superpipe), Daron Rahlves (men's skier X), Andreas Hatveit (men's slopestyle), Sarah Burke (women's superpipe), Ophelie David (women's skier X), Jon Olsson (men's big air), Kees-Jan van der Klooster (monoskier X)

SNOWMOBILING: Levi LaVallee (freestyle), Tucker Hibbert (SnoCross), Levi LaVallee (speed and style)

Extreme Sports

Extreme sports are those that involve a high level of danger, including great speeds, heights, physical exertion and stunts, and may involve the use of specialized equipment. Some extreme sports include ice climbing, hang gliding, bungee jumping and wakeboarding. New extreme sports, such as wingsuit flying, are being invented each year.

HORSE RACING

The three biggest horse races in the United States are the **Kentucky Derby** at Churchill Downs in Louisville, Kentucky; the **Preakness Stakes** at Pimlico Race Course in Baltimore, Maryland; and the **Belmont Stakes** at Belmont Park in Elmont, New York. These three races take place within a five-week period from early May to early June and comprise the Triple Crown of Thoroughbred Racing, or the **Triple Crown,** for short.

2007 Winners

KENTUCKY DERBY **Street Sense**
PREAKNESS STAKES **Curlin**
BELMONT STAKES **Rags to Riches**

Triple Crown Winners

YEAR	NAME
1919	SIR BARTON
1930	GALLANT FOX
1935	OMAHA
1937	WAR ADMIRAL
1941	WHIRLAWAY
1943	COUNT FLEET
1946	ASSAULT
1948	CITATION
1973	SECRETARIAT
1977	SEATTLE SLEW
1978	AFFIRMED

GUESS WHAT?

On May 2, 1970, Diane Crump became the first female jockey to compete in the Kentucky Derby. Twenty-one years later, jockey Julie Krone was the first female to win one of the Triple Crown races: the Belmont Stakes, on a horse named Colonial Affair.

DOG SLEDDING

Known as the "Last Great Race on Earth," the annual 1,150-mile (1,917-km) dog-sled race from Anchorage to Nome, Alaska, is an incredible challenge. Each March, Iditarod competitors race over icy terrain, often through blizzard-like conditions. Teams include a **musher,** or driver, and 12 to 16 husky dogs, who make their way by day and night over the course. It takes them 10 to 17 days to travel the Iditarod Trail, an old supply route used by settlers during Alaska's pioneer and gold-rush days. The race itself commemorates the delivery of diphtheria serum to residents of Nome during an epidemic in 1925. The winner of the 2007 Iditarod was Lance Mackey, who made the run in a total of 9 days, 5 hours and 8 minutes.

OLYMPIC GAMES

Future Olympic Games

Winter 2010	Vancouver, Canada
Summer 2012	London, England
Winter 2014	Sochi, Russia

Begun in 776 B.C. in the Greek city of Olympia, the Olympic Games were played in honor of the gods and goddesses, especially Zeus. At the original games, all free male citizens could participate. (Women could compete in another event, the Herean Games, which took place every four years and honored Zeus' wife, Hera.) Olympic sports included javelin-throwing, boxing, running, long jumping, shot-put throwing, the pankration (a martial art combination of wrestling and boxing) and horse-riding events.

During the Olympic Games, a truce would be declared so that athletes of warring groups could compete in peace.

Olympian winners received a wreath of olive leaves to wear in their hair. In 393 A.D., the games were banned by the Emperor Theodosius, but were restarted in 1894 through the efforts of a French educator, Pierre Frédy, the Baron de Coubertin. Today, the Olympics are divided into Winter and Summer Games, alternating every two years. Greece is still honored as the country that began the tradition. The Greek athletes are always the first to enter the stadium during the opening ceremony's parade of teams.

WACKY SPORTS FROM AROUND THE WORLD

Think you know a lot about sports? Check out a few sporting events that you might have missed.

Dairy cow races, run in Australia, include human jockeys and "urgers," who help the cows down the course.

Elephant polo is played similarly to regular polo (which uses horses) but, as you might expect, a bit more slowly. This sport is played in Thailand, Laos, Nepal and Sri Lanka.

Tossing the caber, or log-tossing, is a traditional Scottish event, played as part of the highland games. Men throw a 90- to 120-pound (40.5- to 54-kg), 16- to 20-foot (4.8- to 6-m) log end over end to see who can toss it the farthest.

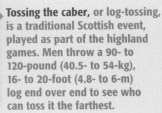

Zorbing involves strapping a person into a plastic sphere 9 feet (2.7 m) wide and rolling him or her down a hill. This sport comes from New Zealand.

Cheese-rolling contests of various kinds, in which players send round-wheeled cheeses along a course to see who can get it to the finish line in the least number of rolls. This sport is practiced in Italy, Holland, Britain and other cheese-making countries.

Underwater hockey, is a lesser-known U.S. sport. Similar to ice hockey, this game is played underwater. Players wear snorkeling equipment, carry foot-long (30-cm) sticks and try to push a 3-pound (1.35-kg) puck around the bottom of a swimming pool.

High-heel racing is a sport in which women compete to see who can run the fastest in shoes with heels at least 3 inches (7.62 cm) high. Originally a Russian pastime, this sport has caught on in other places, such as Germany, Mexico and the United States.

Some Sports Firsts

• The first baseball team to win more than one World Series was the Chicago Cubs, which won in 1907 and 1908. The Cubs haven't won a World Series since.

• The first NBA player to score 38,000 points was Kareem Abdul-Jabbar (33) in 1989.

• The first woman to win an Olympic Gold Medal was singles' tennis player Charlotte Cooper of Great Britain in 1900.

TIME for Fun

- Jackie Robinson is the only player whose number has been retired by Major League Baseball. On April 15, 1997 (exactly 50 years after Jackie Robinson debuted as the first non-Caucasian player in the league), Major League Baseball officials honored him at Shea Stadium. At the ceremony, they retired his number (42) in recognition of his achievements.

- In 1992, Deion Sanders of the Atlanta Falcons played in a football game against the Miami Dolphins. Later that day, he played in baseball's National League Championship Series game as an Atlanta Brave against the Pittsburgh Pirates. He's the only person to have played in two pro sports games on the same day, as well as the only person to compete in both the Super Bowl and the World Series.

- There are only two NASCAR Nextel Cup races that include right turns: the Toyota/Save Mart 350 at Infineon Raceway in Sonoma, California, and the Centurian Boats at the Glen at Watkins Glen International Speedway, in Watkins Glen, New York.

- The Major League Baseball record for the longest hitting streak—56 games—is held by Yankee Joe DiMaggio, who did it in 1941.

Mystery Person

TFK **?** **TFK SPORTS**

CLUE 1: I was born on October 20, 1931, in Spavinaw, Oklahoma.

CLUE 2: I joined the New York Yankees in 1951 as an outfielder. Later, I played first base. I was a switch hitter, which means I batted from both sides of the plate.

CLUE 3: I played in 12 World Series, where I hit a record 18 home runs. I was voted Most Valuable Player in the American League in 1956, 1957 and 1962.

WHO AM I? _____

ANSWERS ON PAGE 244

- The world's most popular spectator sport is soccer. World Cup games can draw a television audience of more than 1 billion people.

- In 2001, PGA golfer Andrew Magee made a hole-in-one on a par 4 hole by hitting his ball more than 330 yards (300.3 m). It accidentally bounced off the club of another golfer, Tom Byrum, who was getting ready to putt.

Super Ballplayer GAME

TFK

ANSWERS ON PAGE 244

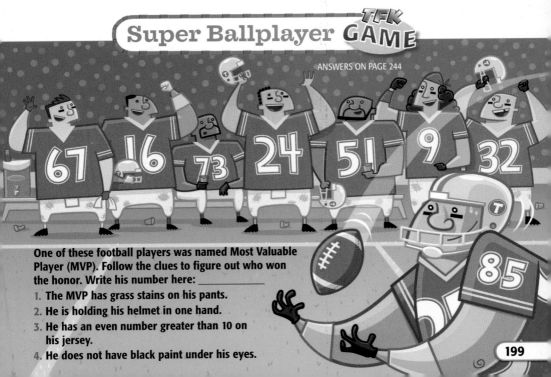

One of these football players was named Most Valuable Player (MVP). Follow the clues to figure out who won the honor. Write his number here: _____

1. The MVP has grass stains on his pants.
2. He is holding his helmet in one hand.
3. He has an even number greater than 10 on his jersey.
4. He does not have black paint under his eyes.

SHOULD THE U.S. REQUIRE VOLUNTEER SERVICE?

A Teach for America training session in Houston, Texas

Community service makes the planet a better place, and Americans always seem to be ready to do their part. Jack McShane, 13, heads to City Park in New Orleans, Louisiana, every Saturday to help mow the grass for free. The city cannot pay people to keep the park looking nice right now, but Jack does it because he loves his hometown. Shelly Jain, 22, teaches sixth-grade math in New York City. She is part of Teach for America, a group that recruits top college graduates to make sure that kids in poor neighborhoods have a chance to learn from a great teacher.

Clearly, good-hearted people have the power to change the world. But should doing good works be a choice for some or an absolute responsibility for all? One idea that is gaining popularity is a system to encourage every able American complete a yearlong service mission.

SHOULD EVERYONE STEP UP?

In some other nations, young people are required to perform a year or more of service. In Israel, every eligible young person must serve in the military for two or three years. In Germany, young men are drafted into the military, but can choose instead to volunteer in hospitals or charities at home or abroad. In South Africa, health-care professionals must spend a year working in poor areas before accepting a permanent job.

Although the U.S. does not have a formal program, millions of Americans do volunteer. In 2006, more than 61 million Americans donated 8.1 billion hours of service. The nation's volunteer rate has increased by more than 6% since 1989. Here are some ideas that government leaders and others are considering.

BABY BOND: The government would give every newborn American a $5,000 bond. At age 18, the person could get the money (with interest) after volunteering for a year.

SUMMER OF SERVICE: Over the summer between middle school and high school, students could earn a $500 college scholarship by volunteering in programs to help younger kids.

RAPID RESPONSE RESERVE CORPS: This volunteer group would be trained to help when disasters strike.

NATIONAL SERVICE ACADEMY: In exchange for promising five years of national service after college, students would get a free four-year education in public-service leadership.

EDUCATION FUND FOR RETIREES: For every 500 hours of community service older volunteers performed, they would get $1,000 to be deposited into an education savings account for their children, grandchildren or any student they choose.

Such programs would require funds from taxes, private donations and corporations. People would have to make sacrifices to make these plans work. But the payoff for our nation could be a future of security, prosperity and pride. The men who signed the Declaration of Independence in 1776 pledged "our Lives, our Fortunes and our sacred Honor" to their new country. Imagine the powerful effect this generation could have by pledging just a little of their time.

—By Richard Stengel

America's Biggest Cities

Top 10 U.S. Cities over Time

New York

For more than 100 years, New York has remained the most populous city in the country. But the list of top 10 most-poplulated U.S. cities has shifted over time.

	1910			1960			2006	
1.	New York	4,766,883	1.	New York	7,781,984	1.	New York	8,214,426
2.	Chicago	2,185,283	2.	Chicago	3,550,404	2.	Los Angeles	3,849,378
3.	Philadelphia	1,549,008	3.	Los Angeles	2,479,015	3.	Chicago	2,833,321
4.	St. Louis	687,029	4.	Philadelphia	2,002,512	4.	Houston	2,144,491
5.	Boston	670,585	5.	Detroit	1,670,144	5.	Phoenix	1,512,986
6.	Cleveland	560,663	6.	Baltimore	939,024	6.	Philadelphia	1,448,394
7.	Baltimore	558,485	7.	Houston	938,219	7.	San Antonio	1,296,682
8.	Pittsburgh	533,905	8.	Cleveland	876,050	8.	San Diego	1,256,951
9.	Detroit	465,766	9.	Washington, D.C.	763,956	9.	Dallas	1,232,940
10.	Buffalo	423,715	10.	St. Louis	750,026	10.	San Jose	929,936

Fastest-Growing American Cities

Between 2000 and 2006, the population of McKinney, Texas (a town near Dallas) grew 97.6%. Here are other cities whose populations are on the rise.

Gilbert, AZ
North Las Vegas, NV
Port St. Lucie, FL
Elk Grove, CA
Miramar, FL
Cape Coral, FL
Henderson, NV
Chandler, AZ
Irvine, CA

Shrinking U.S. Cities

Between 2000 and 2006, New Orleans lost 53.9% of its population. Other major cities whose populations declined are:

*Detroit, MI	lost 8.4%
*Cleveland, OH	lost 6.9%
*Pittsburgh, PA	lost 6.5%
*Flint, MI	lost 6.3%

Most Popular Baby Names in the U.S.

Ten years ago, Jacob and Emily were the most popular names for babies. In 2007 (the most recent year with available data), the most popular names were also Jacob and Emily. Take a look at the other names that topped the list in 1999 and 2007:

RANK	1999 BOYS	1999 GIRLS	2007 BOYS	2007 GIRLS
1.	Jacob	Emily	Jacob	Emily
2.	Michael	Hannah	Michael	Emma
3.	Matthew	Alexis	Joshua	Madison
4.	Joshua	Sarah	Ethan	Isabella
5.	Christopher	Samantha	Matthew	Ava
6.	Nicholas	Ashley	Daniel	Abigail
7.	Andrew	Madison	Christopher	Olivia
8.	Joseph	Taylor	Andrew	Hannah
9.	Tyler	Jessica	Anthony	Sophia
10.	Daniel	Elizabeth	William	Samantha

Source: Social Security Administration

ALL ABOUT THE STATES

ALABAMA

CAPITAL: Montgomery

LARGEST CITY: Birmingham

POSTAL CODE: AL

LAND AREA: 50,750 square miles (131,443 sq km)

POPULATION (2007): 4,627,851

ENTERED UNION (RANK): December 14, 1819 (22)

MOTTO: *Audemus jura nostra defendere* (We dare defend our rights)

TREE: southern longleaf pine

FLOWER: camellia

BIRD: yellowhammer (yellow-shafted flicker)

OTHER: dance: square dance; nut: pecan

NICKNAME: Yellowhammer State

FAMOUS ALABAMIAN: Secretary of State Condoleezza Rice ≫

GUESS WHAT? Huntsville is known as the rocket capital of the world. The U.S. Space & Rocket Center is located there.

Birmingham

Montgomery

ALASKA

CAPITAL: Juneau

LARGEST CITY: Anchorage

POSTAL CODE: AK

LAND AREA: 570,374 square miles (1,477,267 sq km)

POPULATION (2007): 683,478

ENTERED UNION (RANK): January 3, 1959 (49)

MOTTO: North to the future

TREE: Sitka spruce

FLOWER: forget-me-not

BIRD: willow ptarmigan

NICKNAMES: The Last Frontier, Land of the Midnight Sun

FAMOUS ALASKAN: Susan Butcher, four-time winner of the Iditarod

GUESS WHAT? The four-spot skimmer dragonfly is the official state insect.

Juneau

CANADA

Anchorage

Juneau

ARIZONA

CAPITAL: Phoenix

LARGEST CITY: Phoenix

POSTAL CODE: AZ

LAND AREA: 113,642 square miles (296,400 sq km)

POPULATION (2007): 6,338,755

ENTERED UNION (RANK): February 14, 1912 (48)

MOTTO: *Ditat deus* (God enriches)

TREE: paloverde

FLOWER: flower of saguaro cactus

BIRD: cactus wren

NICKNAME: Grand Canyon State

FAMOUS ARIZONAN: Geronimo, Native American leader

GUESS WHAT? The most famous shootout of the "wild west," the gunfight at the O.K. Corral, took place in Tombstone, Arizona.

ARKANSAS

CAPITAL: Little Rock

LARGEST CITY: Little Rock

POSTAL CODE: AR

LAND AREA: 52,075 square miles (134,874 sq km)

POPULATION (2007): 2,834,797

ENTERED UNION (RANK): June 15, 1836 (25)

MOTTO: *Regnat populus* (The people rule)

TREE: pine

FLOWER: apple blossom

BIRD: mockingbird

NICKNAME: Natural State

FAMOUS ARKANSAN: John Grisham, writer

GUESS WHAT? Since 1985, the fiddle has been Arkansas's official state instrument.

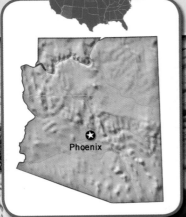

Phoenix

Little Rock

CALIFORNIA

CAPITAL: Sacramento

LARGEST CITY: Los Angeles

POSTAL CODE: CA

LAND AREA: 155,973 square miles (403,970 sq km)

POPULATION (2007): 36,553,215

ENTERED UNION (RANK): September 9, 1850 (31)

MOTTO: *Eureka* (I have found it)

TREE: California redwood

FLOWER: golden poppy

BIRD: California valley quail

NICKNAME: Golden State

FAMOUS CALIFORNIAN: Sally Ride, the first American woman in space

GUESS WHAT? In the United States, almonds, artichokes, figs, olives, raisins, pistachios, prunes, walnuts and kiwi fruits are only grown in California.

COLORADO

CAPITAL: Denver

LARGEST CITY: Denver

POSTAL CODE: CO

LAND AREA: 103,730 square miles (268,660 sq km)

POPULATION (2007): 4,861,515

ENTERED UNION (RANK): August 1, 1876 (38)

MOTTO: *Nil sine numine* (Nothing without providence)

TREE: Colorado blue spruce

FLOWER: Rocky Mountain columbine

BIRD: lark bunting

NICKNAME: Centennial State

FAMOUS COLORADAN: Jack Dempsey, boxer

GUESS WHAT? In 1972, Colorado became the first and only state to reject the Olympics. The winter games had been scheduled for Denver in 1976.

CONNECTICUT

CAPITAL: Hartford

LARGEST CITY: Bridgeport

POSTAL CODE: CT

LAND AREA: 4,845 square miles (12,550 sq km)

POPULATION (2007): 3,502,309

ENTERED UNION (RANK): January 9, 1788 (5)

MOTTO: *Qui transtulit sustinet* (He who is transplanted still sustains)

TREE: white oak

FLOWER: mountain laurel

BIRD: American robin

NICKNAME: Nutmeg State

FAMOUS NUTMEGGER: Harriet Beecher Stowe, novelist and abolitionist who wrote *Uncle Tom's Cabin*

GUESS WHAT? In 1978, "Yankee Doodle" became the state song of Connecticut.

DELAWARE

CAPITAL: Dover

LARGEST CITY: Wilmington

POSTAL CODE: DE

LAND AREA: 1,955 square miles (5,153 sq km)

POPULATION (2007): 864,764

ENTERED UNION (RANK): December 7, 1787 (1)

MOTTO: Liberty and independence

TREE: American holly

FLOWER: peach blossom

BIRD: blue hen chicken

NICKNAME: Diamond State, First State, Small Wonder

FAMOUS DELAWAREAN: Henry Heimlich, surgeon and inventor of the Heimlich Maneuver

GUESS WHAT? The first settlement in Delaware was called *Zwaanendael*, which means "valley of swans" in Dutch. The settlers were killed by Native Americans within a year.

DECEMBER 7, 1787

Wilmington

Dover

205

FLORIDA

CAPITAL: Tallahassee

LARGEST CITY: Jacksonville

POSTAL CODE: FL

LAND AREA: 54,153 square miles (140,256 sq km)

POPULATION (2007): 18,251,243

ENTERED UNION (RANK): March 3, 1845 (27)

MOTTO: In God we trust

TREE: Sabal palm ≫

FLOWER: orange blossom

BIRD: mockingbird

NICKNAME: Sunshine State

FAMOUS FLORIDIAN: Brittany Snow, actress

GUESS WHAT? Florida is known for its sunshine, but snow actually fell in Dade County on January 20, 1977.

GEORGIA

CAPITAL: Atlanta

LARGEST CITY: Atlanta

POSTAL CODE: GA

LAND AREA: 57,919 square miles (150,010 sq km)

POPULATION (2007): 9,544,750

ENTERED UNION (RANK): January 2, 1788 (4)

MOTTO: Wisdom, justice and moderation

TREE: live oak

FLOWER: Cherokee rose

BIRD: brown thrasher

NICKNAME: Peach State, Empire State of the South

FAMOUS GEORGIAN: Martin Luther King Jr., civil rights leader ≫

GUESS WHAT? The first Native American newspaper published in the United States was the *Cherokee Phoenix*. It was first published in 1828 in Echota, Georgia.

Photo: Hawaii

HAWAII

CAPITAL: Honolulu (on Oahu)

LARGEST CITY: Honolulu

POSTAL CODE: HI

LAND AREA: 6,423 square miles (16,637 sq km)

POPULATION (2007): 1,283,388

ENTERED UNION (RANK): August 21, 1959 (50)

MOTTO: *Ua mau ke ea o ka aina i ka pono* (The life of the land is perpetuated in righteousness)

TREE: kukui (candlenut)

FLOWER: yellow hibiscus ≫

BIRD: nene (Hawaiian goose)

NICKNAME: Aloha State

FAMOUS HAWAIIAN: Hiram L. Fong, first Asian-American senator

GUESS WHAT? Hawaii is home to carnivorous caterpillars. They eat snails!

PACIFIC OCEAN

Honolulu ★

IDAHO

CAPITAL: Boise

LARGEST CITY: Boise

POSTAL CODE: ID

LAND AREA: 82,751 square miles (214,325 sq km)

POPULATION (2007): 1,499,402

ENTERED UNION (RANK): July 3, 1890 (43)

MOTTO: *Esto perpetua* (It is forever)

TREE: white pine

FLOWER: syringa

BIRD: mountain bluebird

NICKNAME: Gem State

FAMOUS IDAHOAN: Gutzon Borglum, Mount Rushmore sculptor

GUESS WHAT? The Idaho state fruit is the huckleberry, which is a dark-colored berry somewhat like a blueberry. ≫

Boise ★

ILLINOIS

CAPITAL: Springfield

LARGEST CITY: Chicago

POSTAL CODE: IL

LAND AREA: 55,593 square miles (143,987 sq km)

POPULATION (2007): 12,852,548

ENTERED UNION (RANK): December 3, 1818 (21)

MOTTO: State sovereignty, national union

TREE: white oak

FLOWER: violet

BIRD: cardinal

NICKNAME: Prairie State

FAMOUS ILLINOISAN: Ernest Hemingway, writer

GUESS WHAT? The first Dairy Queen restaurant opened in 1940 in Joliet, Illinois.

Chicago

Springfield ★

INDIANA

CAPITAL: Indianapolis

LARGEST CITY: Indianapolis

POSTAL CODE: IN

LAND AREA: 35,870 sq miles (92,904 sq km)

POPULATION (2007): 6,345,289

ENTERED UNION (RANK): December 11, 1816 (19)

MOTTO: The crossroads of America

TREE: tulip tree

FLOWER: peony

BIRD: cardinal

NICKNAME: Hoosier State

FAMOUS INDIANAN: Michael Jackson, pop star

GUESS WHAT? December 11th is a state holiday known as "Indiana Day." On this day, residents celebrate Indiana becoming a state in 1816.

Indianapolis

Indianapolis ★

Photo: Indiana

IOWA

CAPITAL: Des Moines

LARGEST CITY: Des Moines

POSTAL CODE: IA

LAND AREA: 55,875 square miles (144,716 sq km)

POPULATION (2007): 2,988,046

ENTERED UNION (RANK): December 28, 1846 (29)

MOTTO: Our liberties we prize, and our rights we will maintain

TREE: oak

FLOWER: wild rose

BIRD: eastern goldfinch

NICKNAME: Hawkeye State

FAMOUS IOWAN: William "Buffalo Bill" Cody, "wild west" scout and entertainer

GUESS WHAT? Geode is the official rock of Iowa. Geodes have a hard outer shell, with mineral crystals such as quartz or calcite inside.

Des Moines ★

KANSAS

CAPITAL: Topeka

LARGEST CITY: Wichita

POSTAL CODE: KS

LAND AREA: 81,823 square miles (211,922 sq km)

POPULATION (2007): 2,775,997

ENTERED UNION (RANK): January 29, 1861 (34)

MOTTO: *Ad astra per aspera* (To the stars through difficulties)

TREE: cottonwood

FLOWER: sunflower

BIRD: western meadowlark

NICKNAME: Sunflower State, Jayhawk State

FAMOUS KANSAN: Amelia Earhart, first woman to fly alone across the Atlantic Ocean

GUESS WHAT? Fort Leavenworth, Kansas, is the oldest continuously operated military post west of the Mississippi River. It was established in 1827.

Topeka ★

Wichita ●

LOUISIANA

CAPITAL: Baton Rouge

LARGEST CITY: New Orleans

POSTAL CODE: LA

LAND AREA: 43,566 square miles (112,836 sq km)

POPULATION (2007): 4,293,204

ENTERED UNION (RANK): April 30, 1812 (18)

MOTTO: Union, justice and confidence

TREE: bald cypress

FLOWER: magnolia

BIRD: eastern brown pelican

NICKNAME: Pelican State

FAMOUS LOUISIANAN: Louis Armstrong, jazz musician

GUESS WHAT? The state dog of Louisiana is the Catahoula Leopard Dog, which is a cross between the dog that Native Americans in Louisiana raised and a "war dog" brought by the Spanish in the 1500s.

KENTUCKY

CAPITAL: Frankfort

LARGEST CITY: Louisville

POSTAL CODE: KY

LAND AREA: 39,732 square miles (102,907 sq km)

POPULATION (2007): 4,241,474

ENTERED UNION (RANK): June 1, 1792 (15)

MOTTO: United we stand, divided we fall

TREE: tulip poplar

FLOWER: goldenrod

BIRD: Kentucky cardinal

NICKNAME: Bluegrass State

FAMOUS KENTUCKIAN: Muhammad Ali, boxer

GUESS WHAT? During the Civil War, Kentucky fought with the Union. Frankfort was the only capital in the Union to be occupied by Confederate troops.

MAINE

CAPITAL: Augusta

LARGEST CITY: Portland

POSTAL CODE: ME

LAND AREA: 30,865 square miles (79,939 sq km)

POPULATION (2007): 1,317,207

ENTERED UNION (RANK): March 15, 1820 (23)

MOTTO: *Dirigo* (I lead)

TREE: white pine

FLOWER: white pine cone and tassel

BIRD: chickadee

NICKNAME: Pine Tree State

FAMOUS MAINER: Stephen King, best-selling author

GUESS WHAT? There are more than 5,000 miles of coastline in Maine. That's more than California.

MARYLAND

CAPITAL: Annapolis

LARGEST CITY: Baltimore

POSTAL CODE: MD

LAND AREA: 9,775 square miles (25,316 sq km)

POPULATION (2007): 5,618,344

ENTERED UNION (RANK): April 28, 1788 (7)

MOTTO: *Fatti maschii, parole femine* (Manly deeds, womanly words)

TREE: white oak

FLOWER: black-eyed Susan

BIRD: Baltimore oriole

NICKNAME: Free State, Old Line State

FAMOUS MARYLANDER: Frederick Douglass, freed slave and abolitionist

GUESS WHAT? The first telegraph message was sent from Washington, D.C., to Baltimore, Maryland, on May 24, 1844. It said, "What hath God wrought?"

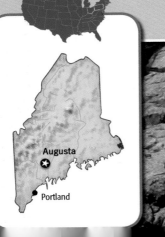

Augusta

Portland

Baltimore

Annapolis

MICHIGAN

CAPITAL: Lansing

LARGEST CITY: Detroit

POSTAL CODE: MI

LAND AREA: 56,809 square miles (147,135 sq km)

POPULATION (2007): 10,071,822

ENTERED UNION (RANK): January 26, 1837 (26)

MOTTO: *Si quaeris peninsulam amoenam circumspice* (If you seek a pleasant peninsula, look around you)

TREE: white pine

FLOWER: apple blossom

BIRD: robin

NICKNAME: Wolverine State

FAMOUS MICHIGANDER OR MICHIGANIAN: Henry Ford, automobile manufacturer

GUESS WHAT? In 1849, the Michigan State Fair became the first state fair in the country.

MASSACHUSETTS

CAPITAL: Boston

LARGEST CITY: Boston

POSTAL CODE: MA

LAND AREA: 7,838 square miles (20,300 sq km)

POPULATION (2007): 6,449,755

ENTERED UNION (RANK): February 6, 1788 (6)

MOTTO: *Ense petit placidam sub libertate quietem* (By the sword we seek peace, but peace only under liberty)

TREE: American elm

FLOWER: mayflower

BIRD: chickadee

NICKNAME: Bay State, Old Colony State

FAMOUS BAY STATER: John Chapman, known as Johnny Appleseed, helped establish apple orchards in the Midwest

GUESS WHAT? Originally called just Newtons, Fig Newtons were named after the town of Newton, Massachusetts.

Photo: Mississippi

MINNESOTA

CAPITAL: St. Paul

LARGEST CITY:
Minneapolis

POSTAL CODE: MN

LAND AREA: 79,617 square miles
(206,207 sq km)

POPULATION (2007): 5,197,621

ENTERED UNION (RANK):
May 11, 1858 (32)

MOTTO: *L'Étoile du nord* (The north star)

TREE: red (or Norway) pine

FLOWER: lady slipper

BIRD: common loon

NICKNAME: North Star
State, Gopher State, Land
of 10,000 Lakes

FAMOUS MINNESOTAN:
Judy Garland, actress best-
known as Dorothy in *The Wizard of Oz*

GUESS WHAT? Two students at the
University of Minnesota wrote "Hail!
Minnesota" in 1904 and 1905. It was
the university song until 1945, when it
became the state's official song.

MISSISSIPPI

CAPITAL: Jackson

LARGEST CITY:
Jackson

POSTAL CODE: MS

LAND AREA: 46,914 square miles
(121,506 sq km)

POPULATION (2007): 2,918,785

ENTERED UNION (RANK):
December 10, 1817 (20)

MOTTO: *Virtute et armis*
(By valor and arms)

TREE: magnolia

FLOWER: magnolia

BIRD: mockingbird

NICKNAME: Magnolia State

FAMOUS MISSISSIPPIAN: Oprah Winfrey,
talk show personality and philanthropist

GUESS WHAT? Elvis Presley's
birthplace in Tupelo, Mississippi, is now
a museum. There is also a chapel on the
site where couples can get married.

Minneapolis
St. Paul

Jackson

MISSOURI

CAPITAL: Jefferson City

LARGEST CITY: Kansas City

POSTAL CODE: MO

LAND AREA: 68,898 square miles (178,446 sq km)

POPULATION (2007): 5,878,415

ENTERED UNION (RANK): August 10, 1821 (24)

MOTTO: *Salus populi suprema lex esto* (The welfare of the people shall be the supreme law)

TREE: flowering dogwood

FLOWER: hawthorn

BIRD: bluebird

NICKNAME: Show-Me State

FAMOUS MISSOURIAN: Edwin Hubble, astronomer

GUESS WHAT? Walter Williams founded the world's first school for journalism at the University of Missouri in 1908.

MONTANA

CAPITAL: Helena

LARGEST CITY: Billings

POSTAL CODE: MT

LAND AREA: 145,556 square miles (376,991 sq km)

POPULATION (2007): 957,861

ENTERED UNION (RANK): November 8, 1889 (41)

MOTTO: *Oro y plata* (Gold and silver)

TREE: ponderosa pine

FLOWER: bitterroot

BIRD: western meadowlark

NICKNAME: Treasure State

FAMOUS MONTANAN: Evel Knievel, motorcycle daredevil

GUESS WHAT? There are seven Indian reservations in Montana: Blackfoot, Crow, Flathead, Fort Peck, Fort Belknap, Northern Cheyenne and Rocky Boy's Reservation.

Kansas City

Jefferson City

Helena

Billings

NEVADA

CAPITAL: Carson City

LARGEST CITY: Las Vegas

POSTAL CODE: NV

LAND AREA: 109,806 square miles (284,397 sq km)

POPULATION (2007): 2,565,382

ENTERED UNION (RANK): October 31, 1864 (36)

MOTTO: All for our country

TREE: single-leaf piñon and bristlecone pine

FLOWER: sagebrush

BIRD: mountain bluebird

NICKNAMES: Sagebrush State, Silver State, Battle Born State

FAMOUS NEVADAN: Andre Agassi, tennis player

GUESS WHAT? There are 49,702 miles (79,988 km) of streets and highways in Nevada. Roughly 40,519 miles (65,209 km) of those are country roads.

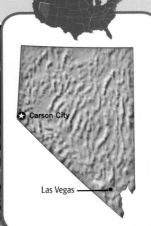
Carson City
Las Vegas

NEBRASKA

CAPITAL: Lincoln

LARGEST CITY: Omaha

POSTAL CODE: NE

LAND AREA: 76,878 square miles (199,113 sq km)

POPULATION (2007): 1,774,5711

ENTERED UNION (RANK): March 1, 1867 (37)

MOTTO: Equality before the law

TREE: cottonwood

FLOWER: goldenrod

BIRD: western meadowlark

NICKNAME: Cornhusker State, Beef State

FAMOUS NEBRASKAN: Malcolm X, civil rights leader

GUESS WHAT? Arbor Day was first celebrated in Nebraska in 1872. More than 1 million trees were planted during the first celebration.

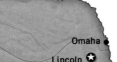
Omaha
Lincoln

NEW HAMPSHIRE

CAPITAL: Concord

LARGEST CITY: Manchester

POSTAL CODE: NH

LAND AREA: 8,969 square miles (23,231 sq km)

POPULATION (2007): 1,315,828

ENTERED UNION (RANK): June 21, 1788 (9)

MOTTO: Live free or die

TREE: white birch

FLOWER: purple lilac

BIRD: purple finch

NICKNAME: Granite State

FAMOUS NEW HAMPSHIRITE: Alan Shepard, first American in space >>

GUESS WHAT? The first free public library in the United States was founded in New Hampshire.

NEW JERSEY

CAPITAL: Trenton

LARGEST CITY: Newark

POSTAL CODE: NJ

LAND AREA: 7,419 square miles (19,215 sq km)

POPULATION (2007): 8,685,920

ENTERED UNION (RANK): December 18, 1787 (3)

MOTTO: Liberty and prosperity

TREE: red oak

FLOWER: purple violet >>

BIRD: eastern goldfinch

NICKNAME: Garden State

FAMOUS NEW JERSEYITE: David Copperfield, magician

GUESS WHAT? The street names in the game Monopoly were named after streets in Atlantic City, New Jersey.

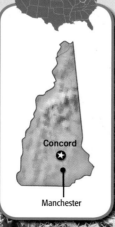

Concord ★

Manchester

Newark

Trenton ★

NEW MEXICO

CAPITAL: Santa Fe

LARGEST CITY: Albuquerque

POSTAL CODE: NM

LAND AREA: 121,365 square miles (314,334 sq km)

POPULATION (2007): 1,969,915

ENTERED UNION (RANK): January 6, 1912 (47)

MOTTO: *Crescit eundo* (It grows as it goes)

TREE: piñon (pine)

FLOWER: yucca

BIRD: roadrunner

NICKNAME: Land of Enchantment

FAMOUS NEW MEXICAN: William Hanna, cartoonist

GUESS WHAT? The official state question of New Mexico is, "Red or green?" which refers to which kind of chiles a person prefers.

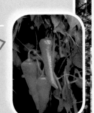

NEW YORK

CAPITAL: Albany

LARGEST CITY: New York

POSTAL CODE: NY

LAND AREA: 47,224 square miles (122,310 sq km)

POPULATION (2007): 19,297,729

ENTERED UNION (RANK): July 26, 1788 (11)

MOTTO: *Excelsior* (Ever upward)

TREE: sugar maple

FLOWER: rose

BIRD: bluebird

NICKNAME: Empire State

FAMOUS NEW YORKER: Eleanor Roosevelt, First Lady and human rights crusader

GUESS WHAT? New York City is known as "The Big Apple." Traveling jazz musicians in the 1930s used to call cities and towns "apples" and New York City was the biggest one of all.

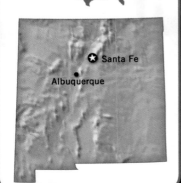

Santa Fe
Albuquerque

Albany

New York

NORTH CAROLINA

CAPITAL: Raleigh

LARGEST CITY: Charlotte

POSTAL CODE: NC

LAND AREA: 48,718 square miles (126,180 sq km)

POPULATION (2007): 9,061,032

ENTERED UNION (RANK): November 21, 1789 (12)

MOTTO: *Esse quam videri* (To be rather than to seem)

TREE: pine

FLOWER: dogwood

BIRD: cardinal

NICKNAME: Tar Heel State

FAMOUS NORTH CAROLINIAN: Fantasia Barrino, *American Idol* winner

GUESS WHAT? In 1718, famous pirate Blackbeard married his fourteenth wife in Bath, North Carolina.

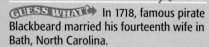

Raleigh

Charlotte

NORTH DAKOTA

CAPITAL: Bismarck

LARGEST CITY: Fargo

POSTAL CODE: ND

LAND AREA: 70,704 square miles (183,123 sq km)

POPULATION (2007): 639,715

ENTERED UNION (RANK): November 2, 1889 (39)

MOTTO: Liberty and union, now and forever, one and inseparable

TREE: American elm

FLOWER: wild prairie rose

BIRD: western meadowlark >>

NICKNAMES: Sioux State, Flickertail State, Peace Garden State, Rough Rider State

FAMOUS NORTH DAKOTAN: Cliff "Fido" Purpur, hockey player

GUESS WHAT? It is not actually known whether North Dakota or South Dakota became a state first. Because it falls first alphabetically, North Dakota is considered the 39th state and South Dakota, the 40th.

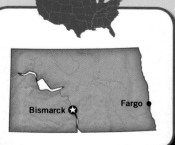

Bismarck

Fargo

OHIO

CAPITAL: Columbus

LARGEST CITY: Columbus

POSTAL CODE: OH

LAND AREA: 40,953 square miles (106,067 sq km)

POPULATION (2007): 11,466,917

ENTERED UNION (RANK): March 1, 1803 (17)

MOTTO: With God, all things are possible

TREE: buckeye

FLOWER: scarlet carnation

BIRD: cardinal

NICKNAME: Buckeye State

FAMOUS OHIOAN: Thomas Edison, inventor

GUESS WHAT? More presidents are from Ohio than any other state. William Henry Harrison, Ulysses S. Grant, Rutherford B. Hayes, James Garfield, Benjamin Harrison, William McKinley, William H. Taft and Warren Harding are all Ohioans.

Columbus ⭐

OKLAHOMA

CAPITAL: Oklahoma City

LARGEST CITY: Oklahoma City

POSTAL CODE: OK

LAND AREA: 68,679 square miles (177,880 sq km)

POPULATION (2007): 3,617,316

ENTERED UNION (RANK): November 16, 1907 (46)

MOTTO: *Labor omnia vincit* (Labor conquers all things)

TREE: redbud

FLOWER: mistletoe

BIRD: scissor-tailed flycatcher

NICKNAME: Sooner State

FAMOUS OKLAHOMAN: Mickey Mantle, baseball player

GUESS WHAT? The parking meter was invented in Oklahoma City.

Oklahoma City ⭐

OREGON

CAPITAL: Salem

LARGEST CITY: Portland

POSTAL CODE: OR

LAND AREA: 96,003 square miles (248,647 sq km)

POPULATION (2007): 3,747,455

ENTERED UNION (RANK): February 14, 1859 (33)

MOTTO: *Alis volat propriis* (She flies with her own wings)

TREE: Douglas fir

FLOWER: Oregon grape

BIRD: western meadowlark

NICKNAME: Beaver State

FAMOUS OREGONIAN: Matt Groening, creator of *The Simpsons*

GUESS WHAT? Oregon's flag is the only one with different images on each side. The front is navy blue and gold and shows the state seal, 33 stars and reads "State of Oregon" and "1859." The other shows an image of a beaver.

Portland
★ Salem

PENNSYLVANIA

CAPITAL: Harrisburg

LARGEST CITY: Philadelphia

POSTAL CODE: PA

LAND AREA: 44,820 square miles (116,083 sq km)

POPULATION (2007): 12,432,792

ENTERED UNION (RANK): December 12, 1787 (2)

MOTTO: Virtue, liberty and independence

TREE: hemlock

FLOWER: mountain laurel

BIRD: ruffled grouse

NICKNAME: Keystone State

FAMOUS PENNSYLVANIAN: Rachel Carson, biologist, ecologist and author of *Silent Spring*

GUESS WHAT? The Great Dane is the official state dog of Pennsylvania. There is even a famous portrait of William Penn with his Great Dane on display in Harrisburg.

Harrisburg ★
Philadelphia

Photo: Oregon

SOUTH CAROLINA

CAPITAL: Columbia

LARGEST CITY: Columbia

POSTAL CODE: SC

LAND AREA: 30,111 square miles (77,988 sq km)

POPULATION (2007): 4,407,709

ENTERED UNION (RANK): May 23, 1788 (8)

MOTTOES: *Animis opibusque parati* (Prepared in mind and resources); *Dum spiro spero* (While I breathe, I hope)

TREE: palmetto

FLOWER: yellow jessamine

BIRD: Carolina wren

NICKNAME: Palmetto State

FAMOUS SOUTH CAROLINIAN: Althea Gibson, tennis player

GUESS WHAT? The South Carolina General Assembly chose an official dance for the state. It is the shag, which is similar to the jitterbug and focuses on footwork rather than turns.

Columbia

RHODE ISLAND

CAPITAL: Providence

LARGEST CITY: Providence

POSTAL CODE: RI

LAND AREA: 1,045 square miles (2,706 sq km)

POPULATION (2007): 1,057,832

ENTERED UNION (RANK): May 29, 1790 (13)

MOTTO: Hope

TREE: red maple

FLOWER: violet

BIRD: Rhode Island red hen

NICKNAME: Ocean State

FAMOUS RHODE ISLANDER: Robert Gray, sea captain who discovered the Columbia River

GUESS WHAT? The Flying Horse carousel in Watch Hill, Rhode Island, is the oldest carousel in the country.

Providence

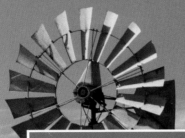

SOUTH DAKOTA

CAPITAL: Pierre

LARGEST CITY: Sioux Falls

POSTAL CODE: SD

LAND AREA: 75,898 square miles (196,575 sq km)

POPULATION (2007): 796,214

ENTERED UNION (RANK): November 2, 1889 (40)

MOTTO: Under God the people rule

TREE: Black Hills spruce

FLOWER: American pasqueflower

BIRD: ring-necked pheasant

NICKNAMES: Mount Rushmore State, Coyote State

FAMOUS SOUTH DAKOTAN: Crazy Horse, Sioux chief

 The official state sport of South Dakota is rodeo. ⟩⟩

Pierre ✪ Sioux Falls •

TENNESSEE

CAPITAL: Nashville

LARGEST CITY: Memphis

POSTAL CODE: TN

LAND AREA: 41,220 square miles (106,759 sq km)

POPULATION (2007): 6,156,719

ENTERED UNION (RANK): June 1, 1796 (16)

MOTTO: Agriculture and commerce

TREE: tulip poplar

FLOWER: iris

BIRD: mockingbird

NICKNAME: Volunteer State

FAMOUS TENNESSEAN: Al Gore, former vice president and environmental activist ⟩⟩

 Of the Confederate states, Tennessee was the last state to secede from the Union during the Civil War. It was also the first to be readmitted at the end of the war.

✪ Nashville

Memphis •

Photo: Texas

TEXAS

CAPITAL: Austin

LARGEST CITY: Houston

POSTAL CODE: TX

LAND AREA: 261,914 square miles (678,358 sq km)

POPULATION (2007): 23,904,380

ENTERED UNION (RANK): December 29, 1845 (28)

MOTTO: Friendship

TREE: pecan

FLOWER: bluebonnet

BIRD: mockingbird

NICKNAME: Lone Star State

FAMOUS TEXAN: Sandra Day O'Conner, first woman Supreme Court justice

GUESS WHAT? Austin, Texas, the live music capital of the world, is known for hosting the South by Southwest (SXSW) Music Festival every March.

UTAH

CAPITAL: Salt Lake City

LARGEST CITY: Salt Lake City

POSTAL CODE: UT

LAND AREA: 82,168 square miles (212,816 sq km)

POPULATION (2007): 2,645,330

ENTERED UNION (RANK): January 4, 1896 (45)

MOTTO: Industry

TREE: blue spruce

FLOWER: sego lily

BIRD: California gull

NICKNAME: Beehive State

FAMOUS UTAHN: Philo T. Farnsworth, inventor of the television

Salt Lake City

GUESS WHAT? Utah's state fossil is that of an allosaurus. More allosaurus fossils have been found in the state than any other dinosaur. Weighing about four tons (3.6 t), an allosaurus would be more than 16 feet (4.9 m) tall and roughly 39 feet (11.9 m) long.

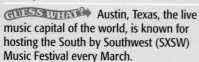

Austin ★ Houston ●

Salt Lake City ★

VERMONT

CAPITAL: Montpelier

LARGEST CITY: Burlington

POSTAL CODE: VT

LAND AREA: 9,249 square miles (23,956 sq km)

POPULATION (2007): 621,254

ENTERED UNION (RANK): March 4, 1791 (14)

MOTTO: Vermont, freedom and unity

TREE: sugar maple

FLOWER: red clover

BIRD: hermit thrush

NICKNAME: Green Mountain State

FAMOUS VERMONTER: Joseph Smith, founder of the Mormon church

GUESS WHAT? Vermont produces more maple syrup than any other state.

Burlington — ● ★ — Montpelier

VIRGINIA

CAPITAL: Richmond

LARGEST CITY: Virginia Beach

POSTAL CODE: VA

LAND AREA: 39,598 square miles (102,558 sq km)

POPULATION (2007): 7,712,091

ENTERED UNION (RANK): June 25, 1788 (10)

MOTTO: *Sic semper tyrannis* (Thus always to tyrants)

TREE: dogwood

FLOWER: American dogwood ⟩⟩

BIRD: cardinal

NICKNAMES: The Old Dominion, Mother of Presidents

FAMOUS VIRGINIAN: Meriwether Lewis and William Clark, American explorers

GUESS WHAT? At the center of Virginia's great seal stands the goddess of virtue. She holds a sword and a spear and stands on top of a figure representing tyranny.

Richmond ● ★

Virginia Beach

WASHINGTON

Photo: Washington

CAPITAL: Olympia

LARGEST CITY: Seattle

POSTAL CODE: WA

LAND AREA: 66,582 square miles (172,447 sq km)

POPULATION (2007): 6,468,424

ENTERED UNION (RANK): November 11, 1889 (42)

MOTTO: *Al-ki* (Indian word meaning "by and by")

TREE: western hemlock

FLOWER: coast rhododendron

BIRD: willow goldfinch

NICKNAME: Evergreen State

FAMOUS WASHINGTONIAN: Bob Barker, game show host

GUESS WHAT? Washington's Grand Coulee Dam is the largest concrete structure in the United States. In addition to being the third largest energy producer in the world, it provides a spot for boaters, water-skiers and fishermen.

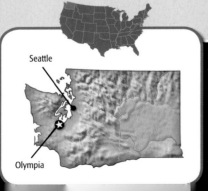

Seattle

Olympia

WEST VIRGINIA

CAPITAL: Charleston

LARGEST CITY: Charleston

POSTAL CODE: WV

LAND AREA: 24,087 square miles (62,384 sq km)

POPULATION (2007): 1,812,035

ENTERED UNION (RANK): June 20, 1863 (35)

MOTTO: *Montani semper liberi* (Mountaineers are always free)

TREE: sugar maple

FLOWER: rhododendron

BIRD: cardinal

NICKNAME: Mountain State

FAMOUS WEST VIRGINIAN: Mary Lou Retton, Olympic gymnast and winner of the 1984 gold medal

GUESS WHAT? The dome on top of the West Virginia State Capitol building is 292 feet (89 km) high. That is higher than the dome on the Capitol building in Washington, D.C.

Charleston

WISCONSIN

CAPITAL: Madison

LARGEST CITY: Milwaukee

WISCONSIN

1848

POSTAL CODE: WI

LAND AREA: 54,314 square miles (140,673 sq km)

POPULATION (2007): 5,601,640

ENTERED UNION (RANK): May 29, 1848 (30)

MOTTO: Forward

TREE: sugar maple

FLOWER: wood violet

BIRD: robin

NICKNAME: Badger State

FAMOUS WISCONSINITE: Frank Lloyd Wright, architect

GUESS WHAT? Wisconsin has a strong German heritage. German words and names can be seen on street signs and in the phone book. German traditions are also reflected in the choice of the polka as the state dance.

Milwaukee
Madison

WYOMING

CAPITAL: Cheyenne

LARGEST CITY: Cheyanne

POSTAL CODE: WY

LAND AREA: 97,105 square miles (251,501 sq km)

POPULATION (2007): 522,830

ENTERED UNION (RANK): July 10, 1890 (44)

MOTTO: Equal rights

TREE: cottonwood

FLOWER: Indian paintbrush

BIRD: meadowlark

NICKNAME: Equality State

FAMOUS WYOMINGITE: Jackson Pollock, artist

GUESS WHAT? In 1906, President Teddy Roosevelt made Devil's Tower the first national monument.

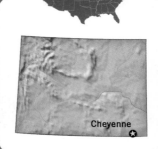

Cheyenne

OUR NATION'S CAPITAL:

WASHINGTON, D.C.

The District of Columbia, which covers the same area as the city of Washington, is the capital of the United States. D.C. history began in 1790 when Congress took charge of organizing a new site for the capital. George Washington chose the spot, midway between the northern and southern states on the Potomac River. The seat of government was transferred from Philadelphia, Pennsylvania, to Washington, D.C., on December 1, 1800, and President John Adams became the first resident of the White House.

LAND AREA: 68.25 square miles
(177 sq km)

POPULATION (2007): 588,292

MOTTO: *Justitia omnibus* (Justice to all)

TREE: scarlet oak

FLOWER: American Beauty rose

FAMOUS WASHINGTONIAN: Duke Ellington, jazz musician

The Capitol

GUESS WHAT? Washington, D.C., is divided into four quadrants: Northwest, Southwest, Northeast and Southeast. The U.S. Capitol building (famous for its dome) sits in the center, where the quadrants meet.

PUERTO RICO AND OTHER U.S. TERRITORIES

Located in the Caribbean Sea, Puerto Rico is about 1,000 miles (1,609 km) southeast of Miami, Florida. A U.S. possession since 1898, it consists of the island of Puerto Rico plus the adjacent islets of Vieques, Culebra and Mona. Both Spanish and English are spoken in Puerto Rico.

CAPITAL: San Juan

LARGEST CITY: San Juan

LAND AREA: 3,459 square miles
(8,959 sq km)

POPULATION (2007): 3,941,459

MOTTO: *Joannes est nomen eius*
(John is his name)

TREE: ceiba (silk-cotton)

FLOWER: maga (Puerto Rican hibiscus)

BIRD: *reinita* (stripe-headed tanager)

FAMOUS PUERTO RICAN: Joaquin Phoenix, actor

GUESS WHAT? Puerto Ricans have been U.S. citizens since 1917.

While Puerto Rico has the largest population of the U.S. territories, there are others.

AMERICAN SAMOA, a group of islands located in the South Pacific, is located about halfway between Hawaii and New Zealand. It has a land area of 77 square miles (200 sq km) and a population of approximately 57,660.

GUAM, located in the North Pacific Ocean, was ceded to the United States from Spain in 1898. It has a land area of 209 square miles (541 sq km) and a population of approximately 173,450.

U.S. VIRGIN ISLANDS, which include St. Croix, St. Thomas, St. John and many other islands, are located in the Caribbean Sea, east of Puerto Rico. Together they have a land area of 136 square miles (353 sq km) and a population of approximately 108,500.

THE NORTHERN MARIANA ISLANDS are located in the North Pacific Ocean. They have a land area of 176 square miles (456 sq km) and a population of approximately 84,550.

San Juan

227

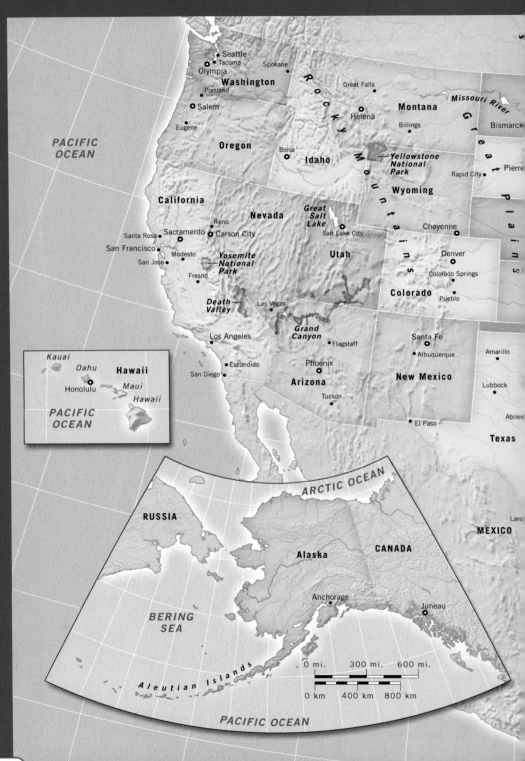

PACIFIC OCEAN

Seattle
Tacoma
Olympia
Spokane
Washington
Portland
Salem
Eugene
Oregon
Boise
Idaho

Great Falls
Montana
Helena
Billings

Missouri River
Bismarck

Rocky Mountains

Yellowstone National Park
Wyoming
Rapid City
Pierre

Great Plains

California
Nevada
Reno
Santa Rosa
Sacramento
Carson City
San Francisco
Modesto
San Jose
Fresno
Yosemite National Park

Great Salt Lake
Salt Lake City

Utah

Cheyenne
Denver
Colorado Springs
Colorado
Pueblo

Death Valley
Las Vegas

Grand Canyon
Flagstaff

Santa Fe
Albuquerque
New Mexico

Amarillo

Lubbock

Los Angeles
Escondido
San Diego

Phoenix
Arizona
Tucson

El Paso

Abilene

Texas

Kauai
Oahu
Hawaii
Honolulu
Maui
Hawaii
PACIFIC OCEAN

ARCTIC OCEAN

RUSSIA

Alaska
CANADA

MEXICO
Lare

Anchorage
Juneau

BERING SEA

Aleutian Islands

0 mi.   300 mi.   600 mi.

0 km   400 km   800 km

PACIFIC OCEAN

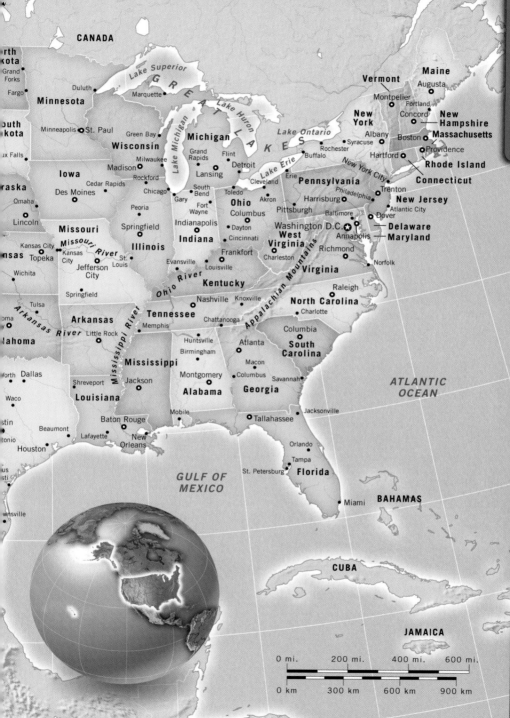

CANADA

Minnesota

Grand Forks

Fargo

rth kota

uth kota

ux Falls

Duluth

Lake Superior

Marquette

G R E A T

Green Bay

Wisconsin

Minneapolis • St. Paul

Iowa

Madison

Milwaukee

Des Moines

Cedar Rapids

Rockford

Chicago

Omaha

raska

Lincoln

Peoria

Springfield

Lake Michigan

Lake Huron

Michigan

Grand Rapids

Flint

Lansing

South Bend

Gary

Fort Wayne

Detroit

Lake Ontario

Lake Erie

Erie

Cleveland

Toledo

Akron

Ohio

Columbus

Dayton

Rochester

Syracuse

Buffalo

Albany

New York City

Harrisburg

Pennsylvania

Philadelphia

Pittsburgh

Baltimore

Vermont

Montpelier

Concord

New York

Hartford

Maine

Augusta

Portland

New Hampshire

Boston

Massachusetts

Providence

Rhode Island

Trenton

Connecticut

New Jersey

Atlantic City

Dover

Indianapolis

Indiana

Cincinnati

Missouri

Missouri River

Kansas City

Topeka

Wichita

ns as

Springfield

Jefferson City

St. Louis

Kansas City

Illinois

Evansville

Frankfort

Charleston

West Virginia

Washington D.C.

Annapolis

Richmond

Delaware

Maryland

Norfolk

Tulsa

Ohio River

Louisville

Kentucky

Nashville

Knoxville

Raleigh

oma y

ahoma

Arkansas River

Arkansas

Little Rock

Memphis

Tennessee

Chattanooga

Huntsville

Birmingham

Charlotte

North Carolina

Appalachian Mountains

Virginia

orth

Dallas

Waco

stin

tonio

Houston

Shreveport

Mississippi River

Mississippi

Jackson

Montgomery

Alabama

Macon

Columbus

Georgia

Savannah

Atlanta

Columbia

South Carolina

Beaumont

Lafayette

Louisiana

Baton Rouge

New Orleans

Mobile

Jacksonville

wnsville

Tallahassee

GULF OF MEXICO

St. Petersburg

Orlando

Tampa

Florida

Miami

ATLANTIC OCEAN

BAHAMAS

CUBA

JAMAICA

0 mi.   200 mi.   400 mi.   600 mi.

0 km   300 km   600 km   900 km

TFK VOLUNTEERING

HE SHOOTS, AFRICA SCORES

FROM TFK MAGAZINE

Austin Gutwein, founder of Hoops of Hope

In 2004, after watching a video about the millions of African children who had lost their parents to AIDS, Austin Gutwein, then 10, vowed to bring them hope. "I didn't know what AIDS was," he told TFK. "I just knew that I had to do something."

HIV is the virus that causes AIDS. People get HIV through bodily fluids, including blood. AIDS destroys the immune system, which is the system that helps the body fight off illness. There is no cure for HIV or AIDS, but there is medication that can help people live longer.

On World AIDS Day 2004, Austin did something for the young victims of HIV/AIDS. He spent seven hours shooting 2,057 free throws, one for each child who would be orphaned that day. He signed up sponsors and raised $3,000. With the help of the relief organization World Vision, the money went to support eight orphans. The next year, 1,000 kids in five states joined Austin. In 2007, kids in at least 26 states

and four European countries signed up to take part in Austin's Hoops of Hope campaign.

In 2006, the program raised $85,000 to help build a school in a small town in Zambia. The Johnathan Sim Legacy School will educate 1,000 students this year. Austin visited the school in November 2007. "It was amazing to actually feel the hands of the people you've helped," he says. "It is something I cannot even describe." Next, Austin hopes to raise $150,000 to build a medical lab in the town.

Austin is calling on kids to take part in events like his. "You don't have to be an adult to make a difference," he says. "You don't even have to be a great basketball player." To help, go to hoopsofhope.org.

—By Claudia Atticot

Important Activists Throughout History

Throughout history, many people have volunteered their time to make the world a better place. Here are a few.

MARTIN LUTHER (1483–1546), a Catholic priest in Germany, protested the abuses of power by the Roman Catholic Church.

HARRIET TUBMAN (about 1820–1913), helped more than 300 people escape from slavery.

CLARA BARTON (1821–1912), a Civil War nurse, founded the American Red Cross in 1881.

MOHANDAS K. GANDHI (1869–1948), led the people of the British colony of India in a nonviolent movement for independence.

MOTHER TERESA (1910–97), a Catholic nun who founded the Order of the Missionaries of Charity, worked tirelessly in India to help the "poorest of the poor."

MAKE A DIFFERENCE

Many non-profit organizations are working hard to make the world a better place. Here are just a few:

HEIFER INTERNATIONAL (www.heifer.org) fights world hunger by helping underdeveloped communities become self-sustaining. Instead of passing money along to hungry families, you can purchase for them a pig, a colony of honeybees or a flock of chicks (that will eventually produce enough eggs to feed a family and generate income). The idea is that when people can grow crops, raise animals and start businesses of their own, they are able to lift themselves out of poverty.

THE UNITED NATIONS INTERNATIONAL CHILDREN'S EMERGENCY FUND (UNICEF) (www.unicef.org) maintains programs around the world that ensure the health and safety of all children. Their efforts include education, immunization, health care and food distribution.

HABITAT FOR HUMANITY INTERNATIONAL (www.habitat.org) provides low-cost housing for those who can't afford to buy a home. Volunteers work alongside the people in need to build new homes.

INTERNATIONAL RED CROSS and **RED CRESCENT** (www.icrc.org, www.redcross.int) offer relief around the world to victims of war and natural disasters. With offices in more than 80 countries around the world, the organization does not take sides politically.

JUST A DROP (www.justadrop.org) is dedicated to bringing simple technology that provides clean and safe water for drinking and washing to underdeveloped communities around the world.

CARE and **CARE INTERNATIONAL** (www.care.org, www.care-international.org) work to alleviate worldwide poverty through programs that help families, and especially women, become self-supporting. The organization works with farmers to increase their crop yields and provides disaster relief aid in the forms of food, medical care and temporary shelter, among others.

NELSON MANDELA (1918–) fought against the South African system of racial discrimination and segregation known as apartheid.

DR. MARTIN LUTHER KING JR. (1929–68) fought for the civil rights of African Americans and all people.

ALBERT GORE (1948–) gives his time to bring the issue of global warming to the world's attention.

CHRISTOPHER REEVE (1952–2004) fought to improve the lives of the paralyzed and to increase funding for medical research.

KIDS HELPING OTHERS

Adults aren't the only ones doing great work around the world. Check out some non-profit charities started by children. Maybe they'll inspire you to fight for a cause you believe in.

ALEX'S LEMONADE STAND
(www.alexslemonade.org) Cancer patient Alexandra Scott was only 4 years old when she set up a lemonade stand to raise money for research into the causes and cures of childhood cancers. Word spread and, by the time she passed away at the age of 8, she had raised more than $1 million. Since her death, her charity has raised more than $16 million.

THE CARE BAGS FOUNDATION
(www.carebags4kids.org) In 2000, 11-year-old Annie Wignall of Iowa realized that many kids in crisis situations are forced to leave their homes suddenly, without any of their belongings. She started an organization that fills homemade bags with age-appropriate toys, games and toiletries for kids ranging from infants to teens. Annie's organization now distributes Care Bags worldwide.

RYAN'S WELL FOUNDATION
(www.ryanswell.ca) Ryan Hreljac of Canada was in first grade when his teacher told the class about the number of people in the world dying from a lack of clean drinking water.

Ryan decided to do something about this using the money he earned doing household chores. It took him four months to raise $70, but he continued until he raised $2,000, which he donated to help build a well in the African country of Uganda. What grew into the Ryan's Well Foundation has built more than 319 wells in 14 countries and has given more than 485,433 people access to clean water.

Want to Lend a Hand?

There are many things you can do to help others in your community and around the country. One place to find out more about volunteer opportunities is the Youth Volunteer Network (networkforgood.youthnoise.com).

Here are 10 things you can do to make the world a better place.

1. **Hold a fund-raising event.** Hold a bake sale or organize a walk (in which people sponsor you for each mile). Donate all of the profits to the organization you wish to support.

2. **Host a clothing drive.** Find a local store that will allow you to leave out a donation box.

Hang up fliers letting people know where and when to bring their extra clothing. Pick up the items regularly and drop them at a nearby shelter.

3. **Make someone's day.** Visit an assisted living or nursing home and spend time with the residents. Share your own interests, work on a craft project or play cards with them.

4. **Donate books and DVDs.** Collect old (gently used) books and DVDs from your friends or classmates and bring them to a children's hospital, shelter or other aid organization.

Small Amounts, Big Rewards

You do not need to make a large contribution in order to make a difference. Here are things your donation can buy:

ORGANIZATION	DONATION AMOUNT	WHAT IT CAN BUY
Just a Drop	about $2	10-year supply of safe drinking water for a child
Heifer International	$10	1/12 share of a goat, sheep or pig
Oxfam America	$18	mosquito nets
Heifer International	$20	a flock of geese, ducks or chicks
Just a Drop	about $20	lifetime supply of safe drinking water for a person
Oxfam America	$20	irrigate a farmer's land for two months
Oxfam America	$25	cooking stove
Oxfam America	$30	plant 50 trees
Heifer International	$30	honeybees

TFK TOP 5

Charities

Here are the charities that received the most donations from individuals in 2005.

1. **United Way of America**
   $4 billion in private donations

2. **Salvation Army**
   $3.59 billion

3. **AmericCares Foundation**
   $1.31 billion

4. **American Red Cross**
   $1.27 billion

5. **American Cancer Society**
   $929 million

Source: THE CHRONICLE OF PHILANTHROPY, 2006

5. Forgo the gifts. For your next birthday party, request that guests donate to a particular charity instead of bringing you a present.

6. Tutor a younger child in reading or math. Ask your teacher to introduce you to a child who needs extra help.

7. Un-pollute! You can tackle a corner of a public park or garden on your own or with friends.

8. Help out—while pursuing a passion. Volunteer to work for an organization that interests you, and it won't feel like work at all! Volunteer at an animal shelter, zoo, theater group, library, YMCA or YWCA.

9. Donate canned goods. Look through your pantry for soups and other canned goods that have not expired and donate these items to a local soup kitchen.

10. Make every penny count. Set up a "giving jar" in your home or classroom, in which you put aside money to give to the charity of your choice.

FIGHTING A FIRESTORM

Special winds called Santa Ana winds make wildfires worse in California.

FROM TFK MAGAZINE

Tom Sollie is the kind of neighbor you want to have around when disaster strikes. In October 2007, a blanket of black smoke covered his neighborhood, Rancho Bernardo, in San Diego, California. Raging flames hopscotched around the houses on his block. But instead of abandoning his neighbors, Sollie, 49, helped them spray their rooftops with water.

Sollie was one of the lucky ones. His house was untouched, even as more than a dozen wildfires roared across Southern California. They blazed a trail of destruction in seven counties, from northwest of Los Angeles through San Diego to the Mexican border. The fires were responsible for at least eight deaths and 58 injuries. More than 500,000 residents were forced to evacuate in San Diego County alone. About 1,500 homes were burned. Some 720 square miles were left charred by the flames.

More than 7,000 firefighters, including volunteers from other states and Mexico, struggled to save lives and contain the fires. At times, it seemed hopeless.

A DEADLY TRIPLE WHAMMY

One of the fires was set on purpose. But all of them were propelled by hot weather, strong winds and a severe drought. Temperatures in Southern California were about 10 degrees above average, reaching 100°F (37.8°C) in some areas. Hot weather and little rainfall dried up grasses, shrubs and trees, turning them into fuel that caught fire easily.

The lethal combination was made worse by the Santa Ana winds. These hot, dry winds blast westward from the desert and down the mountains every autumn. The Santa Ana winds were stronger than usual, with some gusting more than 100 miles (161 km) per hour. These powerful winds acted as nature's blowtorch, shooting 200-foot (61-m) walls of flame in all directions and scattering embers.

As smaller blazes merged into larger, more dangerous ones, firefighters had difficulty keeping up and containing the unpredictable fires. The high winds also prevented emergency workers from flying aircraft that could spray water and firefighting chemicals. As a result, fires were "popping up all over the place," said one San Diego County spokesperson.

DECISIONS, SMALL AND LARGE

As the flames raced closer, Californians had to make spur-of-the-moment decisions. Beckie Samuels, 54, and her son Garrett, 17, quickly gathered a few items from their home before fleeing to safety. "We took photo albums, jewelry and passports," Beckie told TIME. "When you only have a few minutes, you just take what is important."

After Hurricane Katrina devastated the Gulf Coast, the government's handling of that disaster angered many Americans. This time, relief efforts were quick and organized. President George W. Bush quickly declared the seven scorched counties a major disaster. Survivors began looking to the future. When Matt Nowak's family fled their home in the Scripps Ranch area of San Diego, they knew it could be the last time they ever saw it. But they also knew they would survive. "It was scary," he told TIME, "but we have hope."

—By Joe McGowan with TIME reporting by Coco Masters

TEMPERATURE is the amount of heat a solid, liquid or gas contains. This heat is caused by the movement of molecules in that substance. The faster they move, the higher the temperature of the substance is.

THERMOMETERS Thermometers measure temperature. The most common thermometers may contain a column of alcohol or mercury that expands in the presence of heat, or they may be digital and use liquid crystals or electricity.

CELSIUS OR FAHRENHEIT? Temperature is measured in degrees Fahrenheit (°F) or Celsius (°C). These scales are different. Water boils at 212°F and 100°C. Water freezes at 32°F and 0°C. These formulas allow you to convert temperatures:

$$°C = (°F - 32) \times \frac{5}{9} \qquad °F = (°C \times \frac{9}{5}) + 32$$

CLOUDS form when moisture in the air rises and collects in the sky. Clouds vary greatly in appearance and height depending on how much moisture they contain as well as the air pressure conditions surrounding them.

Low-lying stratus clouds blanket the sky.

The **PRECIPITATION** that falls from clouds is determined by the temperature of the water vapor in the clouds and the temperature of the air between the cloud and the earth. **SNOW** falls when the cloud-to-ground air is consistently below 40°F (4.4°C). **RAIN** falls at higher temperatures. **SLEET** and **HAIL** form when the air temperature fluctuates within the cloud and between the cloud and the ground.

Lightning

About 44,000 **THUNDERSTORMS** happen on Earth every day. Thunderstorms occur when a huge mass of warm air collides with a huge mass of cold air. Tall clouds form and the molecules of water vapor in them freeze and collide. These collisions form electrical fields in the clouds. When the electrical fields get big enough, sparks shoot between them, between the clouds and the electrical fields in the air or between the clouds and the electrical fields on the ground. These sparks form long paths, called **LIGHTNING.** Bolts of lightning can get as hot as 50,000°F (27,760°C). That's hotter than the surface of the Sun. Each year in the United States, about 60 people die from being hit by lightning.

WHERE DOES WIND COME FROM?

WINDS are caused by the Sun's heat falling on different parts of the earth at different times of the day and year. The temperatures over water and land change at different rates during the day and night. In addition, warm air rises and cool air sinks. These fluctuations cause the movement of air in different patterns, creating wind.

Wind

EXTREME WEATHER

A **TORNADO** is a column of twisting air that drops from a storm cloud and is powerful enough to lift or destroy houses, cars, trees and anything else in its path. Tornadoes begin when winds meet a center of low atmospheric pressure. The winds naturally curve around it, increasing in speed anywhere from 300 to 500 mph (500 to 833 km/h) until a column of spinning air forms and lowers to the ground. The vacuum in the center of the tornado sucks in anything it touches. On April 3–4, 1974, one of the worst tornado outbreaks in U.S. history occurred when 148 separate tornadoes struck 13 states in the Midwest and South. In all, 330 people were killed and 5,484 were injured.

FLOODS can be caused by many conditions, including hurricanes, heavy rainstorms, earthquakes, broken dams and tsunamis. One of the most famous floods occurred in Johnstown, Pennsylvania. On May 31, 1889, the combination of a powerful rainstorm and the bursting of an old dam caused the flooding of the town 14 miles (22.5 km) away and the deaths of 2,209 people. The wave that hit Johnstown was nearly 40 feet (12 m) high.

HURRICANES

are formed when tropical winds gather moisture as they pass over warm water of at least 80°F (20°C). The category, or strength, of a hurricane is measured on a scale of 1 to 5. A Category 1 hurricane has sustained winds of at least 74 mph (123 km/h). A Category 5 hurricane has sustained winds greater than 155 mph (258 km/h). No hurricane in recent memory has had a greater impact on American lives than Hurricane Katrina. On August 29, 2005, the Category 3 storm hit the Gulf Coast areas of New Orleans and parts of Mississippi and Alabama. The levees in the northern part of New Orleans collapsed, resulting in catastrophic flooding. More than 1,000 people died and there was more than $80 billion in property damage.

DROUGHTS occur when a long-term dry-weather pattern settles in an area. They may last for days, weeks, months and even years. In the 1930s, an eight-year drought occurred in the American and Canadian Midwest. The farmland got so dry that the soil turned to dust, which made people sick. About 350,000 left their homes for other parts of the country.

GUESS WHAT?

During the 1930s, the states experiencing severe drought conditions became known as the "dust bowl." The term, coined by a reporter named Robert Geiger, mostly referred to parts of Colorado, New Mexico, Texas, Oklahoma and Kansas.

BLIZZARDS are snowstorms that are blown by powerful winds of at least 35 mph (58 km/h) and a windchill factor of at least -20°F (-28°C). They are caused when a huge mass of cold air cuts under a huge mass of warm air, forming a giant bank of clouds. If the air from the clouds to the ground is colder than 40°F (4.4°C), the precipitation from the clouds falls as snow instead of rain or sleet. One of the worst U.S. blizzards happened in the West in 1949, lasting for seven weeks and killing more than 100 people. In addition, more than 1 million farm animals died.

Record Breaker

The biggest one-day snowfall in the U.S. occurred in Silver Lake, Colorado, on April 14–15, 1921. A total of 76 inches (193 cm) fell.

AVALANCHES occur when loose, light snow settles over more solidly packed snow on the sides of mountains. Gravity, an earthquake or even the vibrations caused by noise can pull the light snow very quickly down the slope, pushing more snow in front of it. The resulting huge mass of sliding snow is an avalanche.

WILDFIRES are the result of human or natural causes. Playing with matches or failing to extinguish a campfire properly can start a wildfire, but so can the heat of the sun or a lightning strike when grasses and trees are dry from a lack of rain.

MUDSLIDES happen when the ground on a slope gets wet from a rainstorm but can't drain the water quickly enough. The water pushes together the soil and rocks to form a kind of dam. When enough pressure builds, this earthen dam can break, causing the mud to slide quickly downhill, gathering and pushing down even more muddy soil and destroying whatever is in its path.

Atlantic Hurricane Names

Because the location of a hurricane constantly changes, hurricanes are named so that it is easier to describe their tracking. Before 1979, all hurricanes had female names. Since then, their names alternate between male and female ones. The list of names is reused every six years. When a hurricane is particularly devastating, its name is "retired" and never used again. Some retired names are Andrew, Ivan, Katrina, Rita, Stan and Wilma.

2009	2010
Ana	Alex
Bill	Bonnie
Claudette	Colin
Danny	Danielle
Erika	Earl
Fred	Fiona
Grace	Gaston
Henri	Hermine
Ida	Igor
Joaquin	Julia
Kate	Karl
Larry	Lisa
Mindy	Matthew
Nicholas	Nicole
Odette	Otto
Peter	Paula
Rose	Richard
Sam	Shary
Teresa	Tomas
Victor	Virginie
Wanda	Walter

Source: National Hurricane Center of the National Weather Service

Staying Safe in Extreme Weather

• **Do not stay outdoors in a severe thunderstorm.** Find shelter right away. If you can't find shelter, go to the lowest point on the ground (a ditch, for example) or crouch into a ball with your arms covering your head. Do not seek shelter under a tree or near structures like power lines, telephone lines or fences—tall objects may attract lightning.

• **If your area experiences a drought,** follow the instructions of your city or town law enforcement and health-safety officials on how to conserve water. (Conserving water is a great thing to do any time.)

• **If a tornado is nearby,** go to the lowest, most central part of your house (preferably a room without windows such as a basement, closet or bathroom).

• **In the event of a hurricane or flood,** follow the instructions of your city or town law enforcement and health-safety officials. Obey all orders to evacuate your home.

Underwater exploration bases, vacations in space and refrigerators that tell you when it's time to go food shopping are just a few of the wondrous inventions and trends that will greet us in the near future.

Science and Medicine on the Way

SECRETS OF THE SEAFLOOR

The seafloor at the Juan de Fuca plate

It's long been said that the world beneath the sea is the least-explored territory on Earth, but now some scientists are moving ahead to solve more mysteries of the deep. The goal of the National Science Foundation's Regional Scale Nodes program, led by the University of Washington, is to install a series of underwater "base stations" along the seabed at the Juan de Fuca Plate. This is an area of the Pacific Ocean where two massive boundaries of shifting earth meet.

The stations will be loaded with instruments. Cables carrying electricity and communications will connect the stations to one another and to laboratories and classrooms on land. Roving robots controlled from the shore will explore the seabed and the ocean above. Data will be transmitted to students, educators and scientists in near real time. Who knows what they'll discover?

An artist's drawing of what the base station may look like

PRIVATE VENTURES IN OUTER SPACE

The next few years may open new doors to anyone who wants to travel beyond Earth. More and more, corporations and wealthy businesspeople are beginning to invest in building their own spaceships. Eventually, they hope to explore and settle on the Moon or other planets. They are even looking to mine the mineral resources they find in space. In the future, people will be traveling to other parts of the solar system as tourists, much like they now travel around the world.

LIGHTING THE WAY TO TREATING CANCER

Imagine if doctors could light up cancer cells in the human body. That's what some researchers are working on right now. They are developing a liquid material called a "probe" that causes a chemical reaction in cancer cells, making them visible to a special camera.

A new technique makes cancer cells appear red when photographed.

Scientists believe that pinpointing the exact location of cancer cells will eliminate the need for the painful surgeries currently used to determine whether or not cells or tumors are cancerous. Further, these probes will aid in the early detection of cancer, which will save many lives!

New hearts start to beat after about a week in the lab.

GROWING A NEW HEART

In the not-too-distant future, it will be possible to repair faulty human hearts not by transplanting them but by growing new ones! Scientists at the University of Minnesota have already succeeded in creating living, beating hearts in rats by injecting stem cells into the shell of a dead heart. This process may work for more than just hearts. It may even help to solve the problem of patients' bodies rejecting transplants.

Scientists are hopeful that this technique will someday be used to create all kinds of new organs, helping millions of people who suffer from degenerative diseases.

ALLERGEN-FREE PEANUTS

There is good news for allergy sufferers. Scientists have discovered a peanut variety that doesn't contain allergens (the chemical substances that make people react badly). Other scientists have found a way to breed a peanut that doesn't cause an allergic response. Still other scientists have developed a roasting process that wipes out a peanut's allergens. All these developments can make a big difference in the lives of people who cannot eat—or even be near—peanuts. Who knows? These advances might lead to more discoveries that will make more foods allergen-free.

THE BIG-SCREEN WORLD AT YOUR FINGERTIPS

Consider the finger-touch–operated iPhone. Now imagine that screen blown up to 3 feet (90 cm) by 8 feet (240 cm) and hung on a wall. That's the new Media Wall from Perceptive Pixel. It's like a chalkboard, but instead of chalk, all you need to write on it is your finger. You can also move pictures around with a touch of your palm and decrease the size of a picture simply by pinching it. The Media Wall may find its way into classrooms and conference rooms in the near future, and maybe into some people's homes—that is, if they can afford the $100,000 price.

NEW WAYS TO FIND YOUR WAY

The development of the Global Positioning System (GPS) has changed the way people get from one place to another. You can expect many more GPS applications in the near future. For example, a walker or driver will be able to say a destination to a device with voice-recognition software and that device will retrieve the address and directions. In the future, users may be able to see whether there's an open space in a certain parking lot, search the Internet for movie schedules or locate gas stations with the cheapest prices. Look for this GPS boom in the next few years.

GASOLINE FROM GARBAGE?

It's perhaps one of the most stunning technological discoveries of our time: a simple process enables us to transform landfill garbage—and even sewage—into oil, gas and minerals that can be used as fertilizer or to create other products. The thermal depolymerization process (TDP) consists of five easy steps:

1. Chop up garbage into very fine bits and mix them with lots of water.
2. Put the mixture under intense heat (500°F/260°C) and pressure (600 pounds/270 kg) for about 15 minutes to break up the molecules.
3. Lower the pressure greatly so that the water escapes.
4. Send the remaining sludge to another chamber and heat it to an even higher temperature (900°F/482°C) to produce a hydrogen-carbon mixture.
5. Separate the mixture into a clean-burning gas (a methane/propane/butane combination), liquid oil and powdered carbon.

Scientists predict that TDP will be the wave of the future for sustainable, renewable energy. After all, there will always be plenty of garbage and sewage. This process will solve two problems at once!

A NEW KIND OF WATER POWER

Don't throw away that bath water! Remember to collect that dishwasher water, too. That's what scientists will tell us in the future, if a new technology begins to spread. It's called the "biological fuel" cell, and it uses bacteria that eat up pollutants and give off electrons as they feed. The electrons then move along a circuit and produce electricity.

As a result of the process, the water becomes clean again. This could mean that someday homes could generate their own power and clean water by re-circulating all the used water through a biological fuel cell. It will give parents a whole new reason for telling their kids to take a bath!

WE'RE OUT OF MILK.

THE "SMART" HOME

Imagine a home in which your handprint or fingerprint unlocks the front door, your voice turns on lights, your refrigerator tells you when you're low on certain foods, your malfunctioning washing machine calls a repairman and the heating system turns on and off at certain times of the day to save energy when no one is home. That kind of house is coming soon. Called the "networked home," it will have a central computerized system that takes care of all the family's needs.

"SMART" CLOTHES, TOO

In the future, your clothes may do a lot more than cover you and keep you warm and stylish. They will tell you when you need to dry-clean your shirt, which outfit you wore to the dance last week and, best of all, if you need medical attention because of a heart or breathing problem.

A team of Australian researchers at the Wearable Computer Laboratory has developed "garment management" technology in which electrodes are implanted in clothing. These electrodes collect information and send it to be recorded and analyzed. These messages can be read by the wearer or even by a doctor or nurse to see if any treatment is needed.

One day, smart clothing may be able to download music, as well as tell others about the wearer's activities, such as their wake-up and sleep times, if they are walking around or enjoying a meal and more. If you think your clothes already tell a lot about you, just wait a few years.

STEP UP AND BE COUNTED

Every ten years the United States government conducts a census, or count, of everyone living in the country, and 2010 will be the next one. What's the reason for the census? It helps the government provide services for its people based on their needs. The census questionnaire asks each person or family about his or her age, address, gender, marital status, race, citizenship status, ethnic group, level of education, military service, household members, employment, means of transportation and income. By gathering such data, government officials and lawmakers can make changes to national policies based on people's current lifestyles and needs.

Watch for an envelope mailed to your home in 2010. Your family's responses can make a difference in all of our lives.

NO MORE CHECKOUT LINES?

As more and more stores and super markets offer self-serve electronic checkout stations, the need for salespeople and one-on-one customer service decreases. Shoppers scanning their own purchases cuts down on the use of paper receipts and lines, making it an environmentally friendly trend, as well as a time-saver.

COMING TO A THEATER NEAR YOU

Movie studios are busy developing fun flicks for every audience. Be on the lookout for news about:

- *Avatar*
- *Cloudy with a Chance of Meatballs*
- *The Hobbit*
- *Harry Potter and the Deathly Hallows*
- *Spider-Man 4*
- *Shrek 4*

- *The Justice League*
- *The Chronicles of Narnia: Voyage of the Dawn Treader*
- *Thundercats*
- *Toy Story 3*
- *Transformers 2*

ANSWERS

Page 23:

Offspring!:
1. kid
2. chick
3. joey
4. pup
5. fawn

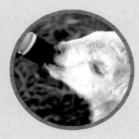

Page 37:

Mystery Person: Arthur C. Clarke. The dinosaur is called the *Serendipaceratops arthurcclarkei.* The asteroid, discovered in March 1981, is known as 4923 Clarke.

By the Book:
Fiction: *The Mystery at Shadow Ranch, The Three Little Pigs*
Science: *Our Solar System, Becoming Butterflies*
Biography: *Rosa Parks' Story, Who Was Ben Franklin?*

Page 41:

Monument Matchup:
1. D, Rainbow Bridge
2. C, Mount Rushmore
3. A, Statue of Liberty
4. E, Muir Woods National Monument
5. B, Washington Monument

Page 45:

Creepy Counting:
1. Odd
2. Three
3. True
4. Two

Page 106:

Explore the Past:
1. 1325
2. False
3. 42

Mystery Person: Ferdinand Magellan

Page 129:

Mystery Person: Benjamin Franklin

Page 143:

Bright Ideas:
1. D
2. C
3. B
4. A

Mystery Person: Thomas Edison

Page 147:

Words in Spanish:

Hello—
I live in Mexico. I have a cat, a bird and a dog.
Your friend,
Pilar

Page 151

Abuzz About Numbers:
1. 36
2. 9
3. 3
4. 21
5. 18

Page 171:

Doodler in Chief:
1. A
2. D
3. C
4. B

Page 199:

Mystery Person: Mickey Mantle

Super Ballplayer: #16

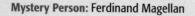

INDEX

CREDITS

News Recap: 8: Associated Press, Mehdi Ghasemi (Ahmadinejad); Associated Press, Vahid Salemi (Iranian students); Associated Press, Adil Al-Khazali (Iraq). 9: Associated Press, B.K. Bangash (Bhutto); Associated Press, Kirsty Wigglesworth (Brown); Associated Press, Riccardo Gangale (Sirleaf); Associated Press, HADJ/SIPA (Sarkozy and Bush). 10: Associated Press, Mel Evans (Live Earth); Associated Press, Damian Dovarganes (wildfires); Photos.com (beekeeper). 11: Associated Press, John Bazemore (scientist); Associated Press, Sam Dean (Virginia Tech); Associated Press, Jose Luis Magana (product recall). 12: Associated Press, Jae C. Hong (for sale); Associated Press, George Widman (immigration march). 13: Associated Press, Harry Cabluck (campaign signs); Associated Press, Elise Amendola (Obama and Clinton); Associated Press, Charlie Neibergall (Huckabee and McCain); Associated Press, Kevin Sanders (Republican candidates). 14: Kevork Djansezian (iPhone); Associated Press, Mark Lennihan (Kindle); Associated Press, George Nikitin (Bonds); Associated Press, Mary Altaffer (Jones). 15: Associated Press, Jeff Roberson (*Harry Potter*); Photos.com (food); Library of Congress, Prints and Photographs Division (Johnson); Associated Press, Anonymous (Kneival); Associated Press, Dima Gavrysh (Ledger).

Animals: 16: OAR/National Undersea Research Program (NURP); 17: Photos.com (all). 18: Photos.com (salmon, frog, snake, wolf, parakeet, sponge, jellyfish, starfish, snail, butterfly); Shutterstock.com (worm). 19: Photos.com (dog, coral reef, cardinal, jaguar); NOAA Restoration Center, Louise Kane (brown pelican). 20: Photos.com (all). 21: U.S Customs and Border Protection Canine Enforcement Training Center photo by James R. Tourtellotte (dog); Photos.com (pigeon, cat); Shutterstock.com (monkey, leech). 22: Photos.com (hedgehog, dog, jockey); USDA Photo by Keith Weller (veterinarian). 23: Photos.com (kangaroo, blowfish, dolphin, baboon, chameleon); Shutterstock.com (baby goat).

Art: 24: SuperStock, Inc./SuperStock (*Aphrodite of Knidos*, Mona Lisa); Photos.com (*Book of Kells*). 25: Shutterstock.com (Church of Invalides); Peter Willi/SuperStock (*Napoleon Crossing the Alps, The Tiger Hunt*). 26: Photos.com (*Girls at the Piano, Wheat Field with Crows*); © 2008 Artists Rights Society (ARS), New York/ADAGP, Paris (*The Man with a Guitar*; photo provided by Peter Willi/SuperStock). 27: Associated Press, Richard Drew (Warhol); ©2008 Salvador Dali, Gala–Salvador Dali/Artists Rights Society (ARS), New York (*The Persistence of Memory*; photo provided by SuperStock, Inc./SuperStock); Associated Press, Mary Altaffer (sculptures).

Body and Health: 28: Shutterstock.com (heart, muscular system); iStockphoto.com/Eraxion (cardiovascular system, skeletal system, immune system, viruses). 29: Shutterstock.com (nerves); iStockphoto.com/Eraxion (brain, intestines, lungs, kidneys); iStockphoto.com/Sonifo (hands). 30: Photos.com (all). 31: Photos.com (sunglasses, soap); Shutterstock.com (skateboard, broken arm, sleeping girls, water bottle, no smoking sign). 32: Shutterstock.com (girl, ear, doctor); Photos.com (eye, gardener, stethoscope); iStockphoto.com/gollykim (hands). 33: Photos.com (feet, baby, peppers, girl, sneezing boy, orange, pirate); Shutterstock.com (crying child).

Books and Literature: 34: Photos.com (books at top of page), Penguin Young Readers Group (*David Copperfield, Death of a Salesman*); Courtesy of Dover Publications (*The Autobiography of Benjamin Franklin*); Courtesy of Mitchell Lane Publishers, Inc. (*Paul Bunyan*). 35: Photos.com (open book); Cover from RUN, BOY, RUN by Uri Orlev, translated by Hillel Halkin. Copyright © 2003 by Uri Orlev. Reprinted by permission of Houghton Mifflin Harcourt Publishing Company. All rights reserved. Penguin Young Readers Group (*The Heart of a Chief, This Land Was Made for You and Me*); *Good Masters! Sweet Ladies!* Text copyright © 2007 Laura Amy Schlitz. Illustrations copyright © 2007 Robert Byrd. Reproduced by permission of the publisher, Candlewick Press, Inc., Cambridge, MA. 36: Library of Congress, Prints and Photographs Division (Whitman, Yeats, Shakespeare); Associated Press, Clifford Skarstedt (bookstore). 37: New York Public Library Humanities and Social Sciences Library, Astor, Lennox and Tilden Foundations (Basho); Photos.com (Bronte); Associated Press, Fiona Hanson (Clarke); Illustration for TIME Eɴ☐☐ʜ☐ɪby David Coulson.

Buildings, Landmarks and Architecture: 38: Associated Press, Steve Ruark (top aquarium); Associated Press, Gail Burton (shark aquarium). 39: Shutterstock.com (background); Photos.com (Empire State Building, Eiffel Tower, Sydney Harbor Bridge, Golden Gate Bridge); Associated Press, Michel Springler (Chunnel). 40: Photos.com (all). 41: Photos.com (Statue of Liberty, Mount Rushmore, Washington Monument, Muir Woods); Shutterstock.com (Rainbow Bridge); Associated Press, Kathy Willens (7 World Trade).

Calendars: 43: Photos.com (fireworks, Easter basket, girl with valentine, Mardi Gras mask, flag, menorah); Shutterstock.com (green river, groundhog, jack-o'-lantern, Santa). 44: Associated Press, John D. McHugh (Guy Fawkes Day); Shutterstock.com (Dia de los Muertos, Holi); Associated Press, Jack Mikrut (Santa Lucia's Day); Associated Press, Koji Sasahara (Shichi-Go-San). 45: Photos.com (dragon background); Shutterstock.com (Chinese New Year dragon, lanterns); Illustration for TIME FOR KIDS by Scott Angle (Creepy Counting).

Computers and Communication: 46: Associated Press, Jim Cole (Internet safety guide); Photos.com (background keyboard); Shutterstock.com (girls). 47: Shutterstock.com (family, girl); Photos.com (login screen). 48: Associated Press (ENIAC, early cell phone); NASA (1953 computer, 1973 computer); Photos.com (microchip, mouse); Associated Press, Sal Veder (Jobs, Scully, Wozniak); Shutterstock.com (floppy disk). 48–49: Photos.com (background). 49: Associated Press, Elise Amendola (Berners-Lee); Shutterstock.com (Apple Macintosh, iPod, Japanese girls); Amazon.com (Amazon's first gateway page); © Google Inc. (Google founders); Associated Press, Jeff Adkins (MySpace.com); Associated Press, Kevork Djansezian (iPhone). 50: The Artist's Toolkit: Visual Elements and Principles/A co-production of the Minneapolis Institute of Arts, Walker Art Center, and Educational Web Adventures (www.artsconnected.org/toolkit); U.S Environmental Protection Agency (www.epa.gov/kids); Dallas Symphony Association/Designer Mike Itashiki (www.dsokids.com); Shutterstock. com (computer keys). 51: TIME Eɴ☐☐ʜ☐ɪ(www.timeforkids.com); © Exploratorium (www.exploratorium.edu); Sports Illustrated Kids (www. SIKids.com); Photos.com (boy). 52: Associated Press, Eckehard Schulz (Wii); Associated Press, D.J. Peters (Guitar Hero); Associated Press, Stephen Chernin (Webby Award); Shutterstock.com (background). 53: Shutterstock.com (cell phone, WiFi zone, communications tower, wireless router, girl); U.S. Air Force photo by Tech. Sgt. Sonny Cohrs (man on satellite phone).

Countries of the World: 54: Associated Press, Richard Vogel. 55: Shutterstock.com (background); Holton Collection/SuperStock (rock art). 56: Shutterstock.com (background); Photos.com (koala, Mozart). 57: Shutterstock.com (background); Photos.com (Bahamanian dollar, Bahrain dollar). 58: Shutterstock.com (background); Photos. com (lace, orchids). 59: Shutterstock.com (background); Photos. com (elephant, Burundi franc). 60: Shutterstock.com (background, Angkor Wat); Photos.com (beaver, gorilla). 61: Shutterstock.com (background, vanilla); Photos.com (Easter Island). 62: Shutterstock. com (background); Photos.com (butterfly); Library of Congress, Prints and Photographs Division (Tesla). 63: Shutterstock.com (background, windmill, blue-footed boobies). 64: Shutterstock.com (background, Tallinn); iStockphoto.com/onfilm (Suez Canal). 65: Shutterstock. com (background, Fiji dollar, sauna, castle). 66: Shutterstock.com (background); Library of Congress, Prints and Photographs Division (Einstein); Photos.com (Rhodes). 67: Shutterstock.com (background, cashews, paprika); Andrea Biraghi/Dreamstime.com (Guyanese dollar). 68: Shutterstock.com (background); Library of Congress, Prints and Photographs Division (Wilde). 69: Shutterstock.com (background); Photos.com (Pompeii, ikebana). 70: Shutterstock. com (background, yurt); iStockphoto.com/Lingbeek (Liberation Tower). 71: Shutterstock.com (background, Freedom Monument). 72: Shutterstock.com (background, lemurs, Lake Malawi). 73: Shutterstock. com (background); Photos.com (coconut palm, Djenné Mosque). 74: Shutterstock.com (background); Photos.com (dodo); iStockphoto. com/fiondavi (Ulaanbaatar). 75: Shutterstock.com (background, Shwezigon temple); New York Public Library Humanities and Social Sciences Library, Astor, Lennox and Tilden Foundations (gusle), Photos. com (dirham, cheetah). 76: Shutterstock.com (background); Photos. com (Mount Everest); iStockphoto.com/Jaap2 (Anne Frank). 77: Shutterstock.com (background, reindeer, hirz, Panama Canal); Photos. com (butterfly). 78: Shutterstock.com (background, pierogi); Photos. com (llama). 79: Shutterstock.com (background); Photos.com (Tepes, bananas), iStockphoto.com/CaraMaria (Pitons). 80: Shutterstock.com (background, cacao, peanuts). 81: Shutterstock.com (background, Seychelles, Bratislava); National Archives and Records Administration (Solomon Islands). 82: Shutterstock.com (background); DigitalStock (olive oil); Paul Cowan/Dreamstime.com (hoppers). 83: Shutterstock. com (background); UN Photo/JO (Hammarskjold); Photos.com (Matterhorn). 84: Shutterstock.com (background, tuk-tuks, harissa). 85: Shutterstock.com (background, Hagia Sofia, Ukraine); Photos. com (Ugandan shilling). 86: Shutterstock.com (background); Photos. com (Big Ben, rose, Samarkand). 87: Shutterstock.com (background, Vietnam); Photos.com (capybara, Victoria Falls). 88: iStockphoto. com/deviousrim (Neuschwanstein Castle); Photos.com (Stonehenge, Chichen Itza, Machu Picchu, Colosseum); iStockphoto.com/rramirez125 (Alhambra); iStockphoto.com/crazycroat (Christ Redeemer). 89: Photos.com (Eiffel Tower, Kiyomizu Temple, Petra, Kremlin, Acropolis, Great Wall of China).

(McKinley, Roosevelt); Library of Congress, Prints and Photographs Division (Taft, Wilson, Harding, Coolidge). 169–170 Library of Congress, Prints and Photographs Division (all). 171: U.S. Department of Defense (George W. Bush); Herbert Hoover Presidential Library and Museum (Hoover doodle); John F. Kennedy Presidential Library and Museum, (Kennedy, Kennedy doodle); Ronald Reagan Presidential Library (Reagan, Reagan doodle); Library of Congress, Prints and Photographs Division (Hoover); LBJ Library photo by Yoichi R. Okamoto (Johnson); LBJ Library (Johnson doodle).

Religion: 172: Photos.com (menorah, Jesus, Torah); Shutterstock.com (crucifix). 173: Shutterstock.com (all).

Science: 174: Clay Bryce (Marsupial lion skeleton). 175: Photos.com (Earth); SuperStock, Inc./SuperStock (cave painting); 175: Shutterstock.com (trilobite, dinosaur fossil, evolution, tree rings); Associated Press, Michael Stravato (*A. africanus*). 176: Shutterstock.com (astronomy background, computer background, chemistry, paleontology, mathematics); Photos.com (geology background, engineering background). 177: Photos.com (all). 178: Shutterstock.com (H_2O, CO_2, molecules, atom, diamond); Photos.com (salt, pencil, Newton, Pasteur); Library of Congress, Prints and Photographs Division (Darwin). 179: U.S. Department of Agriculture (plant scientists); U.S. Department of Agriculture, photo by Scott Bauer (chemist); U.S. Department of Agriculture, photo by Brian Precthel (botanist); U.S. Department of Agriculture, photo by Peggy Greb (entomologist); U.S. Fish and Wildlife Service, photo by John and Karen Hollingsworth (ornithologist); U.S. Fish and Wildlife Service, photo by John and Karen Hollingsworth (ichthyologist); Photos.com (Curie); Library of Congress, Prints and Photographs Division (Einstein); Associated Press, Jean-Marc Bouju (Jane Goodall). 180: Photos.com (landfill, trash, chiles, girl); Shutterstock.com (solar system, greenhouse). 181: Photos.com (police tape, eye); Shutterstock.com (chalk outline, tire mark, thumbprint, biometrics).

Space: 182: NASA (Comet Hale-Bopp, lunar eclipse, spiral galaxy); Photos.com (solar eclipse, crater); iStockphoto.com/njnightsky (meteoroids). 183: NASA (all). 184: NASA (Moon); Photos.com/ChristianAnthony (solar system). 186: NASA: (*Gemini 4*, *Sputnik 1*, Gagarin, White, *Apollo-Soyuz*, *Gemini 6*, *Apollo 11*); Photos.com (Earth); Associated Press (Laika). 187: NASA (all).

Sports: 188: Associated Press, Paul Sancya (Manning); Getty Images Sport, Evan Pinkus (Burress); Associated Press, Matt Slocum (Tyree). 189: Associated Press, Paul Sancya (Brady); Associated Press, Nam Y. Huh (LSU). 190: Associated Press, H. Rumph Jr. (Rollins); Associated Press, Ed Betz (Rodriguez); Associated Press, Mark Humphrey (World Series); Associated Press, Gene J. Puskar (Carriker). 191: Associated Press, Mark Duncan (James); Associated Press, Roy Dabner (Augustus); Associated Press, Rob Carr (Florida vs. Ohio). 192: Associated Press, Eugene Hoshiko (soccer); Associated Press, Mark Avery (hockey). 193: Associated Press, Tom Strattman (race car); Associated Press, Terry Renna (Johnson); Associated Press, Laurent Rebours (Armstrong); Associated Press, Peter Dejong (Tour de France). 194: Associated Press, Kathy Willens (Henin); Associated Press, Mark Duncan (Zach Johnson); Associated Press, Marcio Jose Sanchez (Shawn Johnson). 195: Shutterstock.com (snowboarding background, skiing background, figure skating, cross country skiing); Associated Press, Alessandro Trovati (Paerson). 196: Associated Press, Jens Meyer (Florschutz and Wustlich); Associated Press, Nathan Bilow (Bleiler); Associated Press, Reed Saxon (White); Shutterstock.com (wakeboarding). 197: Shutterstock.com (horse race, Olympics); Photos.com (Iditarod). 198: Associated Press, David Longstreath (elephant polo); Associated Press, Randi Lynn Beach (underwater hockey); Shutterstock.com (tossing the caber, zorbing); Associated Press, Sergey Ponomarev (high-heel racing); Associated Press, Barry Batchelor (cheese rolling); Associated Press, Reed Saxon (Abdul-Jabbar); Illustration for TIME For Kids by Gary Lacoste (Super Baller); Associated Press (Mantle).

United States: 200: Associated Press, David J. Phillip (Teach For America). 201: Photos.com (all). 202: U.S. Department of State (Rice); iStockphoto.com/BergmannD (Juneau). 202–203: Shutterstock.com (background). 203: Library of Congress, Prints and Photographs Division (Geronimo); Photos.com (fiddle). 204: Photos.com (quail, Rocky Mountain columbine). 204–205: Shutterstock.com (background). 205: Photos.com (robin, peach blossom). 206: Shutterstock.com (Sabal palm); LBJ Library photo by Yoichi R. Okamoto (King). 206–207: Shutterstock.com (background). 207: Shutterstock.com (hibiscus); iStockphoto.com/maceofoto (huckleberry). 208: Photos.com (cardinal); Shutterstock.com (Indianapolis). 208–209: Shutterstock.com (background). 209: Photos.com (geode, sunflower). 210: Library of Congress, Prints and Photographs Division (Ali); Shutterstock.com (dog). 210–211: Shutterstock.com (background). 211: Photos.com (moose, black-eyed susan). 212: Photos.com (chickadee,

apple blossom). 212–213: Shutterstock.com (background). 213: Shutterstock.com (lady slipper); Photos.com (magnolia). 214: Photos.com (hawthorn); iStockphoto.com/Gonzuller (bitterroot). 214–215: Shutterstock.com (background). 215: Library of Congress, Prints and Photographs Division (Malcolm X); Photos.com (Las Vegas sign). 216: NASA (Shepard); Photos.com (purple violet). 216–217: Shutterstock.com (background). 217: Photos.com (chile); Library of Congress, Prints and Photographs Division (Roosevelt). 218: Photos.com (blackbeard); U.S. Fish and Wildlife Service, photo by John and Karen Hollingsworth (western meadowlark). 218–219: Shutterstock.com (background). 219: Library of Congress, Prints and Photographs Division (Edison); Photos.com (parking meter). 220: Photos.com (beaver); U.S. Fish and Wildlife Service (Carson). 220–221: Shutterstock.com (background). 221: Shutterstock.com (Rhode Island red hen); Library of Congress, Prints and Photographs Division (Gibson). 222: Shutterstock.com (rodeo); U.S. Department of Defense (Salt Lake City). 222–223: Shutterstock.com (background). 223: Library of Congress, Prints and Photographs Division (O'Connor); Photos.com (Salt Lake City). 224: Shutterstock.com (maple syrup); Photos.com (dogwood). 224–225: Shutterstock.com (background). 225: Photos.com (Grand Coulee dam); Shutterstock.com (rhododendron). 226: Library of Congress, Prints and Photographs Division (Wright); Photos.com (Devil's Tower). 226–227: Shutterstock.com (background). 227: Shutterstock.com (Washingon D.C., San Juan).

Volunteering: 230: Courtesy of Dan Gutwein (Austin Gutwein); Photos.com (Luther, Tubman, Barton); Associated Press (Gandhi); Associated Press, Jeff Robbins (Mother Teresa). 231: Heifer International (women with animals); ICRC/W. Lembryk/CD-E-00466 (background); Habitat for Humanity International (homebuilders); UN Photo/James Bu (Mandela); Library of Congress, Prints and Photographs Division (King); UN Photo/Mark Garten (Gore); Associated Press, Charlaine Brown (Reeve). 232: Image provided by Alex's Lemonade Stand Foundation (Alex's Lemonade); Ryan's Well Foundation (Ryan's Well); Photos.com (books); Shutterstock.com (girls). 233: Heifer International (woman with goat); Associated Press, Pat Little (United Way); Photos.com (tutoring, trash can); Associated Press, Dave Scherbenco (canned food drive).

Weather: 234: FEMA, Andrea Booher (wildfire); Shutterstock.com (thermometer). 235: Ralph F. Kresge/National Oceanic and Atmospheric Administration/Department of Commerce (cloud background); Photos.com (lightning, wind, stratus clouds). 236: Photos.com (tornado, drought, hurricane); FEMA/Marvin Nauman (flood); FEMA/Michael Rieger (blizzard). 237: FEMA/Dave Saville (avalanche); FEMA/Mark Wolfe (wildfire); FEMA/Robert J. Alvey (mudslide); Shutterstock.com (tornado background).

What's Next?: 238: OAR/National Undersea Research Program/NURP (spider crab); Image courtesy of the Regional Scale Nodes program at the University of Washington, produced by the University's Center for Environmental Visualization (base station); Photos.com (tourists, Moon). 239: Matthew Bogyo Laboratory/Stanford University School of Medicine (cancer probe); Emily Jensen, University of Minnesota Academic Health Center (heart); Photos.com (peanuts). 240: Getty Images Entertainment, Noel Vasquez (Media Wall); Shutterstock.com (GPS); 241: Shutterstock.com (gas pump, landfill, faucet, light bulb); Photos.com (dishwasher). 242: Shutterstock.com (handprint, kitchen); The Smart Wardrobe developed by researchers at UniSA's Wearable Computer Laboratory (smart clothes). 243: Shutterstock.com (checkout scanner); Associated Press (*Toy Story*); Dreamworks/The Kobal Collection (*Transformers*).